ALL ABOUT STOCKS

OTHER TITLES IN THE "ALL ABOUT..." SERIES

ALL ABOUT STOCKS

The Easy Way to Get Started

ESMÉ FAERBER

THIRD EDITION

New York   Chicago   San Francisco   Lisbon   London
Madrid   Mexico City   Milan   New Delhi   San Juan
Seoul   Singapore   Sydney   Toronto

CONTENTS

PREFACE

This third edition to *All About Stocks* has been rewritten to include information that will make investors feel more knowledgeable about their investments in stocks. Investing in stocks is not easy because the process is filled with questions, recrimination, and insecurity. Hindsight always provides the clarity as to what stocks should have been purchased, but looking to the future many investors are afraid to make investment decisions to take advantage of opportunities in the market. The aim of this book is to provide a clear understanding of the characteristics of stocks, their risks and returns, the workings of the stock market, valuation of stocks, the use of fundamental and technical analysis in the choice of stocks to buy and sell, the differences between value, growth, and momentum stocks, and the theories of the stock markets.

Among the many changes to this edition are new chapters on the valuation of stocks, investing in foreign stocks, and exchange-traded funds. Each chapter includes many new sections to provide both beginning and sophisticated investors with the tools and knowledge to increase their returns without significantly increasing their risks through the building of a diversified portfolio. As a more informed investor, it will be easier for you to make better decisions regarding your stock investments.

ACKNOWLEDGMENTS

The preparation of this book was facilitated by many people at McGraw-Hill, most notably Daina Penikas.

Thomas Hoens provided me with information on his CFAR research, for which I am especially appreciative.

This book is dedicated to my husband, Eric, and children Jennifer and Michael for their continued encouragement, patience and support.

CHAPTER 1

Why Invest in Stocks?

KEY CONCEPTS

- Why you should invest in stocks
- Developing your financial plan
- What investing in stocks can do for you

Investment Snapshot

- In November 2001, Enron filed for bankruptcy. Investors who bought the stock of this high-profile company at $60 per share at the beginning of that year saw their investments wiped out.
- For the three-year period from March 2000 through 2003, the stock market was in a steep decline. The Nasdaq Index was down 71 percent. To put this in historical perspective, the stock market has not seen such a decline since the Depression of 1929.
- The stock price of Boeing Company was $33.50 a share on November1, 2001, and rose to $85 per share on May 3, 2006, a 155 percent increase over the four-and-a-half-year period.

The preceding Investment Snapshot illustrates the ease with which you can lose money investing in stocks. Yet more than half the households in the United States own stocks either directly or indirectly through retirement accounts. Understanding what stocks are and how stock markets work can help you to avoid the costly mistakes when investing in stocks and to build a portfolio of stocks that include winners such as the Boeing Company example.

WHY YOU SHOULD INVEST IN STOCKS

The Investment Snapshot poses the question: Why invest in stocks when you can lose part of your investment? The answer to this question can be obtained from Figure 1–1, which illustrates why stocks are so compelling an investment.

Over the 19-year period from 1986 through 2004, both large-company and small-company stocks outperformed bonds and Treasury bills and kept well ahead of inflation. In 5 of the 19 years stocks underperformed bonds and Treasury bills. However, an investor with a long time horizon should not be bogged down by a small number of negative yearly returns because the focus should be on accumulating long-term wealth.

FIGURE 1 - 1

Annual Returns of Stocks, Bonds, and Treasury Bills, 1986–2004

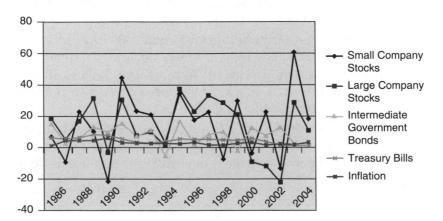

FIGURE 1-2
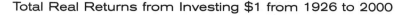

Total Real Returns from Investing $1 from 1926 to 2000

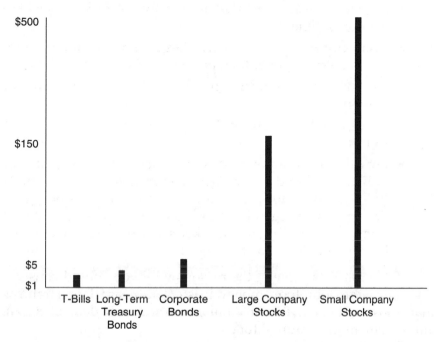

Figure 1–2 illustrates how the total real returns of stocks outperformed significantly returns of bonds and Treasury bills over the time period from 1926 through 2000. One dollar invested in each of the aforementioned investments had markedly different returns when adjusted for inflation. For a one-dollar investment in small-company stocks, the total accumulated value would have increased to over $500, whereas a similar investment in large-company stocks would have returned $150 over the period. Real returns on Treasury bills, long-term Treasury bonds, and corporate bonds were $1.50, $3.79, and $5.50, respectively. These returns illustrate how compelling stock investments are over long time periods.

You can draw the following inferences:

- For stock investors, a long time horizon is needed to reduce the risk of loss.
- In order to earn greater returns over a long time horizon, stock investors should not focus on the volatility of annual

returns, which may be thought of as bumps in the road to larger overall returns.

- Losses in the stock market are hardly noticeable over long periods of time.
- Small-company stocks earn larger returns than large-company stocks over long periods of time.
- For short time horizons, bonds and Treasury bills might outperform stocks.
- Bonds earn larger returns than Treasury bills (money market securities).
- Investing in common stocks offers federal tax benefits not available to bond and money market investors. Dividends from common stocks are taxed at preferential federal rates (lower than marginal tax bracket rates), whereas interest from bonds and money market securities are taxed at the holder's marginal tax bracket rates.

Table 1–1 lists some of the reasons why you should consider investing your long-term money in stocks to earn larger returns than those of bonds, Treasury bills, certificates of deposit (CDs), and money market mutual funds.

Investors with a long time horizon (more than five years) who can withstand the risk of loss owing to down markets should invest in stocks. Investors with shorter time horizons who need to earn current steady streams of income from their investments and

TABLE 1 - 1

Major Reasons to Save More and Invest Wisely

- People are living longer and need more money to fund retirement.
- Health care, education, and insurance costs are rising.
- Real estate and housing prices have risen steadily.
- There is a need to get ahead of inflation and improve standards of living.
- People want to accumulate wealth to pass on to heirs.
- The more you save and invest now, the greater is your purchasing power owing to compounding.
- Investing wisely increases your wealth.

who are risk-averse should invest in bonds. The types of securities that you invest in are determined by your financial objectives and your personal characteristics.

DEVELOP YOUR FINANCIAL PLAN

The investment process begins with a financial plan that lists your financial objectives and the road map to achieving those objectives. If you don't know where you are heading, you won't know how to get there.

1. List Your Financial Objectives

The first step in any investment plan is to determine what you want to achieve from your investments and when you want this money to be available. You probably have many objectives, namely, saving for retirement in 20 years, paying for your children's education in 10 years, and making a down payment on a vacation house in 2 years. Financial objectives are the financial milestones that you would like to achieve through investing. Take a few moments to list your financial objectives and determine how much you want to achieve with each objective in the future. Possible objectives include

- Funding an emergency fund within one year
- Funding the purchase of a car in five years
- Funding a child's college education in 10 years
- Building a retirement fund over the next 25 years

Investing for retirement is not the same as investing for shorter-term objectives owing to the time horizon and risk factor.

Time Horizon

Listing the time horizon is important because it gives you a better idea of how much you will need to fund each objective. The amount of money that you have to fund each objective is directly related to your financial condition or net worth. Table 1–2 illustrates how you can determine your net worth. *Net worth* is the difference between what you own and what you owe.

Reviewing your monthly budget also may assist you in determining how much you have to invest and the level of risk that you can accept.

TABLE 1-2

What Are You Worth?

List What You Own (Assets)		List What You Own (Liabilities)
Bank accounts		Credit card debt
Certificates of Deposit		Bank Loans
Stocks		Other short-term debts
Bonds	Minus	Mortgage
Mutual Funds		Car loans
Retirement Accounts		Others Loans
Real Estate		**Total Liabilities**
Automobiles		
Income minus expenses		
Other assets		
Total Assets		
	=	
	Net Worth	

Risk

Evaluate your objectives with regard to risk, which may be characterized as follows:

- Safety of principal
- Stream of income
- Capital growth

Safety of Principal Money market securities, such as bank accounts, savings accounts, CDs, money market mutual funds, Treasury bills, and commercial paper, offer safety of principal and low rates of return. Short-term objectives such as building an emergency fund and saving for short-term purchases within the year fall into this category of investments. Returns from these securities often do not cover inflation and taxes.

Stream of Income Investments that provide a steady stream of income with higher rates of return than money market securities include bonds and preferred stock. The tradeoff in seeking higher levels of return from bonds and preferred stock is the possible loss of principal. When bonds and preferred stock prices decline below their acquisition costs, investors experience losses of capital (principal loss) should they have to sell their investments. High-risk, high-return bonds (junk bonds) offer the potential of higher streams of income than investment-grade bonds, but junk bonds are also more likely to default on the repayment of principal to their bondholders. Investors looking to fund objectives with one- to five-year time horizons use bonds with matching maturities to their time horizons to earn higher rates of return than money market securities.

Capital Growth Investing for capital growth has the potential to provide an increase in value of the investments also referred to as *capital growth*. Stocks offer the potential for capital growth when stock prices increase above their acquisition prices. The risk is that a stock's price can decline below its acquisition cost, resulting in a *capital loss*. For this reason, you need a longer time horizon (greater than five years) in order to be able to wait out any losses in the stock market. Some stocks pay dividends, thereby providing stockholders with a stream of income. Generally, the yields on dividend-paying stocks tend to be lower than the yields of bonds. However, not all stocks pay dividends, and investors invest in these stocks for their potential capital growth. Stock investments are suitable to fund investors' longer-term objectives (with a time horizon of greater than five years), such as building a retirement fund.

In summary, there is a tradeoff between risk and return. Low-risk investments (money market securities) guarantee principal but provide low returns in the form of income. Fixed-income securities (bonds and preferred stock) provide higher levels of income but carry a risk of loss of principal in the event of default for bonds or having to sell preferred stock at a lower price than the purchase price. Common stocks offer the greatest total return (capital growth and income) over long periods of time but carry a higher risk of loss of principal over short periods of time. Your personal circumstances (age, marital status, number of dependents, net worth, and income) determine your tolerance for risk as a guide to your choice of investments.

2. Allocate Your Assets

Asset allocation is the assignment of your funds to different investment asset classes such as money market funds, bonds, stocks, real estate, gold, options, and futures. Your particular asset allocation

FIGURE 1-3

(a) Asset allocation plan for a married couple in their thirties.
(b) Asset allocation plan for a married couple in their mid-
forties.

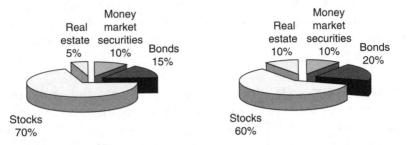

plan depends on several factors such as your time horizon, tolerance for risk, and personal financial situation.

In general, the younger you are, the greater can be your allocation toward capital growth investments (common stocks and real estate). The closer you are to retirement, the greater should be your allocation to bonds and money market securities, which provide income, and the smaller should be your allocation to stocks, which provide growth to the portfolio. Figure 1–3 gives two examples of asset allocation plans: The first is for a married couple in their thirties who are investing primarily to build a retirement fund over 30 years. The second is for a couple who are in their mid-forties, indicating a slightly reduced percentage allocated to stocks with a 20-year time horizon to retirement.

Asset allocation plans are evaluated periodically when your personal financial circumstances change. Table 1-3 illustrates guidelines for determining your particular asset allocation plan.

TABLE 1-3

How to Determine Your Asset Allocation Plan

Financial planners use this rule of thumb method for determining the percentage to allocate to stocks:

Percentage amount to allocate to stocks = 100 − your age

For example, if you are 65 years old, you would allocate 35 percent to stocks and divide up the balance to other investment asset classes (bonds and money market securities). This is the starting point to your plan, where the categories will be adjusted for your financial circumstances and risk tolerance.

3. Identify Your Investment Strategy

Your investment strategy conforms to your objectives and asset allocation plan. Your perception of how efficiently stock and bond markets process relevant information with regard to the pricing of their securities determines your investment strategy. If you believe that securities markets are efficient, meaning that all current and new information is reflected quickly and efficiently in stock and bond prices, you would pursue a passive investment strategy. For example, when there are undervalued stocks, they will be bought immediately, driving up their prices to their fair or intrinsic values. Consequently, there will be very few underpriced or overpriced stocks in an efficient market. An efficient market means that few investors will be able to consistently beat the market returns on a risk-adjusted basis (seeking returns that are greater than the market by investing in securities with the same level of risk). Investors who believe that the markets are efficient would hope to do as well as the market averages, seeing that they cannot beat the market averages. Such investors would pursue a passive investment strategy of buying and holding a diversified portfolio of stocks that resemble market indexes.

If investors believe that the markets are inefficient (slow to reflect pricing information), there will be many under- and overvalued stocks. Consequently, such investors use financial and technical analysis to find those underpriced stocks in order to earn larger returns than those of the market averages. Investors following an active investment strategy buy stocks when they are undervalued and sell those stocks when they are perceived to be overvalued. Asset allocation plans change in response to circumstances in the market, and the percentage allocated to stocks will increase when the stock market is perceived to be undervalued and will be reduced when the stock market is perceived to be overvalued.

4. Select Your Investments

After you formulate your objectives, asset allocation plan, and investment strategy, it is time to select your investments. Your decision as to which stocks to buy is guided by your investment strategy. Investors following a passive investment strategy choose diversified investments in each investment asset class. A *diversified stock portfolio* includes stocks from different sectors of the economy (technology, energy, health care, consumer, industrial, financial, auto, basic materials, manufacturing, and utilities) whose returns are not directly related.

An investor following an active strategy uses fundamental and technical analysis to assemble stocks to buy that are undervalued and then sells them when they become overvalued and replaces them with new undervalued stocks.

Irrespective of whether you are an active or passive investor, you need to even out the risk of loss by having a diversified portfolio. In other words, you should not have all your eggs in one basket.

5. Evaluate Your Portfolio

You should evaluate your portfolio periodically because a change in your circumstances might necessitate a change in your asset allocation plan. In addition, fluctuating economic and market conditions might affect your asset allocation plan. Similarly, a change in a company's business will have a direct bearing on the valuation of that company's stock in your investment portfolio.

WHAT INVESTING IN STOCKS CAN DO FOR YOU

If you have a long investment time horizon and you can sleep well at night when there is a decline in the stock market, you should consider investing in stocks because

- Stocks provide returns in the form of dividends and capital appreciation. Historically, returns from stocks have been greater than the returns received from bonds and money market securities over long time horizons (seven-plus years). Investing in stocks provides growth to an investment portfolio in addition to any dividend income.
- Stocks provide a store of value. Buying and holding appreciated stocks in a portfolio is a tax-efficient way to increase wealth in that if the holding period is longer than a year before selling a stock, the capital gain is taxed at a maximum of 15 percent at the federal level. Gains from stocks held for less than a year are taxed at your marginal tax bracket, which could be as high as 35 percent. Check with your accountant that Congress has not made any changes to the Tax Code for the taxation of capital gains.

- Dividend income from qualified stocks is taxed at lower rates than interest from bonds and money market securities.

The following chapters outline the characteristics of the different types of stocks and the process of choosing stocks that are appropriate for your circumstances. Not all stocks are winners, and even the stocks of good companies decline in value. Understanding the factors that drive stock prices will steer you to assembling stocks for your portfolio that will achieve your financial objectives.

Common Stocks

KEY CONCEPTS

- Characteristics of common stock
- What you need to know about dividends
- Classes and types of common stocks

Investment Snapshot

- The bankruptcies of WorldCom and Enron resulted in shareholders losing their entire investments.
- Shareholders of Home Depot were irate at the $123.7 million pay package (excluding stock options) of CEO Bob Nardelli over a five-year period when Home Depot's stock price declined by 9 percent for the same period. Rival Lowe's stock price increased by 185 percent during that same period.

Both common stocks and preferred stocks represent ownership in a corporation, but as the Home Depot example in the Investment Snapshot indicates, shareholders do not have a say in the management of the company unless they have a majority or significant ownership share of the company. The characteristics of shareholders are discussed in the following section.

CHARACTERISTICS OF COMMON STOCK

- Common stockholders are the residual owners of the corporation because they have voting rights and bear the ultimate risk associated with ownership.
- In bankruptcy, common stockholders are last in line (after bondholders and preferred stockholders) for claims on assets.
- Shareholders' liability is limited to the amount of their investments (limited liability).
- With regard to claims on earnings, common stockholders are entitled to receipt of dividends only after all the corporation's obligations have been met.
- Shareholders receive dividends only when a company's board of directors declares a dividend.

When a new company is formed, common stock is sold to shareholders to raise money for the company. Companies that need additional funds to expand sell more common stock, bonds, and/or preferred stock.

Ownership of common stock is evidenced by stock certificates. The front of a certificate shows the name of the issuing company, the name of the owner of the shares, the number of shares of ownership, the identifying serial number, the name of the register, and the par value of the stock. The back of a stock certificate normally includes an assignment statement, which must be signed by the holder of the stock when the holder transfers ownership of the shares.

Voting Rights

Voting rights are the rights of shareholders to vote. A characteristic of common stock is that shareholders can vote on important issues facing the corporation, such as membership to the board of directors. The board of directors, in turn, selects officers to run the corporation. Common shareholders must approve of any changes to the charter of incorporation. A *charter of incorporation* is a document that the company files with the state when forming a corporation. For example, a corporation's management team that would like to take over another corporation through the issuance of new common shares would have to get approval from their shareholders.

Rather than attend the shareholders' meeting to vote in person, many shareholders use a proxy vote. A *proxy* is a legal document that gives a designated person temporary power of attorney to vote at the shareholder meeting for an absentee shareholder. Most often management chooses both the slate of candidates to stand for the board of directors and the important issues to be voted on by shareholders. The names of these choices are then sent out on proxy cards to be voted on by shareholders.

Corporations use either the majority voting procedure (also known as the *statutory method*) or the cumulative voting procedure. In the *majority voting procedure*, shareholders are allowed one vote for each share held for each director's position. Under the majority voting procedure, the number of votes a shareholder has equals the number of shares he or she holds. The majority of votes cast determines the issue or the director elected.

In the *cumulative voting procedure*, shareholders are entitled to a total number of votes equal to the total number of shares owned multiplied by the number of directors being elected. Shareholders can cast all their votes for a single candidate or split them as they see fit. Cumulative voting gives increased weight to minority shareholders, enabling them to elect at least one director.

The following example illustrates the difference between majority voting and cumulative voting. Assume that a company has 1,000 shares outstanding and that two candidates are to be elected to the board of directors. Under majority voting, a minority shareholder with 300 shares, for example, can cast 300 votes for each of the two candidates. However, under cumulative voting, a minority shareholder with 300 shares could cast all 600 votes (300 $\times$ 2) for one candidate. This method is advantageous for minority shareholders because they can work together to cast all their votes for one candidate who might be more sympathetic to their cause.

Preemptive Rights

Preemptive rights allow shareholders to maintain their constant percentage of a company's outstanding stock by being given the first chance to purchase newly issued stock in proportion to their existing percentage ownership of stock. Not all corporations provide preemptive rights in their charters. For example, if a shareholder owns 10 percent of a company's stock, that shareholder is entitled to purchase 10 percent of new shares being offered. To put it another way, existing shareholders have the first right of refusal in purchasing new shares. Certificates called *rights* are issued to the shareholders, giving them the option to purchase a stated number of new shares at a specific price during a specific period. These rights can be exercised (which allows the purchase of new common stock at below-market price), sold, or allowed to expire.

WHAT YOU NEED TO KNOW ABOUT DIVIDENDS

When the board of directors of a corporation decides to pay out its earnings or part of its earnings in dividends, all its common shareholders have a right to receive them. If the board of directors decides not to declare a dividend, the shareholders receive nothing. Companies are not legally required to pay dividends even if they are profitable and have paid them in the past. In contrast, companies are legally required to pay interest to their bondholders on their debt. This is an important distinction for people who rely on regular income from their investments.

Declaration of Dividends

If the receipt of dividends is important to you, you need to be aware of these four dates:

- *Date of declaration* is the date on which the board of directors declares dividends.
- *Date of record* is the date that determines which shareholders are entitled to receive the dividends. Only shareholders owning shares of the company on the date of record are entitled to receive dividends. If shares are purchased after the record date, the owners are not entitled to receive the dividends.
- *Ex-dividend date* is two business days before the date of record. Stocks traded on the ex-dividend date do not include the dividend. When common stock is bought, the settlement takes three business days to be completed. Thus, if the record date for a company's dividend is Friday, the ex-dividend date is the preceding Wednesday. Investors who buy these shares on Tuesday (the day before the

ex-dividend date) receive the dividend because the transaction is recorded in the ownership books for that company in three working days.

- *Payment date* is the date on which the company pays the dividends.

Companies generally make their dividend policies known to the public. Because investors use dividend payments, rightly or wrongly, as a yardstick or mirror of a company's expected earnings, changes to dividend payments can have a greater effect on the stock price than a change in earnings does. This phenomenon explains the reluctance by management to cut dividends when earnings decline. Similarly, a lag in increasing dividends might occur when earnings increase because members of management want to be sure that they can maintain any increases in dividends.

Shareholders who rely on income from their investments generally purchase the stocks of companies that have a history of paying regular dividends from their earnings. These companies tend to be older and well established; their stocks are referred to as *income stocks* or *blue-chip stocks*. Table 2–1 discusses the importance of dividend-paying stocks.

Young companies that are expanding generally retain their earnings; their stocks are referred to as *growth stocks*. Growth stocks appeal to investors who are more interested in capital appreciation.

Types of Dividends

Following are the various forms of dividends:

- Cash dividends
- Stock dividends and stock splits
- Property dividends
- Special distributions, extra dividends, spin-offs and split-offs

Cash Dividends

A cash dividend is a dividend paid in cash. To be able to pay cash dividends, companies need to have not only sufficient earnings but also sufficient cash. Even if a company shows a large amount of retained earnings on its balance sheet, it may not be enough to ensure cash dividends. The amount of cash that a company has is

TABLE 2-1

Dividends: How Important Are They?

> The average dividend yield on the 500 stocks in the Standard & Poor's (S&P) Index
> was 1.99 percent in May 2006, and the dividend payout ratio was 28 percent. In
> other words, company managers retained 72 percent of company profits for their
> own preferred uses.
>
> So why are dividends important if companies pay such a small percentage in
> dividends? The importance of dividends lies in their tax benefits.
>
> In 2003, federal tax rates on qualified dividends were lowered to a maximum rate
> of 15 percent if held for the required length of time. This lowered tax rate makes
> investing in dividend-paying stocks more advantageous from a tax point of view
> than many taxable bonds, where interest is taxed at the taxpayer's marginal rate,
> which can be as high as 35 percent.

independent of retained earnings. Cash-poor companies still can
be profitable.

Most American companies pay regular cash dividends quarterly; some pay dividends semiannually or annually. Johnson &
Johnson, the pharmaceutical company, pays quarterly dividends,
and McDonald's pays an annual dividend. A company might
declare extra dividends in addition to regular dividends. An *extra
dividend* is an additional, nonrecurring dividend paid over and
above the regular dividends by the company. Microsoft
Corporation paid an extra dividend of $2 per share over and above
its regular dividend to shareholders of record holding the stock on
November 15, 2004. Rather than battle to maintain a higher amount
of regular dividends, companies with fluctuating earnings pay out
additional dividends when their earnings warrant it. Whenever
times were good for the automobile industry, for example, General
Motors declared extra dividends.

Stock Dividends

Some companies choose to conserve their cash by paying *stock dividends,* a dividend paid in stock. The companies then recapitalize
their earnings and issue new shares, which do not affect its assets
and liabilities. Table 2–2 shows an example of a company's balance
sheet before and after a 10 percent stock dividend.

In this table, the "Total equity" section of the balance sheet is
the same before and after the stock dividend ($200,000). The
amounts that are transferred to the different accounts in the equity

TABLE 2-2

Effects of a Stock Dividend on a Company's Balance Sheet

XYZ Company Balance Sheet before a Stock Dividend			
Current assets	$100,00	**Current liabilities**	$ 50,000
Fixed assets	200,00	**Long-term liabilities**	50,000
		Equity: Common stock 100,000	
		$1 par 100,000 shares outstanding	
		Additional paid-in capital 30,000	
		Retained earnings 70,000	
		Total equity	200,000
Total assets	$ 300,000	**Total liabilities & equity**	$300,000
After 10 percent Stock Dividend (Market Price $5 per Share)			
Current assets	$100,000	Current liabilities	$ 50,000
Fixed assets	200,000	**Long-term liabilities**	50,000
		Equity: Common stock 110,000	
		$1 Par 110,000 Shares Outstanding	
		Additional paid-in capital 70,000	
		Retained earnings 20,000	
		Total equity	200,000
Total assets	$ 300,000	**Total liabilities & equity**	$300,000

section depend on the market value of the common stock and the number of new shares issued through the stock dividend. Amounts from retained earnings are transferred to the common stock and additional paid-in capital accounts. In this example there are 10,000 additional shares that have a market price of $5 per share. The "Retained earnings" account is debited (deducted) for $50,000 (market price of $5 × 10,000 shares), and $10,000 (10,000 shares × $1 par value) is added to the common stock account. The other $40,000 ($4 premium over par value × 10,000 shares) is added to the additional paid-in capital account.

Receiving a stock dividend does not increase shareholders' wealth. Shareholders who receive a stock dividend receive more shares of that company's stock, but because the company's assets and liabilities remain the same, the price of the stock must decline to account for the dilution. For shareholders, this situation resembles a slice of cake. You can divide the slice into two, three, or four pieces, and no matter how many ways you slice it, its overall size remains the same. After a stock dividend, shareholders receive more shares, but their proportionate ownership interest in the company remains the same, and the market price declines proportionately.

Stock dividends usually are expressed as a percentage of the number of shares outstanding. For example, if a company announces a 10 percent stock dividend and has 1 million shares outstanding, the total shares outstanding are increased to 1.1 million shares after the stock dividend is issued.

Stock Split

A *stock split* is a proportionate increase in the number of outstanding shares that does not affect the issuing company's assets, liabilities, or earnings. A stock split resembles a stock dividend in that an increase occurs in the number of shares issued on a proportionate basis, whereas the assets, liabilities, equity, and earnings remain the same. The only difference between a stock split and a stock dividend is technical.

From an accounting point of view, a stock dividend of greater than 25 percent is recorded as a stock split. A 100 percent stock dividend is the same as a two-for-one stock split. A company might split its stock because the price is too high, and with a lower price the company's stock becomes more marketable.

The following example illustrates what happens when a company declares a two-for-one stock split. If at the time of the split the company has 1 million shares outstanding and the price of the stock is $50, after the split the company will have 2 million shares outstanding, and the stock will trade at $25 per share. Someone who owns 100 shares before the split (with a value of $50 per share) would own 200 shares after the split with a value of approximately $25 per share (50 ÷ 2). On January 16, 2003, Microsoft Corporation announced a two-for-one stock split that took effect on February 18, 2003. Before the split, Microsoft closed at $48.30 per share. On the morning of the split, it opened at $24.15 per share. An investor with 100 shares before the split would have had 200 shares after the split.

Occasionally, companies announce reverse splits, which reduce the number of shares and increase the share price. A *reverse split* is a proportionate reduction in the number of shares outstanding without affecting the company's assets or earnings. When a company's stock has fallen in price, a reverse split raises the price of the stock to a respectable level. Another reason for raising the share price is to

TABLE 2 - 3

Are there Advantages to Stock Dividends and Stock Splits?

If shareholder wealth is not increased through stock dividends and stock splits, why do companies go to the trouble and expense of issuing them?

The first advantage for the issuing company is a conservation of cash. By substituting stock dividends for cash dividends, a company can conserve its cash or use it for other investment opportunities. If the company successfully invests its retained earnings in business ventures, the stock price is bid up, benefiting shareholders. Consequently, shareholders are better off receiving stock dividends, but there are costs associated with the issue of stock dividends. Shareholders pay the cost of issuing new shares, the transfer fees, and the costs of revising the company's record of shareholders.

Advocates of stock dividends and stock splits believe that a stock price never falls in exact proportion to the increase in shares. For example, in a two-for-one stock split, the stock price might fall less than 50 percent, which means that shareholders are left with a higher total value. This conclusion has not been verified by most academic studies. When the price of the stock is reduced because of the split, the stock might become more attractive to potential investors because of its lower price. The increased marketability of the stock might push up the price if the company continues to do well financially; stockholders benefit in the long run by owning more shares of a company whose stock price continues to increase.

Stock dividends and stock splits do not increase stockholder wealth from the point of view of the balance sheet. Cash dividends, however, directly increase a shareholder's monetary wealth and reduce the company's cash and reinvestment dollars.

meet the minimum listing requirements of the exchanges and the Nasdaq market. For example, a stock trading in the $1 range would trade at $10 with a 1-for-10 reverse split. The number of shares outstanding would be reduced by 10 times after the split. On November 19, 2002, AT&T had a reverse stock split of one-for-five shares. See Table 2–3 for a discussion of whether there are any advantages to stock dividends and stock splits.

Property Dividends

A *property dividend* is a dividend paid in a form other than cash or the company's own stock. A property dividend is generally taxable at its fair market value. For example, when a corporation spins off a subsidiary, shareholders might receive assets or shares of that subsidiary. Distributing the stocks or assets of the subsidiary (rather than cash) allows shareholders to benefit directly from the market value of the dividends received.

Special Distributions

Companies sometimes make special distributions in various forms, such as extra dividends, spin-offs, and split-offs.

Extra Dividends Companies might want to distribute an extra dividend to their shareholders on a one-time or infrequent basis. A company might have had a particularly good quarter financially, or other reasons for this distribution might exist. The company might use a special distribution rather than increase its regular dividends because the distribution is a one-time occurrence. Companies would not want to increase their dividend rates if they could not continue paying those increased rates in the future.

Spin-Offs A *spin-off* is the distribution of shares of a subsidiary company to shareholders. Some companies allocate proportionately to their shareholders some or all of their shares of a subsidiary company as a spin-off. For example, on August 9, 2005, IAC/InterActive Corporation (ticker symbol IACI) spun off Expedia Corporation (ticker symbol EXPE) to shareholders to allow it to focus on its business. Prior to the spin-off (August 8, 2005), InterActive Corporation had a one-for-two reverse stock split. For every two shares of InterActive Corporation common stock owned as of August 8, 2005, shareholders received one share of InterActive Corporation and one share of Expedia common stock. Shareholders have the option of keeping or selling the additional shares they receive. Companies spin off unrelated or underperforming businesses to shareholders so that they can concentrate on their own business. In many cases the shares of spin-off companies outperform their parent companies because the new stand-alone companies can expand in directions where they are no longer hindered by their parent companies.

Split-Offs A *split-off* is the exchange of a parent company's stock for a pro-rata share of the stock of a subsidiary company. Split-offs, which differs from spin-offs, do not occur frequently. In a split-off, shareholders are offered the choice of keeping the shares they own in the existing company or exchanging them for shares in the split-off company. For example, on August 10, 2001, AT&T completed a split-off of Liberty Media Corporation. AT&T redeemed each outstanding share of its class A and class B Liberty Media tracking stock for one share of series A and series B common stock, respectively, from Liberty Media. In a split-off, an exchange of

TABLE 2 - 4

What Are DRIPS?

A *dividend reinvestment plan* (DRIP) allows shareholders to reinvest their dividends in additional stock rather than receiving them in cash. These plans are offered directly by companies or through agents acting on behalf of the corporation. In the former case, a company issues new shares in lieu of cash dividends. You also have the option of purchasing additional shares from the company. The advantage is that you pay no brokerage fees, although some companies charge fees for this service.

The other type of plan is offered by agents, such as banks, that collect the dividends and offer additional shares to shareholders who sign up for the plan. The bank pools the cash from dividends and purchases the stock in the secondary market. Investors are assessed fees, which cover the brokerage commissions and the fee charged by the bank.

The advantage of DRIPs to shareholders is that they act as a forced savings plan; dividends are reinvested automatically to accumulate more shares. This method is particularly good for investors who are not disciplined savers.

A disadvantage of DRIPs is that shareholders need to keep, for tax purposes, accurate records of the additional shares purchased. When additional shares are sold, the purchase price is used to determine whether there is a capital gain or loss. These dividends are considered taxable income whether they are received in cash or automatically reinvested in additional shares. Another disadvantage of DRIPs is that the fees charged to participate in this program can be high.

shares takes place, whereas in a spin-off, shareholders receive additional shares in another company.

Although shareholders obviously benefit from receiving dividends, they also benefit when earnings are not paid out but instead are reinvested in the company. This technique increases the value of the company and hence the value of its stock.

Table 2–4 discusses dividend reinvestment plans for investors wishing to reinvest their dividends directly in the stock of the companies they already own.

CLASSES OF COMMON STOCK

Some corporations issue different classes of common stock that can have different characteristics. For example, Bershire Hathaway, Inc., has class A and class B common stock. One share of class A common stock is convertible (at the option of the shareholder) into 30 shares of class B common stock.

Some companies issue *tracking stocks,* which are a class of shares tied to the performance of a part of the business of the company. A tracking stock is a separate class of stock that tracks the performance of a part of a business within a company. General Motors was the first company to issue this type of share in 1984 and 1985 for its subsidiaries Electronic Data Systems and Hughes Electronics. In 1999, Donaldson, Lufkin & Jenrette (ticker symbol DLJ) issued a tracking stock for its Internet brokerage business DLJ Direct. The Internet brokerage company competed with DLJ for business; this created a potential conflict for the board of directors of DLJ, which served both sets of shareholders. Despite the potential conflicts when the same board of directors serves two sets of shareholders with different interests, several companies (such as General Electric Co., Walt Disney Co., and DuPont Co.) have issued tracking stocks. The other disadvantage for shareholders is that some tracking stocks do not come with voting rights.

The advantages of tracking stocks are that companies retain certain tax advantages, and the tracked businesses are connected to their less risky parent companies. Tracked businesses have the necessary room to conduct their business operations and also have the support of their parent corporations.

TYPES OF COMMON STOCK

Companies have different characteristics that make their stock prices react differently to economic data. Consequently, you should know the types of stocks that you invest in. *Blue-chip stocks* pay dividends, and *growth stocks* generally do not pay dividends. Stocks can be classified into various categories, which is useful for investors because different types of stocks vary with regard to their returns, quality, stability of earnings and dividends, and relationship to the various risks affecting the companies and the market.

Blue-Chip Stocks

Blue-chip stocks refer to companies with a long history of sustained earnings and dividend payments. These established companies have developed leadership positions in their respective industries and, because of their importance and large size, have stable earnings and dividend records. Most companies in the Dow Jones Industrial Average are considered to be blue-chip companies. However, some financially troubled stocks such as AT&T, for example, cut their dividends and were removed from the Dow and replaced with other, more solid companies.

Not all blue-chip companies are the same. For example, Wal-Mart, the largest retailer in the world, pays an annual dividend of $0.88 per share, whereas Merck, the pharmaceutical company, pays an annual dividend of $1.52 per share, and the ExxonMobil annual dividend is $1.40 per share (as of May 2007). Wal-Mart sales and earnings grew rapidly in its early years, during which time it retained its earnings to fuel its growth. In later years it began paying a small dividend. Wal-Mart does not fit into the typical definition of a blue-chip company because it does not pay much of a dividend and has not had a long history of paying out dividends. Merck and ExxonMobil historically also have had growing sales and earnings, but they have elected to pay out a higher percentage of their earnings in dividends and have longer histories of paying dividends.

Blue-chip companies appeal to investors who seek quality companies with histories of growing profits and regular dividend payouts. These types of companies tend to be less risky in periods of economic uncertainty because of their dependable earnings. In bear markets, the stock prices of blue-chip companies tend to decline less than those of growth companies that do not pay dividends. Investors are attracted to blue-chip stocks because they not only provide a store of wealth in anticipation of capital appreciation but also deliver regular dividend income.

Income Stocks

Income stocks have high dividend payouts, and the companies are typically in the mature stages of their industry life cycles. Stocks of companies that have established a pattern of paying higher-than-average dividends can be defined as income stocks. Income stocks tend not to appreciate in price as much as blue-chip stocks do because income stock companies are more mature and are not growing as quickly as are blue-chip companies. This statement does not mean that income stock companies are not profitable or are about to go out of business. On the contrary, they have stable earnings and cash flow, but they choose to pay out much higher ratios of their earnings in dividends than other companies do. Utility companies and real estate investment trusts (REITs) are examples of income stocks. American Electric Power (ticker symbol AEP) has a current dividend of $1.56 and a dividend yield of 3.2 percent; Ameren Corporation (ticker symbol AEE) has a current dividend of $1.52 and a dividend yield of 4.7 percent; and NiSource (ticker symbol NI) has a current dividend of $0.92 and a dividend yield of 3.7 percent. These dividends and dividend yields, quoted as of May 11, 2007, were based on the stock prices on that day. The average dividend yield for stocks on the S&P 500 Index was 1.81 percent over the same period. REITs are also classified as income stocks because they are required to pass on most of their earnings to shareholders because they are pass-through entities for tax purposes.

Growth Stocks

Growth stocks are issued by companies expected to have sustained high rates of growth in sales and earnings. These companies generally have high price/earnings (P/E) ratios and do not pay dividends. Companies such as Home Depot (ticker symbol HD) and Intel (ticker symbol INTC) grew at high double digits rates during the 1990s; the growth in these companies was curtailed shortly after that for different reasons. Home Depot faced increased competition from Lowe's, which has newer, smaller, and more manageable stores. Intel saw sharp declines in its sales because of reductions in capital equipment spending by business, a decline in computer replacement sales by consumers, and increased competition from Advanced Micro Devices. Nevertheless, Intel still managed to keep its gross profit margins above 50 percent for most quarters during the first half of the 2000 decade.

An indication that these two companies have passed through their sustained high-growth periods is that they no longer retain all their earnings. Both pay out small amounts of their earnings in dividends. In addition, because of their leadership positions in their respective industries, they also could be classified as blue-chip companies. Most growth companies pay no dividends, such as Cisco Systems (ticker symbol CSCO), which saw annual sales growth in the 30 to 50 percent range during the 1990's technology boom. Cisco's stock price soared around 130,000 percent from its initial public offering (IPO) in February 1990 to March 2000. Cisco expects growth to continue in the high single digits to low teens for revenue and earnings over the next five years. Rather than pay out their earnings in dividends, growth companies retain their earnings and reinvest them in the expansion of their businesses. Google is a good example of a growth company with a price-to-earnings ratio of 71. Investors are willing to buy Google at $404 per share, paying 71 times earnings of $5.70 per share.

Growth stocks are often referred to as *high P/E ratio stocks* because their greater growth prospects make investors more willing to buy them at higher prices. Investors do not receive returns in the form of dividends, so they buy these stocks for their potential capital appreciation.

Value Stocks

Value stocks are stocks that have lower prices relative to their fundamental values (growth in sales and earnings). Value stocks tend to have low P/E ratios, low price-to-book ratios, low price-to-sales ratios, and high dividend yields, and they also may be out of favor with investors. One reason might be disappointing quarterly earnings. For example, at the end of the economic expansion period, auto companies trade at lower P/E ratios than the stocks of other companies because investors' expectations for the companies' growth prospects are low. Because investors have relatively low expectations for the immediate growth of these companies, their stocks trade at lower prices relative to their earnings and dividends. Patient investors with longer time horizons are willing to purchase these stocks and wait for their prospective earnings to increase.

Table 2–5 compares some of the characteristics of growth stocks and value stocks. Investors are willing to pay 71 times earnings for Google, Inc., because of its potential future sales and earnings growth. Cisco had similar growth rates to Google in the late 1990s, but growth

TABLE 2-5

Characteristics of Growth and Value Stocks

Company	Symbol	Stock Price*	P/E Ratio	1-year Earnings Growth	5-year Earnings Growth	Dividends per Share
Growth stocks						
Cisco Systems, Inc	CSCO	$19	22	13%	14.7%	$0
Google Inc.	GOOG	$404	71	37%	33.2%	0
Starbucks	SBUX	$35	51	18%	8%	0
Value stocks						
Citigroup	C	$47	9.8	8.3%	8%	$1.96
D.R. Horton	DHI	$23	4.7	−4.66%	15%	0.40
ExxonMobil	XOM	$60	10	5.6%	7.3%	1.28

*Prices as of June 28, 2006

rates have stabilized, resulting in a decline in price from $40 per share to $19. Starbucks Corporation is also seeing a slowdown in its growth rate, resulting in a decline in its P/E ratio from 63 to 51 over the past two years. What you need to be aware of is that if growth stocks cannot sustain their high growth rates, their stock prices fall by amounts greater than the corresponding fall of value stocks.

The potential strengths of value stocks are not always evident or visible. D. R. Horton, Inc., a home builder, was trading at a low P/E ratio because of rising interest rates, which accounted for the decline in earnings growth for the next year. Patient investors with a five-year time horizon would find value in this stock with a projected 15 percent growth rate over the next five years. Citigroup's stock price was supported by a dividend of $1.96 per share (close to a 4 percent yield), which protected the stock's decline in price owing to rising interest rates. Value investors are interested in stocks whose prices are trading at less than their intrinsic value and are willing to buy stocks of companies experiencing temporary setbacks in the hope that they will overcome their earnings and asset valuation setbacks. Table 2–6 shows how you can use the Internet to find value and growth stocks.

Cyclical Stocks

Cyclical stock prices move with the economy. Cyclical stocks often reach their high and low points before the respective peaks and troughs of the economy. When the economy is in recession, these stocks see a decline in sales and earnings. During periods of expansion, these stocks grow substantially in sales and earnings. Examples of cyclical stocks are stocks issued by capital equipment companies, home builders, auto companies, and companies in other sectors tied to the fortunes of the economy as a whole. The economic growth in 2005–2006 has seen the stocks of John Deere (ticker symbol DE), the farm equipment maker, and Cummins Engine (ticker symbol CMI),

TABLE 2-6

How to Use the Internet to Find Value and Growth Stocks

Use a stock screener on www.finance.yahoo.com or www.moneycentral.msn.com to see a list of some current growth and value stocks. For growth stocks, enter *higher P/E ratios* and *higher earnings per share growth* estimates. For value stocks, enter *lower P/E ratios* and *lower earnings per share growth* estimates.

the diesel engine manufacturer, rise to their 52-week highs. During a recession, stocks of this type are beaten down and are considered value stocks for patient investors who are willing to buy them and hold them until the next economic turnaround. Cyclical stocks appeal to investors who like to trade actively by moving in and out of stocks as the economy moves through its cycle.

Defensive Stocks

Defensive stocks are the stocks of companies that tend to hold their price levels when the economy declines. Generally, these stocks resist downturns in the economy because these companies produce necessary goods (food, beverages, and pharmaceutical products). However, during periods of economic expansion, defensive stocks move up more slowly than other types of stocks. Defensive stocks are the stocks of companies whose prices are expected to remain stable or do well when the economy declines because they are immune to changes in the economy and are not affected by downturns in the business cycle. Examples of stocks of this type are drug companies, food and beverage companies, utility companies, consumer goods companies, and even auto parts manufacturers. In a recession, people generally wait to replace their cars and are more likely to spend money to repair them. Similarly, during periods of inflation, the prices of gold stocks tend to rise. Drug companies have predictable earnings, which puts them in the defensive category and also the growth stock category because of their pipelines of new drugs. If the economy goes into a deflationary environment, the stocks of some supermarket chains, which are viewed as defensive-type stocks, might fall out of this category because supermarket chains generally have low profit margins and cannot pass higher prices on to consumers.

Many investors buy defensive stocks ahead of an economic downturn and hold them until better economic times.

Speculative Stocks

Speculative stocks have the potential for above-average returns, but they also carry above-average risk of loss if the company does poorly or goes bankrupt. Speculative stocks are stocks issued by companies that have a small probability for large increases in the prices of their stocks. These companies do not have earnings records and are considered to have a high degree of risk. In other words, these companies are quite likely to incur losses and not as likely to experience profits, so they have a higher possibility of larger price gains or losses than other types of stocks. Speculative stocks are more volatile than the other stock types.

Speculative stocks are often issued by new companies with promising ideas that are in the development stages. With oil above $70 per barrel in 2006, the stocks of many alternative energy companies with low sales and no earnings rose to high prices with investors speculating on their potential relevance in providing alternative sources of energy.

The requisite quality for buying speculative stocks, because of their high risk, is a strong stomach—you have to be able to sleep well at night under any circumstances. These stocks deliver either large capital gains or large capital losses.

Penny Stocks

Penny stocks are speculative, low-priced stocks that generally trade on the over-the-counter markets and pink sheets. [The pink sheets provide the listings, the quotes (bid and ask) of the lower-priced, thinly traded over-the-counter domestic stocks and foreign stocks.] Penny stocks are low-priced stocks ($1 or less) in companies whose future operations are in doubt. "Boiler room" (illegal) sales operators have promoted some penny stocks by cold calling unsophisticated investors on the telephone to stress how much money they could make by buying these low-priced stocks. To paraphrase the old saying, "There are no free lunches on Wall Street." If a share is trading at 25 cents per share, it is probably trading at its fair value and for good reason. If the stock goes up to 50 cents, an investor makes a 100 percent return; if the company goes out of business, the investor loses his or her entire investment.

Foreign Stocks

Foreign stocks are stocks issued by companies outside the country of origin. Although the U.S. stock markets still account for the largest market capitalization of all the stock markets in the world, the foreign stock markets are growing in market share. Foreign stocks provide you with the opportunity to earn greater returns and to diversify your portfolio. You can buy foreign stocks directly in the foreign markets or buy American depository receipts of the stocks of foreign companies. An *American depository receipt* (ADR) is a negotiable receipt on stocks held in custody abroad. These receipts

TABLE 2-7

Foreign ADR Stocks

Company	Symbol	Price*	Country	Exchange
Sony Corporation	SNE	$38.41	Japan	NYSE
Royal Dutch Petroleum	RD	$56.97	Holland	NYSE
ASML Holding NV	ASML	$15.76	Holland	Nasdaq
Nokia Corporation	NOK	$15.80	Finland	NYSE

* Prices are as of July 5, 2006.

are traded in place of foreign stocks. Many large foreign companies trade as ADRs on the U.S. markets (New York Stock Exchange and the over-the-counter market). Table 2–7 provides an example of some of the foreign stocks trading as ADRs on the U.S. markets.

Large-, Medium-, and Small-Cap Stocks

Stocks also can be classified by size: small-cap stocks, medium-cap stocks, and large-cap stocks. *Cap* is short for "market capitalization," which is the market value of a company (determined by multiplying the company's stock price in the market by the number of outstanding shares). Market capitalization changes all the time, and although the definitions include a market value for each category, these market value threshold classifications also change over time. Below are the differentiating values for the groupings of companies by size:

Large-cap stocks are the stocks of large companies with considerable earnings and large amounts of common stock outstanding. This group has a market capitalization of greater than $5 billion. Large-cap stocks represent the companies in the Dow Jones Industrial Average and the S&P 500 Index. These large-cap companies account for more than half the total value of the U.S. equity markets. These are blue-chip, established companies that can be either growth or value companies. Some examples are Intel, Microsoft, IBM, General Motors, ExxonMobil, and many other large leading companies in their respective industries.

Medium-cap stocks are the stocks of medium-sized companies with market capitalizations of between $1 billion and $5 billion. Medium-cap companies have the safety net of having significant assets in terms of their capitalization, but they also may not be so well known to average investors. Some examples of well-known medium-cap companies are Tyson Foods, Outback Steakhouse, Starbucks, and Borders.

Small-cap stocks are the stocks of small-sized companies with a market capitalization of less than $1 billion. Small-cap companies generally are not household names, although they offer the most attractive return opportunities. This group of stocks has, according to studies, outperformed the large-cap stocks over long periods. Small-cap stock prices tend to be more volatile than those of large- and medium-cap companies because of their greater exposure to risk. Some small-cap companies are potentially the Intels and Microsofts of tomorrow. Many small-cap companies go out of business, whereas others are successful and grow to become medium- and large-cap companies. Because small-cap stocks are riskier investments, you should diversify your holdings of them to reduce your overall risk of loss.

Figure 2–1 shows how small-cap and foreign stocks outperformed medium- and large-cap stocks for the year ended March 31, 2006. For the same-period, medium-cap growth stocks outperformed medium-cap value stocks. The strategies for which types of stocks to choose are discussed in Chapters 10, 11, and 12.

What also becomes apparent from these classifications of common stock types is that a company can have multiple classifications. The pharmaceutical company Johnson & Johnson can be classified as a blue-chip stock, a growth stock, a large cap-stock, and a defensive stock. These classifications are useful when you plan your portfolio

FIGURE 2-1

Total Returns of the Russell 2000 Index (Small-Cap), S&P 400 Index (Medium-Cap), S&P 500 Index (Large-Cap), MSCI EAFE Index (Foreign Stocks), Medium-Cap Value and Medium-Cap Growth for the Year Ended March 31, 2006.

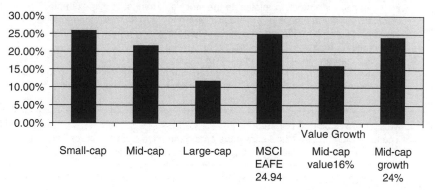

to determine which types of stocks you want to own and the
percentage of each that you want to hold in your portfolio.

HOW TO READ COMMON STOCK QUOTATIONS

Table 2–8 shows how to read common stock quotations.

TABLE 2-8

How to Read Common Stock Quotations

The format for reading stock price quotations is much the same for stocks listed on
the New York Stock Exchange (NYSE), the American Stock Exchange (AMEX),
and the Nasdaq. The amount of company information listed varies somewhat; the
listing of NYSE companies is the most comprehensive. Market prices of listed
stocks are quoted daily in the financial pages of major newspapers. For example,
a typical listing of a common stock from the financial pages looks like this:

365-Day High	Low	Stock	Sym	Div	Yld., %	P/E	Vol, 100s	Close	Net Chg.
53.15	44.67	General Mills	GIS	1.40	2.7	18	27645	51.95	0.08

As of July 6, 2006.

The following list describes what is in the example, from left to right across the
columns:

- The "High" and "Low" columns indicate the yearly range of trading of the stock. General
  Mills traded at a 365-day high of $53.15 per share and a low of $44.67 per share.
- The "Stock" column shows the name of the stock, General Mills Company, and the
  "Sym" column shows that its trading symbol is GIS.
- The "Div" column indicates the amount of the annual dividend, $1.40 per share.
  A corporation might, from time to time, change the amount of dividends it pays
  based on its last quarterly or semiannual dividend payment.
- The "Yld" column is the *dividend yield* for General Mills, which is 2.7 percent. You
  can calculate the yield by dividing the expected dividend by the last, or closing,
  price of the stock (1.40/51.95).
- The "P/E" column is the price-earnings ratio and indicates the price investors are
  willing to pay for a stock in relation to the stock's earnings. In this example,
  investors buying the stock at $51.95 are willing to pay 18 times General Mills'
  earnings. High P/E ratios indicate that buyers are willing to pay more for a dollar of
  earnings than for low P/E ratio stocks.
- The "Vol" column indicates the number of shares traded for that day. In this case,
  2,764,500 shares of General Mills were traded that day. By following the average
  daily volume, you can tell if any unusually heavy trading activity has taken place
  on a particular day.
- The "Close" column indicates the closing price of the stock for that day. General
  Mills closed at $51.95 per share.
- The last column, "Net Chg," shows the change in price from the preceding day.
  In this case, General Mills closed up $0.08 from the preceding day's close.

CHAPTER 3

Preferred Stocks

KEY CONCEPTS

- What preferred stock is
- Reasons to invest in preferred stock
- Characteristics of preferred stock
- How to evaluate preferred stock
- Trust preferred stock derivatives

Investment Snapshot

- Preferred stock yields can be three to four times greater than common stock yields.
- Preferred stocks bear a greater resemblance to bonds than common stocks.
- Not all preferred stock issues share the tax advantages of common stocks.
- Chesapeake Energy Corporation issued a mandatory convertible preferred stock offering with a dividend yield of 6.25 percent.

The Investment Snapshot shows that preferred stocks appeal to investors seeking current income because of their higher yields over common stocks. In order to share in the lower federal tax rates on dividends, investors need to make sure that the preferred issues they purchase qualify for the lower tax rates. Convertible preferred stock can earn shareholders capital appreciation should the price of the common stock of the company rise above the conversion price.

WHAT IS PREFERRED STOCK?

Preferred stock is classified on a balance sheet as equity, but it has many features that resemble debt securities. *Equity* is defined as capital invested in a company by its owners; *debt* is capital lent to the corporation, which must be repaid. Preferred stock is a hybrid type of security in that it has characteristics resembling both debt and equity. Generally, preferred stocks have a fixed dividend, but owners of preferred stock do not have voting rights. Although preferred stock is classified as equity, preferred stockholders do not have ownership interests in the company. The failure of a company to pay dividends to preferred stockholders does not result in bankruptcy, as it would with the default of interest on bonds. Instead, the company does not pay common stockholders any dividends until the preferred stockholders are paid their dividends. Unlike common stock, the dividend rate on preferred stock is usually fixed. It might be stated as a percentage of the par value of the preferred stock or as a fixed dollar amount. The *par* value is a stated value, and hence a preferred stock issue with $100 par value that has a dividend of 8 percent would pay a dividend of $8 per share (8 percent of $100).

In the event of bankruptcy, the claims of preferred stockholders are senior to the claims of common stockholders on the earnings and assets of a company. If a preferred stock issue has a call provision, it may be retired by the company.

REASONS TO INVEST IN PREFERRED STOCK

The fixed dividend of preferred stock appeals to investors who seek regular payments of income, but in exchange for regular income, preferred stocks do not experience large capital gains (or losses). The downside to a fixed dividend rate is that the price of preferred stock is sensitive to changes in market rates of interest similar to bonds. For example, if you buy preferred stock for $100 a share that pays a dividend of $4, and market rates of interest subsequently go up to 6 percent, there will be downside pressure on the price of this preferred stock issue. New investors will not want to buy this preferred stock for $100 when the dividend is only $4 (a return of 4 percent, 4/100) and new preferred stock issues return a higher yield. Prices of adjustable-rate preferred stock issues do not fluctuate as much as the prices of fixed-rate preferred stock issues with changes in interest rates. Thus preferred stock is appealing to investors if interest rates remain stable or decrease.

Another advantage to owning preferred stock is the changes to the tax code enacted in 2003. Dividends from preferred stock are taxed at favorable rates, 5 percent for taxpayers in the 15 percent or lower marginal tax brackets and 15 percent for all other taxpayers. However, not all preferred stock issues benefit from this favorable tax treatment. A majority of the preferred stock issues, namely, trust preferred stock issues, do not qualify for this favorable tax treatment These trust preferred stock issues are created by trusts that technically pay interest, and therefore, the payments are taxed at taxpayers' marginal tax rates (can be as high as 35 percent).

CHARACTERISTICS OF PREFERRED STOCK
Multiple Classes of Preferred Stock

Most companies issue one class of common stock, but it is quite common to see companies with more than one series of preferred stock. Table 3–1 lists some of the different preferred stock issues of Citigroup, Inc. (listed on the New York Stock Exchange).

Each class of preferred stock has different features. For example, Citigroup's preferred F series pays a dividend of $3.18 per share with a yield of 6.3 percent at a closing price of $50.25 per share and was down $0.25 from the preceding day's closing price. Citigroup has several *cumulative preferred* stock issues, which give holders the right to receive all missed dividend payments before common shareholders are paid. *Convertible preferred* stock can be converted, by holders, into a fixed number of shares of common stock of the underlying company. A *call provision* gives the issuing company the right to call the preferred stock at a specific price (normally a premium over its par value). These issues also might be differentiated in their priority status with regard to claims on assets in the event of bankruptcy.

TABLE 3·1

Different Preferred Stock Issues of Citigroup, Inc.

Stock	Div	Yld.	Close	Net Chg.	Type of Stock
Citigroup pfF	3.18	6.3	50.25	−0.25	Cumulative preferred
Citigroup pfH	3.12	6.2	50.35	−0.50	Cumulative preferred
Citigroup pfM	2.93	5.9	49.70	0.40	Cumulative preferred
Citigroup pfS	1.50	6.7	22.39	−0.01	Noncumulative preferred
Citigroup pfV	1.78	7.1	25.07	−0.03	Trust preferred

Prices as of July 6, 2006.

Claims on Income and Assets

Preferred stock has a preference over common stock with regard to claims on both income and assets. Companies are required to pay dividends on preferred stock before they pay dividends to common stockholders. In the event of bankruptcy, preferred stockholders' claims are settled before the claims of common shareholders. This makes preferred stock less risky than common stock but more risky than bonds because bondholders have priority in claims to income and assets over preferred stockholders. Companies must pay the interest on their debt, and in the event of a default, bondholders can force the defaulting corporation into bankruptcy, whereas dividends on preferred stock (and common stock) are declared only at the discretion of the board of directors. In the case of multiple classes of preferred stock, the different issues are prioritized in their claims to income and assets.

Cumulative Dividends

Most preferred stock issues carry a *cumulative feature*, which is a provision requiring a company to pay any preferred dividends that have not been paid in full before the company can pay dividends to its common stockholders. In other words, if the company fails to pay dividends to its cumulative preferred stockholders, it will have to pay all the missed dividends before the company can pay any dividends to its common shareholders. A company that fails to pay its dividends is said to be *in arrears*, which is defined as having outstanding preferred dividends that have not been paid on a cumulative preferred stock issue. Before the company can pay dividends to its common stockholders, it would have to pay the dividends in arrears to its cumulative preferred stockholders first. This cumulative feature protects the rights of preferred stockholders. A preferred issue that does not have a cumulative feature is called a *noncumulative preferred stock*. Dividends on such stock do not accumulate if they are not paid.

Convertible Feature

Some preferred stock issues have a convertible feature that allows holders to exchange their preferred stock for common shares. The conditions and terms of the conversion are set when the preferred stock is issued. The terms include the *conversion ratio,* which is the number of common shares the preferred stockholder will get for each preferred share exchanged, and the *conversion price* of the common stock.

For example, Chesapeake Energy Corporation issued a mandatory convertible preferred stock issue that will automatically convert on June 15, 2009, into a range of Chesapeake's common stock (no fewer than 7.1715 shares of Chesapeake's common stock and no more than 8.6059 shares depending on the then market price of Chesapeake's common stock). If the price of Chesapeake's common stock rises above the conversion price before June 15, 2009, holders can convert at their option.

The decision to exercise the conversion option depends on three factors:

- *The market price of the common stock.* It must be greater than the conversion price for the holder to share in capital gains.
- *The amount of the preferred dividend.*
- *The amount of the common dividend.*

The conversion feature provides the investor with the possibility of sharing in the capital gains through the appreciation of the common stock, as well as the relative safety of receiving the preferred dividends before conversion. If the preferred dividend is much greater than the common dividend, holders would weigh this into the amount of the appreciation as to whether to hold the preferred stock or convert to common stock.

Call Provision

A preferred stock issue with a *call provision* entitles the issuing company to repurchase the stock at its option from outstanding preferred stockholders. The call price generally is more than the preferred stock's par value.

The call provision is advantageous to the issuing company and not to the holder of the preferred stock. When market rates of interest decline significantly below the dividend yield of the preferred issue, companies are more likely to exercise the call provision by retiring the issue and replacing it with a new preferred stock issue with a lower dividend yield. Citigroup redeemed for cash all the outstanding shares of its 8.4 cumulative preferred stock series K at a redemption price of $25 per share plus accrued dividends in October 2001. In January 2003, Citigroup called in its adjustable-rate cumulative preferred stock series Q and series R for a cash price of $25 per share plus accrued dividends.

When a preferred issue is called, the savings to the issuing company represents a loss of income to preferred stockholders. Thus not only do preferred stockholders suffer a loss of income when their high-dividend-rate preferred stock issues are called in, but the call provision also acts as a ceiling limit on the price appreciation of the preferred stock. When interest rates decline, there is an upward push on the price of high-dividend-rate preferred stock issues, but the price of the preferred stock will not rise above the call price. For example, if a preferred stock issue has a call price of $55, potential buyers of the preferred stock would be unlikely to pay more than this amount when interest rates decline significantly. This is so because investors who pay more than this ceiling price would lose money if the issue were called.

To entice investors to buy preferred stock issues during periods of high interest rates, companies include a *call protection* feature. This prevents the company from calling the issue for a period of time, generally five years, but this varies. After the call protection period, the issue is callable at the stated call price per share.

Participating or Nonparticipating

Participating preferred issues allow holders to receive additional dividends (over and above regular dividends) if they are declared by the board of directors. These additional dividends generally are less than the extra amounts paid to common shareholders. The majority of preferred stocks are *nonparticipating.*

HOW TO EVALUATE PREFERRED STOCK

Investors invest in preferred stock primarily for the dividends, but dividends can be suspended by the board of directors. Therefore, it is important to understand the type of business the company is in and whether the company can earn enough cash to cover its dividend payments. When you find a company's preferred stock you are interested in, read the preferred stock prospectus (usually a 423B prospectus filing).

Most preferred stock issues are rated by rating agencies such as Standard & Poor's, Moody's, Fitch, or Duff & Phelps. The rating categories are slightly different from those for bonds. Ratings above B are considered to be investment grade, with AAA being higher than AA and A. Below B are considered to be speculative or junk.

Before investing in preferred stock, compare the yield (dividend divided by the stock price) of the preferred stock with the yield of comparable bonds. The yield of the preferred stock should be higher than the yield of comparable bonds.

Most preferred stock issues do not benefit shareholders from the lower federal tax dividend treatment. Check that the issue you are interested in purchasing qualifies for the favorable tax rate on dividends. If the issue is a preferred trust stock or a derivative, it does not qualify for the lower tax rates on dividend income for investors.

TRUST PREFERRED STOCKS

There is very little difference (other than the tax treatment) for investors in whether they invest in a regular stock issue or a trust preferred stock issue, but for issuers, there is a considerable difference. Issuers of trust preferred stock issues gain the tax advantages of being able to deduct the interest payments on the subordinated debt, thereby negating the favorable tax treatment on dividends for preferred trust shareholders. Of the Citigroup preferred stock listed in Table 3–1, Citigroup's preferred V series is a trust preferred stock. This is how preferred trust stocks work:

- A bank holding company forms a wholly owned trust which sells the trust preferred stock issue to investors. The proceeds from the sale of the trust preferred stock is used by the trust to purchase the subordinated debt issue of the bank holding company. The terms of the subordinated debt issue and trust preferred stock issue are identical.
- The bank holding company deducts the interest payments on the subordinated debt as well as the dividend payments from taxes. In order to qualify for the latter, the trust preferred issue must have a cumulative feature.
- When the financial statements are consolidated, the subordinated debt is eliminated, and the trust preferred stock is shown as "minority interest in equity accounts of consolidated subsidiaries" on the bank holding company balance sheet.

Trust Preferred Derivatives

There are different trust preferred issues with different names depending on the sponsor or investment bank, each with its own acronym: monthly income preferred shares (MIPS), trust-originated preferred shares (TOPrS), quarterly income debt securities (QUIDS), quarterly income preferred shares (QUIPS), and corporate-backed trust securities (Corts).

The common features of these securities are as follows:

- They have a par value of $25 instead of the traditional $1,000 par for a bond.
- They are listed on the stock exchanges as opposed to the bond exchanges or over-the-counter markets.
- They pay regular interest.
- Most have a maturity date. There are some issues that are perpetual, like common stock.
- Many of these issues have call provisions.

Generally, these are easier to buy than regular preferred stocks and bonds because they are listed on the stock exchanges, where prices are available, and they do not require as large a capital outlay as bonds with the lower par value. Table 3–2 lists some of these securities.

TABLE 3-2

Trust Preferred Derivative Preferred Stocks

Stock	Symbol	Div	Yld	Close	Net Chg
Cort JC Penney	KTP	1.91	7.5%	25.58	0.18
Cabco JC Penney	PFH	1.91	7.6%	25.26	0.06

The first of the issues listed is JC Penney's corporate-backed trust securities (Corts) with a coupon of 7.625 and maturity on March 1, 2097. The closing price of this issue as of July 2006 was $25.58, which is a slight premium to its par value. The rating of this trust preferred issue is the same as the JC Penney 7.5/8 percent bonds in the trust. There is a call provision for this issue that puts a ceiling on the appreciation of the issue when interest rates decline. If this issue is bought at $25.58 per share and held to maturity in the year 2097, the yield to maturity will be 7.5 percent.

JC Penney's corporate asset–backed corporate (Cabco) securities also were issued with a 7.625 percent yield and trade under the ticker symbol PFH, pay a dividend of $1.91, and were trading at $25.26 per share. In the early years of 2000, JC Penney was not as financially sound as it is in 2006, and its Cabco securities were listed as junk bonds.

There are some caveats that investors should be aware of:

- Be cautious when paying a premium for an issue with a call provision. If the issue is called, you will receive the par value, $25, or the call price, which means that you can lose some of your capital.
- These companies can suspend their dividends during times of financial hardship.
- Companies with balance sheets that may be overleveraged might use this type of security to raise funds. Consequently, you should look for issues with strong credit ratings.

Preferred and trust preferred stock issues appeal to investors seeking income and sacrifice the potential for long-term growth through capital gains.

Understanding the Risks of Investing in Stocks

KEY CONCEPTS

- Types of investment risk and what you can do about risk
- The relationship between risk and return
- Measures of risk
- What you can do about risk

Investment Snapshot

- The greatest risk of investment in common stock is losing your entire investment.
- Historically, the volatility of common stocks is highest over a one-year holding period and declines as the length of the holding period increases.
- Holding a diversified portfolio of common stocks over long holding periods reduces the risk of loss significantly.

From the Investment Snapshot you might think that investing in common stocks is the same as gambling. Yes, you can invest in a stock that goes bankrupt and lose your investment, such as the case for shareholders of Enron and the original WorldCom. However, you also could have invested in Hansen Natural, whose stock price increased by 293 percent over the one-year period from

June of 2005 to June of 2006. Over long periods of time, investments in a diversified portfolio of common stocks have earned positive returns, whereas long-term gambling results in negative returns. Understanding what the risks of investing in common stocks are and what you can do about them will help you to manage your investments to earn positive returns. In essence, your objectives, personal characteristics, and time frame outline the level of risk you can absorb, which then determines the choice of investments to make.

TYPES OF INVESTMENT RISK AND WHAT YOU CAN DO ABOUT RISK

Risk is defined as the variability of returns from an investment. Risk is the uncertainty related to the outcome of an investment, and all investments are subject to risk of one type or another. The greater the variability in the price, the greater is the level of risk. Understanding the risks associated with different securities is critical to building a strong portfolio. Risk is probably what deters many investors from investing in stocks and prompts them to keep their money in so-called safe bank accounts, CDs, and bonds. Returns from these passive savings vehicles often have lagged the rate of inflation. Although investors will not lose their capital, they risk losses in earnings owing to inflation and taxes when they merely hold cash and cash equivalents.

Business Risk

Business risk is the uncertainty that pertains to a company's sales and earnings, namely, that a company generates poor sales and earnings for a period of time. By their nature, some companies are riskier than others, and the riskier companies see greater fluctuations in their sales and earnings. If a company's sales and earnings decline significantly, its stocks experience downward pressure. Deterioration in sales and earnings, at worst, could move the company into bankruptcy, which would make its securities (stocks and bonds) worthless. A company with stable sales does not have this problem of not being able to cover its regular expenses.

Investors' expectations of a company's earnings affect the prices of its stocks. Shareholders who anticipate a decline in earnings will sell their shares, which can cause a decline in the stock's price. Similarly, if investors anticipate an increase in earnings, they are willing to pay higher prices for the stock.

Common stocks of auto, home building, construction, and durable goods companies are referred to as *cyclical stocks*, and their earnings and stock prices move directly up and down with the expansion and contraction of the economy. Business risk for a cyclical company increases when changes in the economy result in reduced consumer or business spending for that company's products. This occurred in 2001 and 2002 when the telecommunications equipment sector (companies such as Lucent, Nortel Networks, and Ciena) experienced a downturn owing to an economic recession, which caused the telecom companies (AT&T, Sprint, and WorldCom) to reduce their spending on new equipment.

By investing in the common stocks of companies with stable earnings rather than those of cyclical companies, you can reduce business risk. *Stable stock* is the stock of a company whose earnings are not influenced by changes in the activity of the economy. Some examples are electric utility and consumer goods companies.

Financial Risk

Financial risk is the inability of a company to meet its financial obligations, and the extent of a company's financial risk is measured by the amount of debt the company holds in relation to its equity. A company with a high proportion of debt relative to its assets has an increased likelihood that at some point in time it may be unable to meet its principal and interest obligations. The greater the debt-to-equity ratio, the higher is the financial risk because the company will need to earn at least enough to pay back its fixed-interest and principal payments. When a company carries a high ratio of debt to equity, the company becomes a *default risk* (*credit risk*). In addition to financial risk, business risk also can increase default risk.

Companies that have little or no debt have little or no financial risk. Looking at a company's balance sheet reveals the amount of debt relative to total assets and equity. At worst, financial risk, like business risk, can lead a company to bankruptcy, making the securities worthless. To reduce financial risk, invest in the securities of companies with low debt-to-equity or low debt-to-total-asset ratios. Table 4–1 lists the steps to determine the financial risk for a company using the Internet. Figure 4–1 shows the categories of total risk, which can be broken down into unsystematic and systematic risk.

TABLE 4-1

How to Determine the Financial Risk of a Company Using the Internet to Obtain the Information

You can determine the financial risk of companies that interest you by reviewing their financial statements using the Internet.

1. Go to www.yahoo.com and click on "Finance."

2. In the Enter Symbol(s) box, type the ticker symbols of the company or companies that you want to research. If you want to know the financial risk of General Electric Company, Intel Corporation, and Applied Materials, Inc., type "GE, INTC, AMAT." Make sure to separate each symbol with a comma. If you do not know the symbol for a company, click "Symbol Lookup."

3. Click the "Summary" view.

4. Click "Profile" for information on that company.

5. In the left column, click "Income Statement" in the Financials section. A screen with an income statement appears. Look for "Earnings before interest and taxes" (operating income) and "Interest expense" for the year (or quarter). Determine the company's coverage of its interest expense as follows:

    Coverage ratio = earnings before interest and taxes/interest expense

    Low coverage indicates that a sales decrease or an operating expense increase may result in the company being unable to meet its interest payments.

6. Go to the left of the screen and click on "Balance Sheet." Scroll down to "Liabilities," and add the total current and long-term liabilities. Look for the "Total Assets," and determine the debt ratio for the year or quarter as follows:

    Debt ratio = total current and long-term liabilities/total assets

    A large debt ratio with low coverage indicates high financial risk.

7. Evaluate the financial risk for each of the companies that you researched.

FIGURE 4-1

Breakdown of Total Risk

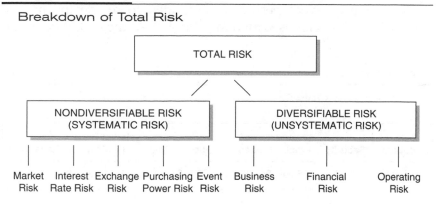

Unsystematic risk is the risk specific to a company or industry. This risk pertains to a company's business, its operations, and its finances. *Operating risk* refers to contingent risks such as the death of a CEO, a labor strike, or litigation. Unsystematic risk is also known as *diversifiable risk.*

Systematic risk is caused by factors that affect all securities. Systematic risk includes risks external to the company such as market risk, event risk, interest-rate risk, exchange-rate risk, liquidity risk, and purchasing-power risk. You cannot reduce market risk through diversification.

Alleviating Business and Financial Risk

You can lessen your exposure to business and financial risk in your portfolio of investments through *diversification*, which refers to the purchase of different investment assets whose returns are unrelated. By building a diversified portfolio, you reduce the variability in returns (risk).

For example, if you invested your savings of $1 million in the common stock of Intel Corporation on July 15, 2005, at $28.30 per share, a year later your loss would have been 37 percent of your investment. Intel stock fell to $17.88 per share. Intel's stock performance was dismal when compared with the market for the same period, July 15, 2005 to July 14, 2006. The Dow Jones Industrial Average (DJIA) increased by 1 percent, the Standard & Poor's (S&P) 500 Index increased by 1 percent, and the Nasdaq Composite Index was down by 6 percent for the same one-year period. Table 4–2 shows the loss in a portfolio with an investment in Intel Corporation's stock.

Suppose that instead of investing the entire $1 million in Intel stock for the one-year period, you decided to divide the money equally into 10 stocks, as shown in Table 4–3. At the end of the same

TABLE 4-2

Portfolio with Only One Stock

Date Bought	Security	Share Price	No. of Shares	Symbol	Cost	Market Price (7/14/06)	Loss
7/15/05	Intel	$28.30	35,335	INTC	$1 million	$631,802	($368,198)

TABLE 4-3

Portfolio with 10 Stocks

Transaction (7/15/05)	Stock Price	Symbol	Cost	Stock Price 7/14/06	Market Value	Gain/ Loss
Buy 1,544 shares Boeing	$64.75	BA	$100,000	$77.25	$119,305	**$19,305**
Buy 1,572 shares Johnson & Johnson	$63.60	JNJ	$100,000	$60.46	$95,063	**($4,937)**
Buy 1,803 shares PepsiCo	$55.45	PEP	$100,000	$61.80	$111,452	**$11,452**
Buy 1,685 shares Conoco Philips	$59.35	COP	$100,000	$67.45	$113,648	**$13,648**
Buy 2,123 shares Walgreens	$47.10	WAG	$100,000	$45.99	$97,643	**($2,357)**
Buy 3,533 shares Intel	$28.30	INTC	$100,000	$17.88	$63,170	**($36,830)**
Buy 922 shares Goldman Sachs	$108.50	GS	$100,000	$140.10	$129,172	**$29,172**
Buy 2,154 shares Citigroup	$46.42	C	$100,000	$47.58	$102,512	**$2,512**
Buy 3,614 shares BHP Billiton	$27.67	BHP	$100,000	$42.20	$155,000	**$55,000**
Buy 2,675 shares Ingersol Rand	$37.39	IR	$100,000	$37.24	$99,643	**($357)**
TOTAL			$1 million		$1,086,608	**$86,608**

one-year period, your diversified portfolio would have increased by 8.6 percent as opposed to the loss of 37 percent from investing the entire amount in Intel. The gains in the portfolio came from aerospace, beverage, oil, financial, and mining stocks (Boeing, Conoco-Philips, Goldman Sachs, Citigroup, BHP Billiton, and PepsiCo). The largest loss was from Intel in the technology sector of the economy.

The importance of diversification can be looked at another way. With a portfolio consisting of one stock, a 50 percent decline in that stock results in a 50 percent decline in the total value. In a portfolio of 10 stocks with equal amounts invested in each stock, a decline of 50 percent in one stock's value, results in a 5 percent decline in the total value. Thus too few stocks in a portfolio means that you have too much risk placed on each stock. Too many stocks in a portfolio dilutes the potential upside appreciation in the total value of the portfolio.

Investing in a number of stocks from different sectors of the economy rather than investing in one stock the risk of loss decreases. The returns on stocks from different sectors of the economy are not perfectly correlated, thereby reducing the variability in the returns. For example, the two financial stocks in the portfolio, Citigroup and Goldman Sachs, have returns that generally move together, a high correlation. Stocks from different sectors of the economy have returns that are not related; they have a low or negative correlation. By increasing the number of stocks in your portfolio to 30 or 40 that have low or negative correlations, you can effectively eliminate all company-related risks. Thus, of the total risk, you can reduce unsystematic risk (operating, business, and financial risk) through diversification.

Market Risk

Market risk refers to the movement of security prices, which tend to move together in reaction to external events that are unrelated to a company's fundamentals. Market risk is the risk that market pressures will cause an investment to fluctuate in value. Although you can diversify investments to virtually eliminate business, financial, and operating risks, you cannot do the same with market risk. Diversification does not provide a safety net when an external event causes a landslide in the stock markets. For example, when the stock market goes up, most stocks go up in price, including those with less-than-spectacular sales, growth, and earnings. Similarly, if a sell-off occurs in the stock market, stocks with better-than-average sales, growth, and earnings will be included in the downslide.

External events that move stock prices are unpredictable. Such an event could be a terrorist incident or news of a war, death of a prominent leader of a foreign nation, changes in the inflation rate, labor strikes, or floods in the Midwest. Investors have no control over these volatile, short-term fluctuations in stock prices.

Over long periods of time, however, stock prices tend to appreciate in relation to their intrinsic value (their growth and earnings). In other words, a stock's long-term returns are determined by a company's investment fundamentals. Market risk highlights the dangers for investors who invest short-term money in the stock market. If you need cash when the market has declined, you will need to sell your stocks, which may produce a loss. For stock investments, you should have a long time horizon so that you are not forced to sell in down markets.

Reducing Market Risk

Investors cannot do much about the volatility of the markets with a short time horizon because the risk of potential loss is high with stocks and other real investment assets. Stocks are more volatile in price than bonds. Table 4–4 shows the historic returns of different financial securities over a 78-year period from 1927 through 2005. With a holding period of 78 years, annual returns averaged 10.34 percent for stocks, 5.2 percent for Treasury bonds, and 3.9 percent for Treasury bills. Stocks clearly outperformed bonds and Treasury bills. However, stocks also have the greatest risk, as measured by their standard deviations, and small-cap stocks have greater risk than large-cap stocks. The table illustrates the variability of returns; stocks can range from a gain of 30.64 (10.34 + 20.3) percent to a loss of 9.96 (10.34 – 20.3) percent. The variability of returns for Treasury bonds is considerably less (a range of 11.3 percent gain to a loss of 0.6 percent).

With a short time horizon, the potential risk of loss from investing in stocks increases. Table 4–5 shows historic returns for stocks, bonds, and Treasury bills during the five-year period 1999–2004 and the 10-year period 1995–2004. Large-cap stocks earned negative returns, but small-cap stocks, long-term corporate bonds, and Treasury bills produced positive returns over the five-year period. The significance of this table is that it shows the importance of having long time horizons of greater than five years for stock investments. Large-cap stocks, which carry less risk than small-cap stocks, saw a decline in the five-year holding period,

TABLE 4-4

Historic Returns, 1927–2005

	Return (Risk) (Standard Deviation)
S&P 500 stocks	10.34% (20.3%)
Treasury bonds	5.2% (5.8%)
Treasury bills	3.9% (3.2%)
Inflation	3.9% (4.4%)

TABLE 4-5

Historic Returns during the 5- and 10-Year Periods
1999–2004 and 1995–2004

	5-Year Returns	10-Year Returns
Small-cap stocks	14.3%	16.4%
Large-cap stocks	−2.3%	12.1%
Long-term corporate bonds	10.7%	9.5%
Treasury bills	2.7%	3.9%
Inflation	2.5%	2.4%

whereas when the holding period is increased to 10 years, both large- and small-cap stocks outperform bonds. When inflation is factored into returns, risk, as measured by the standard deviation, is lower for stocks than bonds and Treasury bills with holding periods of greater than 30 years (Siegel, 2002, p. 32).

The risk of loss through market risk is reduced further with a 20-year holding period, which is not all that long when looked at in terms of the average life expectancy, which is more than 80 years in the United States. The long time horizon for retirement funds is suitable for stock investments.

Another factor that improves overall returns over a long holding period is the reinvestment of dividends and capital gains. Using asset allocation to choose a balanced portfolio of different investments also reduces the effects of market risk, as shown in Table 4–6. A mix of half large-cap stocks and government bonds would have returned less than stocks alone, but the risk of loss is reduced. The lowest five-year return for this mix over the 74-year period was −3.2 percent for bonds and stocks versus −12.5 percent for large-cap stocks. Bond markets, stock markets, and money

TABLE 4-6

Historic Returns from Asset Allocation, 1926–2000

	Return	Greatest 5-Year Return	Minimum 5-Year Return
100% large-cap stocks	11%	28.6%	−12.5%
50% bonds, 50% large-cap stocks	8.7%	18.5%	−3.2%

markets do not always rise and fall in tandem. During a stock market decline, the bond and real estate markets could be rising, and this provides some form of balance for shorter-term objectives.

Interest-Rate Risk

Interest-rate risk is the rise or fall in interest rates that affects the market value of investments. Interest-rate risk refers to changes in market rates of interest, which affect all investments. Fixed-income securities (bonds and preferred stocks) are affected most directly. In periods of rising interest rates, market prices of fixed-income securities decline to make them competitive with yields of new issues that come to the market. This decline in price causes a loss of principal for fixed-income security holders. Similarly, in periods of declining interest rates, prices of fixed-income securities increase, resulting in capital appreciation. Rising and declining interest rates have the same effect on real estate prices.

Changes in interest rates have a lesser effect on common stocks than on fixed-income securities. High interest rates tend to depress stock prices, and low interest rates tend to go hand in hand with bull markets. High interest rates prompt many investors to sell their stocks and move into the bond markets to take advantage of the higher coupon rates of bonds. When interest rates come down, investors move from bond and money market securities to stocks.

Purchasing-Power (Inflation) Risk

Purchasing-power risk is the risk that changes in consumer prices will erode the future purchasing power of returns from investments. If prices in the economy rise (inflation), your future dollars will purchase fewer goods and services than they do today. This is called *purchasing-power risk*, and it has the greatest effect on investments with fixed returns (bonds, savings accounts, and CDs) and no returns (non-interest-bearing checking accounts and the hoard under the mattress).

Assets with values that move with general price levels, such as common stocks, real estate, and commodities, perform better during periods of slight to moderate inflation. To protect against purchasing-power risk, choose investments with anticipated returns that are higher than the anticipated rate of inflation.

Of all the financial assets, common stocks have fared the best during periods of low to moderate inflation. During periods of high inflation, all financial assets, including common stocks, do poorly. However, common stocks perform less poorly than bonds and money market securities under these circumstances.

Event Risk

Event risk is broadly defined as the possibility of the occurrence of an event specific to a company that could affect that company's bond and stock prices. For instance, Taiwan Semiconductor's stock dropped after an earthquake in Taiwan because investors feared that the firm's production facility had been damaged. Because external events are difficult to predict, investors can do little to prevent this type of risk. They can, however, estimate the effect that an event would have.

Exchange-Rate Risk

Exchange-rate risk is the risk that the exchange rate of a currency could cause an investment to lose value. An increase in the value of the dollar against a foreign currency could decimate any returns and result in a loss of capital when the foreign securities are sold. This is called *exchange-rate risk.* For example, a 10 percent rise in the price of the dollar to the British pound negates a 10 percent increase in the price of British stocks. A declining dollar hurts not only U.S. bond and stock markets but also the U.S. economy because imported goods become more expensive, which is inflationary. To temper potential increases in inflation, the Federal Reserve does not hesitate to raise interest rates. This has a negative effect on both the bond and stock markets. Bond prices decline when interest rates rise, and investors sell their stocks when they can get higher returns by moving into bonds.

Liquidity Risk

Liquidity risk is the risk of not being able to convert an investment into cash quickly without the loss of a significant amount of the invested principal. Certain securities are more liquid than others; the greater the liquidity, the easier it is to buy and sell the investment without taking a price concession. When investing in a particular security, you should consider the following two factors:

- The length of time you will need to hold the investment before selling it
- The relative certainty of the selling price.

If you plan to use the funds in a short period of time, invest in securities that are high in liquidity (savings accounts, Treasury bills, money market mutual funds). A Treasury bill can be sold quickly with only a slight concession in selling price, whereas a 20-year-to-maturity junk bond not only may take time to sell but also may sell at a significant price concession.

Common stocks of actively traded companies on the stock exchanges are marketable because they will sell quickly. They also may be liquid if the selling price is close to the original purchase price. However, inactively traded common stocks on the stock exchanges and on the over-the-counter markets may be marketable but not liquid because the spreads between the bid and ask prices may be wide, and the sale price may be significantly less than the purchase price. This could be a problem when you need to sell inactively traded common stocks unexpectedly, and there are no buyers for the stocks. You would have to sell the stocks at a lower price to entice a buyer.

THE RELATIONSHIP BETWEEN RISK AND RETURN

By now you should understand that even with the most conservative investments you face some element of risk. However, not investing your money is also risky. For example, putting your money under the mattress invites the risk of theft and the loss in purchasing power if prices of goods and services rise in the economy. When you recognize the different levels of risk for each type of investment asset, you can better manage the total risk in your investment portfolio.

A direct correlation exists between risk and return and is illustrated in Figure 4–2. The greater the risk, the greater is the potential return. However, investing in securities with the greatest return and, therefore, the greatest risk can lead to financial ruin if everything does not go according to plan.

FIGURE 4-2

Risk and Return

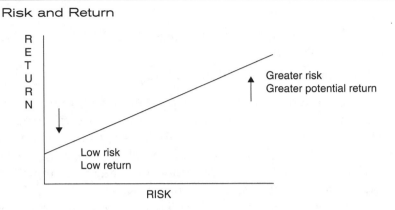

Understanding the risks pertaining to the different investments is of little consequence unless you're aware of your attitude toward risk. How much risk you can tolerate depends on many factors, such as the type of person you are, your investment objectives, the dollar amount of your total assets, the size of your portfolio, and the time horizon for your investments.

How nervous are you about your investments? Will you check the prices of your stocks daily? Can you sleep at night if your stocks decline in price below their acquisition prices? Will you call your broker every time a stock falls by a point or two? If so, you do not tolerate risk well, and your portfolio should be geared toward conservative investments that generate income through capital preservation. The percentage of your portfolio allocated to stocks may be low to zero depending on your comfort zone. If you are not bothered when your stocks decline in price because with a long holding period you can wait out the decline, your portfolio of investments can be designed with a higher percentage of stocks. Figure 4–3 illustrates the continuum of risk tolerance.

A wide range of returns is associated with each type of security. For example, the many types of common stocks, such as blue-chip stocks, growth stocks, income stocks, and speculative stocks, react differently. Income stocks generally are lower risk and offer returns mainly in the form of dividends, whereas growth stocks are riskier and usually offer higher returns in the form of capital gains. Similarly, a broad range of risks and returns can be found for the different types of bonds. You should be aware of this broad range of risks and returns for the different types of

FIGURE 4-3

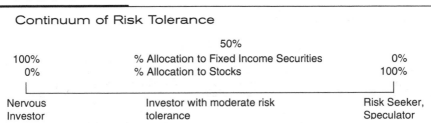

Continuum of Risk Tolerance

securities so that you can find an acceptable level of risk for yourself.

MEASURES OF RISK

Measuring risk is only helpful for a portfolio of stocks rather than for an individual stock, and this is so because investing in a diversified portfolio reduces the overall risk of the individual stocks in the portfolio. As pointed out earlier in this chapter, a diversified portfolio of greater than 20 to 40 stocks reduces the unsystematic portion of risk in the portfolio, leaving only the systematic risk in the portfolio. Reducing some of the risk should reduce the variability of the returns in that portfolio. However, market risk is not reduced by diversification, but having a long time horizon can lessen a portion of this risk. If the market declines with a short time horizon, you would have to sell your stocks at lower prices, whereas with a long time horizon you are able to liquidate your stocks when they have appreciated in value.

Standard Deviation

The *standard deviation* measures the amount by which a stock's or portfolio's returns vary around its average return, which provides a measure of volatility. Measuring the standard deviation of stocks can show you which stocks are the least volatile. For example, consider Table 4–7, which presents the monthly returns for Citigroup and Amgen over a one-year period.

The first step in determining the relative volatility of the two stocks, Citigroup and Amgen, is to find the average monthly returns for each stock. This is based on the closing price at the end of every month. The monthly return is calculated as follows:

$$\text{Monthly return} = [(\text{ending price} - \text{beginning price}) + \text{dividend}]/\text{beginning price}$$

TABLE 4-7

Determination of Risk and Return

Month	Citigroup Price	Return	$(x - \bar{x})^2$	Amgen Price	Return	$(x - \bar{x})^2$
	51.25			66.38		
1	52.84	3.1%	16.72	60.68	−8.58%	38.33
2	50.21	−4.97	15.84	62.71	3.34	32.80
3	45.80*	−8.46	55.81	64.30	2.53	24.19
4	40.50	−11.57	111.95	58.77	−8.6	38.58
5	45.52	12.39	179.01	56.82	−3.31	0.85
6	47.90*	5.57	43.03	66.43	16.91	372.44
7	50.48	5.38	40.57	56.44	−15.03	159.80
8	47.40*	−5.78	22.95	55.50	−1.66	0.53
9	45.25	−4.53	12.53	57.98	4.46	46.91
10	47.52	9.43	108.57	59.68	2.93	28.29
11	43.30	−12.56	133.87	52.88	−11.72	87.07
12	43.18†	0.13	1.25	47.63	−9.92	56.72
Total		**−11.87**	**742.10**		**−28.65**	**886.51**
Mean ($\bar{x}$)		**−0.99%**			**−2.39%**	
SD		**7.86%**			**8.60%**	
Highest monthly return		**12.39%**			**16.91%**	
Lowest monthly return		**−12.56%**			**−15.03%**	

* Dividend $0.16.
† Dividend $0.18.

For example, the following is the return for Citigroup for the first month:

$$\text{Return} = [(52.84 - 51.25) + 0]/51.25 = 3.1\%$$

The standard deviation is a quantitative measure of the stock's risk. The lower the standard deviation, the lower is the variability or risk of the investment.

In a normal distribution of data, two-thirds of the monthly returns in the distribution fall within plus or minus one standard deviation from the mean. For example, Citigroup has a mean of −0.99 percent and a standard deviation of 7.86 percent, so two-thirds of the monthly returns should fall between 6.87 and −8.85 percent. Amgen has a mean of −2.39 percent and a standard deviation of

8.6 percent, so two-thirds of the monthly returns should fall between 6.21 and −10.99 percent.

Another indication of volatility and risk is the range of a stock's high and low returns. Citigroup has a high return of 12.39 percent and a low of −12.56 percent. Amgen has a high return of 16.91 percent and a low of −15.03 percent. Within the 12-month period, Citigroup had five months of negative returns, and Amgen had seven.

So which of these two stocks is less volatile? Citigroup stock is less volatile than Amgen stock on all three indications of volatility. Table 4–8 illustrates how to use Excel software to determine the mean and standard deviation for the returns of a stock. Excel calculates the mean and standard deviation for the entered data field.

The disadvantage of the standard deviation as a measure of risk is the assumption that returns will be normally distributed as in a bell-shaped curve. Stock markets can have crashes that would not be predicted in the normal distribution of data. However, the standard deviation is a useful measure to compare the volatility of different stocks and portfolios.

Beta

The *beta coefficient* is a measure of the sensitivity of the rate of return on a stock in relation to the movement of the market. In other words, it measures the stock's systematic risk.

To determine the beta coefficient, you plot or graph the monthly returns for a stock in relation to the monthly returns

TABLE 4-8

How to Compute a Mean and Standard Deviation Using Excel Software

Use Excel to calculate these statistical measures by entering the monthly returns in a column.

1. Click on "f*" in the toolbar near the top of the screen.
2. In the left box, highlight "Statistical."
3. In the right box, highlight "Average" for the mean and "STDEVPA" for the standard deviation for a population of data.
4. Enter the data field for your column. For example, if the monthly returns are in the C1 through C12 columns, you would type "C1: C12."

for the market (the S&P 500 Index or any other measurement of the market). This shows the average movements in the price of the stock relative to the price movements in the market index. The slope of the line is the beta coefficient, which determines how the stock will react to the movement in the market.

The market always has a beta coefficient of 1, so a stock with a beta coefficient of 1 has systematic risk equal to that of the market. If a stock's beta coefficient is 1.2, for example, this means that the stock is 20 percent more volatile than the market. A stock with a beta coefficient of 0 has no systematic risk; a stock with a beta coefficient of less than 1 is less volatile to changes in the price movements of the market. Beta coefficients for stocks generally range between 0.6 and 1.6, but this does not mean that beta coefficients cannot be more or less. At one point in time, Johnson & Johnson, for example, had a beta coefficient of 0.07, which indicated a miniscule amount of market risk. Table 4–9 shows how to use the Internet to obtain beta coefficients for listed stocks.

The beta coefficient seems like a simple and easy way to measure market risk. When you invest in stocks with beta coefficients higher than the market (>1), the returns in rising markets should be greater than the market returns. Similarly, when you invest in stocks with beta coefficients lower than the market (<1), your potential losses in a declining market should be less than the market losses. Unfortunately, the beta coefficient does not provide a foolproof way to measure market risk because of the following four factors:

1. The beta coefficient for a company's stock varies if you use different measures of the market (for example, the Value Line Index instead of the S&P 500 Index).
2. The beta coefficient for a company's stock varies if you use different time frames (12, 24, 36, 48, or 60 months).

TABLE 4-9

How to Use the Internet to Obtain Stock Beta Coefficients

1. Go to Yahoo (www.yahoo.com).
2. Click the "Finance" link.
3. Type the stock symbols (separate each with a comma) of the companies you are interested in, and then click on each individual symbol for more information.
4. Click the "Profile" link, which appears beneath the detailed information, and then click "Key Statistics," where you find the beta measure for that particular stock.

3. The risk-return relationship may differ from that predicted by the theory. Low-risk stocks have earned higher returns than expected, and high-risk stocks have earned lower returns than expected.
4. Relationships between stock prices and market prices change and do not always reflect past relationships (Malkiel, 1990, pp. 243–255).

Portfolio Beta

Even though a perfect measurement of market risk does not exist, you can use the beta coefficient to determine whether the risk for a portfolio of stocks is greater or less than the risk of the market. The beta coefficient of a portfolio of stocks is the weighted average of the beta coefficients of the individual stocks. For example, a portfolio consisting of 32 stocks in which 8 stocks each have a beta of 1.2, 16 stocks each have a beta of 1.1, and 8 stocks each have a beta of 0.8 has a portfolio beta of 1.05. This calculation appears below:

$$\text{Portfolio beta} = \sum_{K=1}^{n} \frac{\text{number of stocks}}{\text{total number of stock}} \times \text{beta coefficient } k$$

$$= \left(\frac{8}{32} \times 1.2\right) + \left(\frac{16}{32} \times 1.1\right) + \left(\frac{8}{32} \times 0.8\right)$$

$$= 1.05$$

A portfolio beta of 1.05 means that if the market rises or falls by 1 percent, the portfolio rises or falls by 1.05 percent. The portfolio has slightly more risk than the market. Although individual beta coefficients may not accurately predict price movements relative to the market, they do provide an attempt for assessing the market risk of a portfolio.

Sharpe Ratio

The Sharpe ratio is a measure of a risk-adjusted return of a portfolio. The risk-free rate is measured by the 90-day Treasury bill rate, and this rate is deducted from the portfolio's return, which is then divided by the standard deviation of the portfolio. When comparing the Sharpe ratio of different portfolios, the larger the Sharpe ratio, the better are the returns per unit of comparable risk. In other words, by holding the risk of different portfolios constant, you can use the Sharpe ratio to find the portfolio that provides the higher return.

You can analyze the risk of your stocks and portfolio by using the Web site www.riskgrades.com.

WHAT YOU CAN DO ABOUT RISK

An analysis of and an awareness of risk are important for two major reasons. First, you can determine how much risk you can tolerate through asset allocation (how much of your portfolio to allocate to stocks, bonds, and money market securities). Second, you need to have a diversified portfolio of stocks, which reduces the individual risk of specific stocks, and a long time horizon (holding period) for your portfolio of stocks.

REFERENCES

Faerber, Esmé. *All About Investing.* New York: McGraw-Hill, 2006.

Malkiel, Burton G. *A Random Walk Down Wall Street.* New York: W.W. Norton, 1990.

Siegel, Jeremy J. *Stocks for the Long Run*, 3d ed. New York: McGraw-Hill, 2002.

CHAPTER 5

Returns of Stocks

KEY CONCEPTS

- What returns can you expect from stocks?
- Calculating a rate of return
- Risk-return tradeoff
- Asset allocation and the selection of investments

Investment Snapshot

- On the day Caterpillar announced record second-quarter earnings in 2006, its stock price declined by 1.2 percent.
- Alcoa reported a 62 percent quarterly increase in net income, and the stock price declined by a few dollars on the day of the announcement.
- Citigroup reported an increase of 4 percent in quarterly earnings, and the stock price did not change much on the day of the announcement.

The Investment Snapshot illustrates that stock prices bear a relationship to earnings, but in many cases the short-term relationship can be quite volatile. The price that an investor is willing to pay for a stock depends on the expected return from that stock, which is the present value of both the cash flows from dividends and the expected future selling price of the stock. When a company's earnings increase, the company can increase the dividends that it pays as well as expand its retained earnings, thereby causing the stock price to rise.

WHAT RETURNS CAN YOU EXPECT FROM STOCKS?

What is the rate of return that you can expect from your stocks? The answer depends on many factors, one of which is the time frame over which question is asked. If you ask the question during a bull market, the rate of return is often quoted to be in the double digits (above 10 percent), whereas during a bear market it is in the 6 to 7 percent range. This discrepancy is not as important as understanding how returns are made up and that stocks generally outperform bonds and money market securities over long holding periods. Professor Jeremy Siegel says that in every 10-year holding period from 1802, stocks outperformed bonds and Treasury bills and that during the same holding period, the worst performance of stocks was better than that of bonds and Treasury bills (2002, p. 26). During short holding periods, stocks are riskier than bonds and Treasury bills, but over long holding periods, the returns from a portfolio of stocks exceed those of bonds and Treasury bills.

Returns from stocks are from two sources: income in the form of dividends (if the company pays dividends) and capital appreciation. When companies are able to increase their earnings, they can then raise the dividends they pay out to shareholders. Companies do not pay out their entire earnings in dividends. The amount of earnings retained (not paid out to shareholders) is invested in the business to increase future earnings. Thus shareholders of companies that do not pay dividends can benefit when these companies grow their earnings. The disappointment when companies fail to grow their earnings at expected rates accounts for the decline in the prices of their stocks. This volatility of stock prices over short periods results in fluctuating returns for stocks, but over long holding periods, investors in stocks are able to earn higher returns than those from bonds and Treasury bills.

CALCULATING A RATE OF RETURN

A *rate of return* is a measure of the increase (or decrease) in an investment over a period of time. You invest to earn a return in the form of income (interest and dividends) and/or capital appreciation (when the price of the investment sold is higher than the purchase price). Some investments, such as savings accounts and CDs, offer only income with no capital appreciation; others, such as common stock, offer the potential for capital appreciation and may or may not pay dividends. If the price of a stock declines below the purchase price and you sell the stock, you have a capital loss. The simple definition of total return includes income and capital gains and losses.

Calculating a return is important because it measures the growth or decline of your investment, and it provides a yardstick for evaluating the performance of your portfolio against your objectives. You can calculate the total rate of return as follows:

Rate of return for the holding period =
[(ending value − beginning value) + income]/gross purchase price

You should include spreads and commissions in the calculation. For example, if you bought a stock at the beginning of the year for $1,000 (including the commission), sold it at the end of the year for $1,500 (net proceeds received after deducting the commission), and earned a dividend of $50, the rate of return is 55 percent:

$$\text{Rate of return} = [(1{,}500 - 1{,}000) + 50]/1{,}000 = 55\%$$

This rate of return is simple and easy to use, but it is somewhat inaccurate if the investment is held for a long period of time because the time value of money is not taken into account. The *time value of money* is a concept that recognizes that a dollar today is worth more in the future because of its earnings potential. For example, if you invested a dollar at 5 percent for one year, it would be worth $1.05 at the end of one year. Similarly, if you expect to receive a dollar at the end of one year, it would have a present value of less than a dollar (now).

This simple average rate of return of 55 percent does not take into account the earnings capacity of the interest. In other words, you would reinvest the $50 of dividends you received, which would increase the rate of return above 55 percent owing to compounding of the interest.

Using the time value of money to calculate the rate of return gives you a more accurate rate-of-return figure. However, it is more difficult to calculate because the rate of return on a stock equates the discounted cash flows of future dividends and the stock's expected sale price to the stock's current purchase price. This formula works better for bonds than for common stocks because the coupon rate for bonds is generally fixed, whereas dividend rates on common stocks fluctuate (and you therefore need to make assumptions). When companies experience losses, they might reduce their dividend payments, as Ford Motor Company did to preserve its cash in 2006. If a company's earnings increase, the company might increase the amount of its dividend payments. The future sale price of a stock has even less certainty. Bonds are retired at their par price ($1,000 per bond) at maturity; but when a stock eventually is sold, the future sale price is anyone's guess.

How do you calculate a return for a portfolio? It is useful to be able to compute a return for a portfolio of investments. The following example illustrates the steps to determine such a return. The portfolio has five stocks with the following returns:

Stock	Return
A	7.5%
B	6.2%
C & D	2.0%
E	−3.1%

The returns for the stocks are weighted and then summed to give the portfolio weighted average return:

To be able to compare your portfolio return with the return of the market, you need to be able to determine your return accurately.

Stock	Weighting		Rate		Weighted Average Return
A	1/5	×	0.075	=	1.5%
B	1/5	×	0.062	=	1.24%
C & D	2/5	×	0.02	=	0.8%
E	1/5	×	−0.031	=	−0.62%
					2.92%

Weighted average portfolio return = 2.92%

This process may not be easy if you add funds to purchase securities and withdraw funds during the holding period. You may recall that a few years ago the Beardstown Ladies Investment Club had a problem calculating its returns accurately. The members claimed to have earned average annual returns in the low 20 percent range for an extended period, beating annual market averages, only to find that they had computed their returns incorrectly. In fact, an audit by a prominent accounting firm showed that their average annual returns were in single digits during that same period.

For a portfolio where you have not added or withdrawn any funds, the simple holding-period return discussed earlier is sufficient:

Holding-period return = (ending balance − beginning balance)/
beginning balance

Table 5–1 illustrates how to calculate a return for a portfolio where funds have been added and withdrawn.

TABLE 5-1

Measuring a Portfolio Return with Additions and Withdrawals to the Portfolio

If you had $100,000 in your portfolio at the beginning of the year, and at the end of the year your portfolio had increased to $109,000, you had a 9 percent return [($109,000 − 100,000)/100,000].

For additions and withdrawals during the year, the holding-period return for a portfolio is calculated as follows:

$$\text{Holding Period Return} = \frac{\text{Interest} + \text{Dividends} + \text{Capital gains} + \text{unrealized capital gains}}{\text{Beginning Investment} + [\text{New Funds} \times (\text{number of months in portfolio}/12)] - [\text{Funds withdrawn} \times (\text{number of months not in portfolio}/12)]}$$

For example, a portfolio that began with $110,500 at the beginning of the year, received dividends of $8,600 and capital gains of $12,000, suffered unrealized losses of $6,000 during the year, had new funds of $10,000 added at the beginning of April, and had $4,000 withdrawn at the end of October had an annual return of 12.44 percent:

This portfolio earned a 12.44 percent return before taxes and can be compared with a comparable benchmark index for the same period of time.

$$\text{HPR} = \frac{\$8,600 + \$12,000 - \$6,000}{\left[\$110,500 + \$10,000 \times \dfrac{9}{12}\right] - \left[\$4,000 \times \dfrac{2}{12}\right]}$$

$$= 12.44\%$$

THE RISK-RETURN TRADEOFF

When you use the standard deviation, range of returns, and the beta coefficient to measure risk, you can get a better sense of investment risk and expected rates of return. However, you already know that choosing riskier investments does not necessarily mean that you will always receive greater returns. The *risk-return tradeoff* relates directly to your expected or required rate of return on the investments you purchase and hold. In order to invest in a riskier investment, you would expect a greater rate of return. The *required rate of return* is the minimum rate of return necessary to purchase a security. This minimum rate of return includes the rate earned on a risk-free investment, which is typically a Treasury security, plus the risk premium associated with that investment. The *risk premium* is the added return that is related to the risk for that particular investment:

Required rate of return = risk-free rate + risk premium

For example, you may require a 10 percent rate of return for all stock investments. If the risk-free rate is 3 percent, the risk premium for the stocks you purchased is 7 percent. Figure 5–1 shows that the stocks you are willing to purchase must have a beta coefficient equal to that of the market in order to obtain the 10 percent expected return (market beta is 1 multiplied by the risk premium of 7 percent plus the risk-free rate of 3 percent to equal the required or expected rate of return of 10 percent). If you purchased stocks with a beta coefficient of 1.5, the risk premium would be 10.5 percent (1.5 × 7 percent), which is one and a half times the market risk. The preceding equation on the required rate of return can be expanded to include the beta coefficient:

Required rate of return = risk-free rate + beta coefficient
× (market rate − risk-free rate)

Historic returns for stocks, as quoted in Chapter 1, confirm the risk-return tradeoff. That is, over long periods of time, the greater the risk taken, the greater are the expected returns.

However, this rule may not always hold over short periods of time and in down markets. Large- and small-cap stocks had real average annual returns of 7.7 and 9.1 percent over a 74-year period respectively from 1926 to 2000 versus 2.2 percent for intermediate-term government bonds, as quoted by Ibbotson and Sinquefield (1994). *Real rates of return* are nominal rates minus the rate of

FIGURE 5-1

Relationship between Risk and Expected Returns

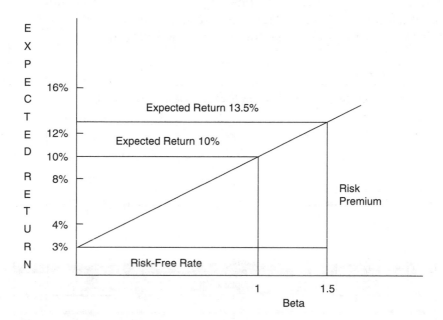

inflation. Risk, however, is greatest for stocks of small companies, followed by large-company stocks, as evidenced by the standard deviations of returns.

ASSET ALLOCATION AND THE SELECTION OF INVESTMENTS

Diversification can reduce some of the risks inherent in investing. For example, when the stock of one company in your portfolio declines, other stocks might increase and offset your losses. However, diversification does not reduce market risk. If the stock market declines, the stocks of a diversified portfolio decline also. When the bond and stock markets move together, even a diversified portfolio during down markets is not immune from market risk. Another element that can help to combat market risk is time. When selecting securities with long time horizons, you can wait for stock prices to recover from down markets to sell.

The securities you select depend on your objectives, your circumstances (marital status, age, family, education, income, net worth, and the size of the portfolio), level of risk, expected rate of return, and the economic environment. *Asset allocation* is the assignment of funds to broad categories of investment assets, such as stocks, bonds, money market securities, options, futures, gold, and real estate. The asset allocation model in Figure 5–2 shows how some of these asset allocation factors determine the selection of investments.

FIGURE 5-2

Asset Allocation and the Selection of Investments

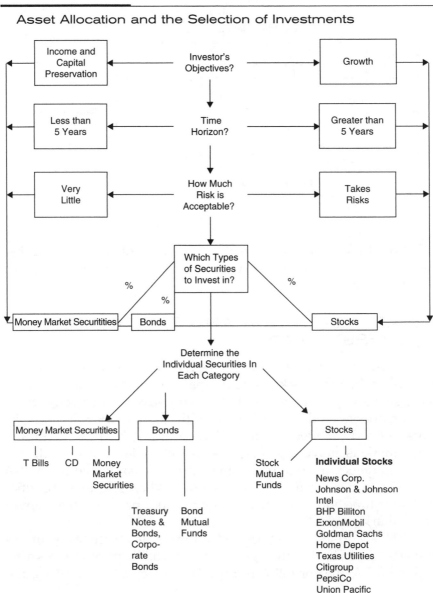

For example, if you are seeking capital growth and are young, single, and a professional with an excellent salary, you may be able to tolerate greater risk in order to pursue higher returns. With a long time horizon and less need for income generation from investments, a greater portion of your portfolio can be invested in common stocks. Such an asset allocation in this case could be as follows:

Stocks	75%
Real estate	10%
Bonds	5%
Money market equivalents	10%

If, however, you do not tolerate risk as well, a more conservative asset allocation model would be as follows:

Stocks	60%
Bonds	30%
Money market equivalents	10%

An older, retired couple with limited net worth whose objectives are income generation and capital preservation would have a different allocation of their assets. They cannot tolerate much risk, and their time horizon is shorter. To generate regular receipts of income, a greater portion of their investment portfolio would go into fixed-income securities with varying maturities. Generally, the longer the maturities, the greater are the returns, even though risk increases with the length of the maturities. Depending on their circumstances, a small percentage of their portfolio might be allocated to common stocks to provide capital appreciation. A suggested asset allocation model might be set up as follows:

Stocks	15%
Bonds	65%
Money market equivalents	20%

As you can see, the percentage allocated to stocks, bonds, and money market equivalents varies depending on your circumstances and the size of your portfolio.

What works for one investor may not be appropriate for another. For example, the financial characteristics of two investors may be identical, but one investor may need to set aside greater amounts in money market securities to meet ongoing medical bills or some other expected expenditure.

An asset allocation plan should be flexible enough to accommodate changes to fit personal and economic circumstances. For example, when market rates of interest are declining, a greater percentage of the portfolio may be allocated to stocks. Similarly, when interest rates are rising, you could put more of your funds in money market equivalents, and when conditions become more favorable, you can move some money back into stocks (see Table 5–2).

TABLE 5-2

Guidelines for Asset Allocation

---

1. Review your objectives and personal financial circumstances. To generate current income and preserve capital, the asset allocation model should be weighted more toward bonds and money market securities. If current income is not needed and you are investing for capital growth in the future, the weighting would be allocated more toward stocks and real assets (real estate, precious metals, and collectibles).
2. Determine your tolerance for risk. If you have a long time horizon and can accept the risks of the stock and real estate markets, a greater amount can be invested in stocks and real estate. If you cannot tolerate risk, the allocation should be weighted more toward bonds and money market securities.
3. Consider the time frame. If you are young and have a long time horizon (about 25 years), allocate a larger percentage to stocks. If you have a short time frame, the allocation would be weighted more toward bonds, with a smaller percentage in stocks.
4. You should not be unrealistic in your expectations of your investments. The returns of the past two decades have been quite spectacular. Long-term bonds in the decade of the 1980s returned, on average, around 13 percent annually. Stock returns were abnormally high during the late 1990s owing to the technology boom and the Internet bubble, only to decline to more realistic levels of valuation in the early 2000s. For example the Standard & Poor's (S&P) 500 Index earned, on average, around 37 percent in 1995, 22 percent in 1996, and 33 percent in 1997. The decades of the 1980s and 1990s were abnormally good for both the bond and stock markets owing to the decline in interest rates, from around 17 percent in 1980 to the current low of 3 to 5 percent in the early 2000s. You should lower your expected returns to more realistic levels into the future.
5. Consider the risk-return tradeoff in the asset allocation model. How you allocate your assets can affect both risk and returns. For example, according to Ibbotson and Sinquefield (1994), diversification among different classes of investment assets lowered the levels of risk and improved returns. The three portfolios in the study used data during the 1926–1993 time frame. The first portfolio consisted solely of long-term government bonds and had an average annual return of 5.5 percent with a risk (standard deviation) of 11.3 percent. A second, more diversified portfolio consisted of 63 percent Treasury bills, 12 percent long-term government bonds, and 25 percent common stocks of large companies. This portfolio had the

(continued)

same annual returns as the first portfolio, 5.5 percent, but the risk fell to 6.1 percent. A third portfolio consisted of 52 percent stocks of large companies, 14 percent long-term government bonds, and 34 percent Treasury bills. This portfolio returned 8 percent annually with a risk of 11.3 percent. This is the same risk as the first portfolio of bonds, but the returns are much greater.

6. After determining your asset allocation model, the next step is to determine your individual investments. In a speech to the American Association of Individual Investors National Meeting, July 10, 1998, John J. Brennan used the example of a portfolio invested in 100 percent international stocks for the five-year period ending 1990. This portfolio, based on the Morgan Stanley EAFE Index, would have outperformed a portfolio of stocks based on the S&P 500 Index. However, in the five-year period from 1992 to 1997, a 100 percent portfolio of stocks based on the S&P 500 Index would have outperformed this portfolio of foreign stocks. To reduce overall risk, you should divide your stock allocation into different sectors of the economy and then choose the individual stocks for each sector. Foreign stocks should be included. You can do the same for a bond portfolio.

After you've determined an asset allocation mix of the broad categories of investments (stocks, bonds, money market funds, and other asset types), your next step is to make your selection of individual investments and amounts to allocate to each. For stocks, it may be useful to review the different categories of common stocks. For example, allocating equal amounts of money to value stocks, growth stocks, foreign stocks, blue-chip stocks, and small-cap stocks reduces the total risk of your stock portfolio. The same process applies to division of the total amount allocated to bonds. The portfolio of individual stocks listed in Figure 5–2 can be classified into sectors and types, as illustrated in Table 5–3.

This table presents a broad representation of the different industry sectors, and most of the companies listed are leaders in their respective sectors. Noticeably absent from this portfolio are small-cap stocks and foreign stocks, which are riskier investments. This portfolio was chosen with the following considerations in mind:

- Large-cap stocks instead of mid- or small caps
- Equal emphasis on growth stocks and value stocks
- U.S. stocks instead of foreign stocks

The easiest way to lose money is to make a few bad investments in stocks and bonds. Nonetheless, many people continue to invest in stocks suggested by friends and associates without even looking at the financial statements of the companies. Rather than relying on a "hot tip" you hear at the hairdresser's, you should be more scientific about your choice of investments.

TABLE 5-3

Portfolio of Stocks

Stock	Sector or Industry	Type of Stock
News Corp.	Media	Growth stock
Johnson & Johnson	Pharmaceuticals	Defensive stock
Intel	Semiconductors	Technology growth stock
BHP Billiton	Mining	Growth stock
ExxonMobil	Oil	Energy blue-chip stock
Goldman Sachs	Financial services	Value stock
Home Depot	Discount retailer	Value stock
Texas Utilities	Utilities	Income stock
Citigroup	Financial services	Blue-chip stock
PepsiCo	Beverages	Defensive stock
Union Pacific	Transportation	Cyclical stock

Note: This is not a recommendation to buy any of these stocks. Some stocks may be trading at high multiples of earnings owing to increases in price, whereas others may be depressed in a bear market.

You can use *fundamental analysis* to choose your investments. Using fundamental analysis, you identify industries in the economy that have the potential for doing well. Then you evaluate the companies within those industries for their earnings and growth capacities. Using *technical analysis*, another method for choosing individual securities, you use past information about prices and volume movements to identify buying and selling opportunities.

REFERENCES

Brennan, John J. "Strategic Asset Allocation in Today's Market," speech given to the American Association of Individual Investors National Meeting, Washington, DC, July 10, 1998.

Faerber, Esmé. *All about Stocks*, 2d ed. New York: McGraw-Hill, 2000.

Ibbotson, Roger G., and Rex A. Sinquefield. *Stocks, Bonds, Bills and Inflation: Historical Return (1926–1993)*. Chicago: Dow Jones–Irwin, 1994.

Siegel, Jeremy J. *Stocks for the Long Run*, 3d ed. New York: McGraw-Hill, 2002.

CHAPTER 6

Stock Market Indexes

KEY CONCEPTS

- Returns as measured by stock market indexes
- Determining which index to use in evaluating your portfolio
- The importance of stock market indexes

Investment Snapshot

- The Dow Jones Industrial Average increased by 212 points on one day of trading, indicating stock market euphoria.
- In July 1998, the Nasdaq Composite Index reached 5,000, and eight years later, the index hovered around the 2,000 level.
- Citigroup has developed a market sentiment index model that indicates whether stock market investors are euphoric or in a state of panic

---

The stock market indexes are viewed as the vital signs for predicting the direction of the stock market. Not only do the stock market indexes influence the investment behaviors of individual investors, but they also influence the investment decisions of investment professionals (fund managers).

RETURNS AS MEASURED BY THE STOCK MARKET INDEXES

A number of stock market indexes give you different measures of the stock market. You can use these indexes in the following ways:

1. To determine how the stock markets are doing
2. As comparison benchmarks for the performance of your individual portfolios, mutual funds, and exchange-traded funds
3. As forecasting tools for future trends

These market indexes give you a glimpse into the movement of individual stock prices. However, you should understand the relationship between the indexes and individual stocks before taking any action. In general, the different stock market indexes move up and down together by greater or lesser amounts, although they sometimes diverge. Figure 6–1 presents a comparison of the three major stock market indexes. These differences are due to the composition of stocks in each index, the manner in which each index is calculated, and the weights assigned to each stock.

An aggregate measure of the market is calculated as an average or an index. An *average* is calculated by adding stock prices and then dividing by a weighted number to give an average price. An *index* is a weighting of stock prices related to a base year's stock prices. Examples are the Standard & Poor's (S&P) 500 Composite Index, the New York Stock Exchange Composite Index, and the OTC Index (over-the-counter stocks).

FIGURE 6-1

Comparison of Market Indexes, 1988–2005

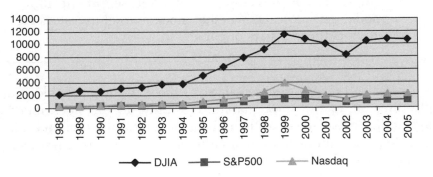

The relative weighting of the individual stocks in each index differs. A *price-weighted* index is composed by adding the share price of each stock in the index and then dividing by a number that is adjusted for stock splits. The Dow Jones Industrial Average is calculated on a price-weighted average. A *market-value-weighted* index is compiled using the market value of each company in the index. The weighting of each company is determined by its *market capitalization*, which is the market price of the stock multiplied by the number of shares outstanding. Consequently, a company with a larger market capitalization will have a greater weighting in the index. Stock splits do not affect the index. The S&P 500 Index is a market-value-weighted index.

An *equally weighted index* is computed by giving each stock the same weight regardless of price or market capitalization. The equal-weighting method places an equal dollar value on each stock, in contrast to price weighting, which uses an equal number of shares of each stock, and market-value weighting, which views stocks in proportion to their market capitalization. An equally weighted index can be calculated using an arithmetic or geometric method. The Value Line Index uses the geometric method.

These differences explain the discrepancies between the rates of return of the different indexes. Following is a discussion of the most widely used stock indexes.

Dow Jones Industrial Average

The *Dow Jones Industrial Average* (DJIA) is the oldest and most widely quoted measure of the stock market. The DJIA is composed of the stock prices of 30 large blue-chip companies. The closing stock prices of each of the 30 stocks are added and then divided by an adjusted divisor. This divisor is a very small number (e.g., 0.123051408 as of May 11, 2007), which makes the DJIA a greater number than the average of the stock prices. When the DJIA was first introduced, it was calculated using a simple average of the number of stocks in the calculation. However, because of stock splits and the addition of new stocks to replace stocks that were dropped, an adjusted divisor was used to keep the average from changing for stock splits and the addition of new stocks. This adjusted divisor explains why the DJIA can be a large number such as 10,800 with the addition of only 30 share prices of the companies in the average.

Given the small number of companies in the DJIA, care has been taken over the years to make sure that these companies are broadly representative of the market. Thus, in 1997, four companies [Bethlehem Steel, Texaco, Westinghouse (now Viacom), and Wool-worths (now Venator Group)] were dropped and were replaced by Hewlett-Packard, Johnson & Johnson, Citigroup, and Wal-Mart. Later changes included the addition of Microsoft Corporation and Intel Corporation.

Much criticism surrounds the DJIA. First, the stocks are not equally weighted; consequently, an increase in a higher-priced stock has a greater impact on the DJIA than an increase in a lower-priced stock. Second, with a sample of only 30 large blue-chip stocks, the DJIA is hardly a representative measure of the market.

Yet the DJIA still can be of use to investors. First, by looking at a chart of the DJIA over a period of time, investors can see the ups and downs of the market, which can help you to decide when to buy and sell stocks. Second, the DJIA can be used as a yardstick for comparing how your blue-chip stocks and blue-chip mutual funds have performed in comparison with the DJIA for the same period of time. However, because the DJIA is composed of only 30 stocks, you also should look at more broad-based measures of the market. Table 6–1 presents a comparison of the DJIA, the S&P 500 Index, and the Dogs of the Dow for the past 16 years.

The *Dogs of the Dow* is an offshoot of the DJIA. It involves a strategy of investing in the 10 highest dividend-yielding stocks in the DJIA at the beginning of the year and then replacing the stocks with the 10 highest-yielding stocks the next year.

Other Dow Jones averages are the *Dow Jones Transportation Average* (DJTA), which is composed of the stocks of 20 major trans-portation companies, the *Dow Jones Utility Average* (DJUA), which consists of 15 major utility stocks, and the *Dow Jones Composite Average*, which combines the three Dow Jones averages and all their stocks.

Standard & Poor's 500 Index

Standard & Poor's 500 Index (S&P 500) consists of 500 stocks listed on the New York Stock Exchange and the Nasdaq. The 500 compa-nies included in the S&P 500 Index also can be broken down into the following indexes:

TABLE 6-1

Performance of the Indexes

Year	DJIA	S&P 500	Dogs of the Dow
1989	31.7%	31.5%	26.5%
1990	−0.4%	−3.2%	−7.6%
1991	23.9%	30.0%	34.3%
1992	7.4%	7.6%	7.9%
1993	16.8%	10.1%	27.3%
1994	4.9%	1.3%	4.1%
1995	36.4%	37.6%	36.5%
1996	28.6%	23.0%	27.9%
1997	24.9%	33.4%	21.9%
1998	18.1%	28.6%	10.7%
1999	27.2%	21.1%	4%
2000	−4.7%	−9.2%	6.4%
2001	−5.4%	−11.9%	−4.9%
2002	−14.9%	−22.1%	−8.9%
2003	28.3%	28.7%	28.7%
2004	5.3%	10.8%	4.4%
2005	1.7%	4.9%	−7.8%
10-year return	12.4%	12.6%	8.2%*

* Ten years ended December 31, 2005.

- S&P Industrial Index, which consists of 400 industrial stocks
- S&P Transportation Index, which consists of 20 transportation companies
- S&P Utilities Index, which consists of 40 utilities companies
- S&P Financial Index, which consists of 40 financial companies

The most often cited of the S&P indexes is the S&P 500 Index. The S&P 500 is a market-value-weighted index that is computed by calculating the total market capitalization (value) of the 500 companies in the index, dividing that by the total market capitalization of the 500 companies in the base year, and then multiplying the number by 10. The percentage increase or decrease in the total market value from one day to the next represents the change in the index.

With 500 stocks, the S&P 500 Index is more representative of the market than the DJIA with only 30 stocks. The S&P 500 Index occasionally adds and drops stocks to maintain a broad representation of the economy. The S&P 500 Index is an important measure of the performance of larger stocks in the market, which is further confirmed by the growing popularity of S&P 500–indexed mutual funds (mutual funds that hold portfolios of stocks designed to match the performance of the S&P 500 Index). These mutual funds outperformed most of the actively managed funds in 1998 primarily because many actively managed mutual funds invested in value stocks and small-capitalization stocks, which all underperformed the 50 large growth stocks in the S&P 500 Index. From 1995 to 1999, both the DJIA and S&P 500 Index more than doubled, only to decrease by about half in the bear market of 2000–2002. The broader market of small-capitalization stocks lagged and did not participate in the four-year rally from 1995 to 1999. Small-cap stocks outperformed large-cap stocks in the five-year period from July 2001 to July 2006.

New York Stock Exchange Composite Index

The *New York Stock Exchange Composite Index* is a more broad-based measure than the S&P 500 Index because it includes all the stocks traded on the New York Stock Exchange (NYSE). It is a market-value-weighted index and, like the S&P 500, relates to a base period, December 31, 1965. On that date, the NYSE Composite Index was 50. In addition to the NYSE Composite Index, the NYSE also has indexes for industrials, utilities, transportation, and financial stocks.

Nasdaq Composite Index

The *Nasdaq Composite Index* is a measure of all the stocks traded on the National Association of Securities Dealers Automated Quotations (Nasdaq) System. The Nasdaq Index is more volatile than the DJIA and the S&P 500 because companies traded on the over-the-counter (OTC) market are smaller and more speculative than the larger companies that trade on the NYSE. Thus an increase in the Nasdaq Composite Index can be interpreted as investor enthusiasm for small stocks.

Other Indexes

The *American Stock Exchange* (AMEX) *Index* is value-weighted and includes all stocks listed on that exchange.

The *Wilshire 5000* is the broadest index and includes all companies listed on the NYSE and the AMEX, as well as many of the larger stocks traded on the OTC market.

The *Value Line Composite Index* differs from the other indexes in that it is calculated with a geometric averaging method using 1,700 stocks listed on the NYSE, AMEX, and OTC markets.

The *Russell 3000 Index* is a broad-market index that offers investors access to 98 percent of the U.S. market. The largest 1,000 stocks in the Russell 3000 Index make up the Russell 1000 Index, and the smallest 2,000 stocks in the Russell 3000 make up the Russell 2000 Index (a measure of the performance of small-cap stocks).

The *EAFE Index* is the benchmark for foreign stocks and foreign stock mutual funds. The EAFE is the Morgan Stanley Capital International Europe, Australasia, Far East Index, which includes 1,026 stocks from 20 countries.

DETERMINING WHICH INDEX TO USE

Studies have shown that all the indexes are correlated; that is, they all move together in the same direction. However, there are some differences. The Nasdaq and the AMEX indexes are not as highly correlated with the S&P 500 and the DJIA. This makes sense because companies in the Nasdaq and AMEX indexes are younger, smaller, and riskier than the companies in the DJIA and S&P 500 Index. The best approach is to choose the index that closely resembles the makeup of your stock portfolio.

Individual measures of the market are convenient indicators or gauges of the stock market. These market indexes are convenient gauges of the stock market that also indicate the direction of the market over a period of time. By using these market indexes, you can compare how well individual stocks and mutual funds have performed against comparable market indicators for the same period.

THE IMPORTANCE OF STOCK MARKET INDEXES

Although the stock market is much more dynamic than the indexes suggest, along with the fact that there are different ways to calculate the indexes, causing calculation bias, the stock market indexes are useful in a number of ways to stock investors. First, the market indexes provide an historical perspective of stock market performance, giving investors more insight into their investment decisions. Investors who do not know which individual stocks to invest in can use indexing as a method of choosing their stock investments. By wanting to match the performance of the market, investors can invest in index mutual funds or index exchange-traded funds (ETFs) that track the performance of the indexes with which they are aligned. This form of investing gives investors the opportunity to do as well as the markets and not significantly underperform the markets.

The second benefit of stock market indexes is that they provide a yardstick with which investors can compare the performance of their individual stock portfolios. Individual investors with professionally managed portfolios can use the indexes to determine how well their managers are doing in managing their money.

The third major use of stock market indexes is as a forecasting tool. Studying the historical performance of the stock market indexes, you can forecast trends in the market. The Internet bubble is a prime example, which in hindsight provides 20/20 vision. The price-to-earnings (P/E) ratio of the stock markets was in the high 20s to low 30s in 1999–2000, indicating that the markets could not sustain the rapid increase in stock prices. The P/E ratio for the market historically has ranged between the high single digits and the low 30s, with an average around 15. The P/E ratio for the S&P 500 was 17 on August 4, 2006, an indication that the stock market was not particularly overvalued. Consequently, the market indexes provide investors with a useful tool for forecasting trends in the market.

CHAPTER 7

How Stocks Are Traded

KEY CONCEPTS

- The stock exchanges
- How the securities markets work
- The primary markets and how new issues are brought to the market
- The secondary markets and how securities are traded
- The different types of orders
- The different types of brokerage accounts
- The mechanics of short selling

Investment Snapshot

- Investors can trade stocks before and after the stock exchanges open and close for the day
- The spreads between the bid and ask price on a stock can be as low as 1 cent.
- With real-time quotes, prices of stocks are transparent.

THE STOCK EXCHANGES

A *stock exchange* is a marketplace where stocks of companies are bought and sold. The stock markets in the United States consist of the two major exchanges and an over-the-counter (OTC) market: the New York Stock Exchange (NYSE) and the American Stock Exchange (AMEX), which have trading floors where stocks are traded, and the National Association of Securities Dealers Automated Quotations System (Nasdaq), which is an OTC market that trades primarily new, small-cap stocks of companies over telephone lines and computer networks. A public company lists its shares on one exchange by meeting the listing requirements of that particular exchange. Stocks listed on one exchange can be bought and sold on many exchanges, including the electronic computer networks (ECNs), which are Internet-only exchanges.

The stock markets have changed significantly because of advances in technology. The widespread use of personal computers and, more specifically, the Internet has given investors direct access to information that was unavailable previously. In addition, daily trading hours for investors have been lengthened. Whereas the stock markets were once open for trading only during specific hours, after-hours trading now takes place. The exchanges still close at the end of the official trading day (4:00 p.m., Eastern Standard Time), but after-hours trades transpire via ECNs before the market opens at 9:30 a.m. and after the market closes at 4:00 p.m. Eastern Standard Time (EST).

Trades on the NYSE are matched by specialists on the floor through open-outcry auction (see "Auction Market" later in this chapter), but the NYSE is moving toward allowing widespread automatic matching of buy and sell orders like its rival Nasdaq.

One of the many advantages for investors using the Internet is that they can trade securities online without directly contacting a broker. Another advantage of the Internet is the greater stock-pricing transparency offered. In other words, you can see the price that buyers and sellers are willing to settle on for a particular stock.

The function of the security markets is to provide continuous and fair pricing. Buying and selling financial securities are auction processes. A specialist submits a *bid* price (the amount he or she is willing to pay), and a specialist submits an *ask* price (the amount at which he or she wants to sell). If these prices do not match, the bid and ask prices from other buyers and sellers are sought so that trades can be made.

Efficient markets provide up-to-date prices for certain securities. For stocks, you can get instantaneous prices through real-time pricing on the Internet or by calling your broker. You can easily obtain spreads between the bids and ask quotes for stocks. The *spread* is the difference between the bid and ask prices.

The security markets in the United States are large, in that they have many buyers and sellers. The larger the number of buyers and sellers in a market, the more investors are assured of receiving fair pricing. Use of the Internet, along with the viewing of stock information on television stations (such as on CNBC and Bloomberg), has provided stock-price transparency, where investors can see changing prices from trade to trade, as well as the rapid transmittal of information that affects stock prices. In efficient markets, stock prices reflect all relevant information. Because stock prices in efficient markets reflect all relevant information, little likelihood exists that investors will trade their stocks at unfair prices.

The NYSE, also referred to as the "Big Board," is the largest and the oldest stock exchange in the United States. It has the most stringent listing requirements. In addition to maintaining the requirements for listing on the exchanges, companies are expected to comply with certain regulations administered by the Securities and Exchange Commission (SEC), such as publishing quarterly and annual reports and releasing any information that affects the company's ongoing operations. Companies that do not meet the listing requirements can be delisted. Generally, the largest, best-known, and most financially secure companies that meet the listing requirements are listed on the NYSE.

When a buy or sell order is placed for a company listed on the NYSE, the broker or registered representative transmits the order electronically to the floor of the exchange. The order is then taken to the trading post for that stock, where a specialist executes the order. The ticker tape reports executed transactions. You can watch the trades on the ticker tape, which is shown on television networks such as CNBC during the trading session. After you place an order to buy or sell shares, you receive a confirmation of your executed trade from your brokerage firm.

The AMEX has less stringent listing requirements than the NYSE and generally has the listings of younger, smaller companies. The exchange has added the trading of stock options, stock indexes, and exchange-traded funds (ETFs). The AMEX, like the NYSE, has a physical trading floor, whereas the Nasdaq is an electronic exchange. The AMEX uses a specialist system like the NYSE. A company can be listed on the NYSE or the AMEX as well as on a regional exchange.

Five regional exchanges (Philadelphia, Boston, Cincinnati, Chicago, and the Pacific Exchange) list the stocks of companies in their geographic areas that are not large enough to qualify for listing on the two larger exchanges. These exchanges also can dual-list the same company. For example, General Electric is listed on the NYSE and on several regional exchanges. The advantage of these regional exchanges is that local brokerage firms that do not have memberships on the NYSE have access to these dual-listed shares. The Pacific Exchange has given up its physical trading floor and has become an *electronic communications network* (ECN). An ECN is a privately owned trading network that matches investors' buy and sell orders electronically. The Pacific Exchange accounts for a large percentage of the options traded. The Philadelphia Exchange trades in options, stock, bond, and currency indexes. If trades are not transacted on the NYSE or the AMEX, they can be routed to the regional exchanges in order to get better prices.

A number of companies that issue stocks to the public may not be listed on any of the exchanges described in this section for a variety of reasons. Rather, they are traded over-the-counter. The OTC market is linked by a network of computers and telephones and can include stocks listed on the NYSE or the AMEX. The most actively traded issues are listed on the Nasdaq. The least actively traded issues that do not meet the listing requirements trade on the OTC Bulletin Board. These thinly traded stocks tend to be those of companies that may be more speculative with regard to their future survival. A stockbroker can provide the bid and ask prices for these bulletin board stocks by entering a company's code into the Nasdaq computer system. Many large, reputable companies, such as Intel, Microsoft, Cisco, and Dell, have chosen to remain on the OTC market rather than move up to the AMEX or the NYSE. The listing fees are lower on the OTC market, which is another reason why a majority of the companies listed there are small-cap companies.

In the OTC, orders are executed differently from the way they are executed on the exchange floor. A customer's order to buy is sent to the trading desk of the brokerage firm. From there, a trader at the brokerage firm contacts market makers (in the case of an OTC stock) or dealers (for a stock exchange–listed stock) in that stock to determine the lowest ask price. *Market makers* are the firms that buy stocks for or sell stocks from their own inventories. A *markup* is added to the ask price; you can determine this amount from the stock listings in the Nasdaq National Market Issues in the newspaper or online. Similarly, whenever a stock is sold, an amount called a *markdown* is subtracted from the bid price. In OTC trades, a brokerage firm cannot charge a commission and also act as the market maker. The brokerage firm has to choose between charging a commission and earning a markup or markdown. Market makers or dealers buy and sell securities for and from their own accounts.

Some structural flaws in the Nasdaq trading system encouraged the growth of ECNs. Not a single clearinghouse for OTC trades existed, so buy and sell orders were not always available to interested parties. This lack of centralization led to the charging of high spreads, which resulted in a $1 billion fine against the Nasdaq in 1997. In 1997, the SEC allowed ECNs to display their orders on the Nasdaq electronic trading bulletin board along with the orders of Nasdaq market makers in a system known as *level 2 quoting*. Level 2 quotes are bid and ask prices provided by all market makers of securities carried on the Nasdaq system.

ECNs provide individual and institutional investors with alternative trading systems. ECNs match trades (buy and sell orders) electronically and have increased their trading volume by lowering spreads. Trading on ECNs is advantageous for large institutional investors who want to trade large blocks of shares. If these institutional investors used the Nasdaq market makers (or the exchanges), the general investing public would see their trades, and the stock prices would change based on that knowledge. ECNs allow these institutional investors to trade their stocks anonymously. ECNs also allow individual investors to trade stocks before the stock market opens for the day and after the stock market has closed for the day.

The diversion of trades from the Nasdaq to the ECNs reduces Nasdaq's revenue in that it cannot resell the quotes and trade data to brokers and investors (McNamee, 2002, p. 81). Sustained competition between the Nasdaq and the ECNs can only produce better prices for investors.

The NYSE acquired the ECN Archipelago in April 2005, which allowed the NYSE to broaden its position in options and futures markets, as well as being able to compete with the automated transaction market for Nasdaq-listed stocks and ETFs. .

Foreign stock exchanges list and trade the stocks of their respective markets. Financial newspapers and online financial Web sites, such as Yahoo!, quote the prices of the most actively traded foreign companies listed on the major European, Asian, Australian, South African, and Canadian exchanges (foreign exchanges).

HOW THE SECURITY MARKETS WORK

New issues of common stock and preferred stock are sold in the *primary markets*. In other words, the primary market is the market in which new securities are sold to the market. The *secondary markets* are where existing securities are traded among investors through an intermediary.

PRIMARY MARKETS AND INITIAL PUBLIC OFFERINGS (IPOS) FOR COMMON STOCKS

New issues of stocks that are sold for the first time are *initial public offerings* (IPOs). If a company that has already issued stock on the market wants to issue more stock, it is referred to as a *new issue.* eBay, Yahoo!, and Google were extremely successful IPOs on the market in the late 1990s and early 2000s.

Most IPOs and new issues of stocks are marketed and sold through underwriters (brokerage firms). Most of the underwriting of common stocks takes one of three forms: negotiated arrangement, competitive bid, or best-efforts arrangement. These different arrangements are due to different terms and conditions agreed to between the issuing company and the brokerage firm and do not have a direct effect on the individual purchaser of the securities. What you should know about buying new issues or IPOs is that you do not pay a commission to buy the securities from underwriters. The issuing company pays these fees.

Companies issuing securities in the primary market are required to provide investors with a legal document, called a *prospectus,* so that they can make prudent investment decisions. The prospectus is a formal document related to the offering of new securities that provides information to investors interested in purchasing the securities.

Returns from IPOs

IPOs generally give investors a wild ride in terms of returns. In September 1998, eBay, an Internet company, was brought to market at an issue price of $18 per share, and $3\frac{1}{2}$ months later the stock was trading at $246. This 1,267 percent return took place over $3\frac{1}{2}$

months. Not all IPOs are like eBay, though. Generally, many IPOs increase in price on the first day of trading owing to the heavy demand for the stocks, but over long periods of time they tend to underperform secondary issues. A study done by Christopher B. Barry and Robert H. Jennings (1993) showed that the greatest return on an IPO is earned, on average, on the first day the stock comes to the market. Professor Jay Ritter (1991) concluded that an IPO's long-term performance is much poorer than that of companies trading on the secondary markets (existing shares traded on the markets). Ritter updated his research to include returns from IPOs during the five years after issuance from 1970 to 2002, indicating that IPOs underperformed other firms of the same market capitalization by an average of 4.2 percent, excluding the first-day return. In addition, the Wall Street practice of imposing penalties on brokers who sell their clients' shares immediately after issue is disadvantageous for small investors (Zweig, Spiro, and Schroeder, 1994, pp. 84–90). Table 7–1 offers an explanation of how IPO shares are allocated and who gets them.

One reason for a decline in price of IPO shares after a period of time might be that company insiders sell their shares. Executives, managers, and employees of a company can purchase their own stock or are granted options on the stock. Insiders usually must hold the stock for a period of time, known as a *lock-up period*, which typically ranges from three months to a year. When the lock-up

TABLE 7-1

How IPO Shares Are Allotted and Who Gets Them

Investors of all types have tried diligently to obtain IPO shares because of the spectacular returns earned by many IPOs over short periods. Therefore, if individual investors have a hard time getting these shares at issue, who does get them?

The issuing company distributes a portion of the IPO to its friends and family members. The underwriter also allocates its shares to privileged investors, such as institutional investors and mutual funds. Smaller allocations go to the brokerage firms' wealthy investors. The average small investor is positioned low on the institutional totem pole.

No rules or regulations govern the allocation process. The National Association of Securities Dealers (NASD) bars investment banks from selling these IPO shares to senior officers who are in a position to direct future business back to their investment banks (underwriters).

period expires, company insiders can sell their shares, which can cause the share price to fall.

The IPO market has some disadvantages that you should be aware of before investing:

- Institutional investors get very large allocations of shares, leaving a small percentage available for individual investors.
- Institutional investors are privy to better information than individual investors.
- Individuals rely on information primarily from a prospectus; institutional investors can attend road shows and meet company executives. *Cheat sheets*, provided by brokerage firms to their preferred institutional clients, contain management forecasts and income projections that are not part of a prospectus. Companies are reluctant to include cheat sheets in their public documents; if a company misses its published projections, it might be vulnerable to lawsuits.
- Individual investors are penalized for selling their shares immediately after issue, although institutional investors are allowed to quickly "flip" their shares.

If you want to participate directly in the IPO market, you should be aware of these disadvantages. You might consider instead investing in mutual funds that concentrate on IPOs.

Protecting Against Losses in Choosing IPOs

If you are interested in buying an IPO, you should investigate the company before you buy to limit your risk of loss. Although paying attention to a prospectus does not ensure success, it certainly is a good defensive measure.

Check the prospectus for the following:

- *The underwriters.* Is the underwriting company well known? Large, well-known underwriting firms generally are busy enough to screen out the more speculative IPOs. Even so, some new issues of immature companies are still underwritten by top underwriters, and the stock prices have fallen into oblivion after being brought to the market. Check the underwriter's record by asking the broker for a list of recent underwritings or by checking on the Internet at www.iporesources.org.

- *The number of underwriters in the syndicate.* Large syndicate groups generally give an IPO more exposure. Additionally, large syndicates provide more brokerage firms to trade the new stock, supporting its price (Barker, 1997, pp 168–169).
- *Financial statements.* Look at the financial statements in the back of the prospectus. From the *balance sheet*, determine who has provided the capital for the assets. Is it primarily from debt or equity? If total liabilities exceed shareholders' equity, this is a red flag and requires further investigation. If the company has a downturn in revenues, can it still service its debt? If the shareholders' equity is negative, look carefully at the financial details of the company. Companies that have posted losses that exceed the amount of their retained earnings have negative retained earnings. If these negative retained earnings exceed the amounts in the capital accounts, the company has a negative shareholders' equity. Determine whether this company has the ability to turn its losses into profits in the not too distant future to maintain its business. Lazard company had sizable debt and negative book value, explaining its lackluster share price performance

Related to the income and losses is the cash flow a company generates. For example, Friendly Ice Cream, the restaurant chain, chalked up losses from operations since 1992, but this company had positive cash flows (Barker, 1997, p. 169). You can calculate whether *cash flow* is positive by starting with net income or loss and adding back the noncash items such as depreciation and amortization.

From the *income statement*, determine whether sales and earnings are growing. If a company experiences growth in sales but shows a loss in income, examine its prospectus for comments about profits in the foreseeable future. If profits are not anticipated soon, another red flag is raised. A note of irony: If investors had listened to this advice, they would never have bought any of the new Internet IPOs in October and November 1998, whose share prices mostly went up in the same trajectory as a rocket taking off for Mars. Most of these companies did not anticipate having earnings for years to come and were trading at rich multiples of sales. You should not assume that every company with an idea and no earnings will always be successful, however.

- *Discussion and analysis by management.* See if there is any cushioning of future trouble signs ahead. Take a step back and ask: what could go wrong with this company? What are its risks? Who are its competitors? Who are its customers? Assess the overall risks of the company. If it is too risky, walk away from it.

These precautions can help you to limit the risk of loss from investing in IPOs.

New Issues of Securities

New issues of securities occur whenever exchange-listed companies want to raise new capital by issuing more securities. The procedure for issuing new securities to the public is roughly the same as with an IPO. Before securities are sold to the public, they must be registered with and approved by the SEC. The prospectus, called a *shelf registration*, is less detailed than that for an IPO because the company has already filed the necessary reports with the SEC, in addition to quarterly and annual statements and the necessary initial reports. The price of the issue approximates the market price of the company's securities, and less fine-tuning of that point takes place between the investment bankers and the company.

SECONDARY MARKETS AND HOW SECURITIES ARE TRADED

After new stocks have been sold, investors can trade them on the secondary markets. The company (original issuer of the securities) does not receive any proceeds on these trades. Instead, the trades are made between the buyers and sellers of the securities. The secondary markets are important for providing not only liquidity and fair pricing for securities but also a baseline for the pricing of new issues and IPOs.

How Stocks Are Traded

Individual investors place their orders for stocks through their brokers, who buy and sell stocks for their investors. These orders can be filled in two major trading systems: the auction market and the dealer market.

Auction Market

An *auction market* is a centralized location where bid and ask prices are given for stocks. Bid and ask prices are matched by specialists and floor brokers in an open-outcry auction; shares with the lowest ask price are bought from investors, and shares with the highest bid prices are sold to investors. This process takes place on the NYSE and the AMEX. A *specialist* is a member of an exchange who makes a market in one or more of the securities listed on the exchange.

An example best illustrates the process of order execution on the NYSE. Suppose that you are an interested in buying 200 shares of Home Depot, Inc. You call your broker for a quote or go online for this information. The bid price is $34.90 per share, and the ask price is $34.91 per share. The *bid* means that the specialist is willing to buy Home Depot shares at $34.90 per share, and the *ask* means that the specialist is willing to sell Home Depot shares at $34.91 per share. The *spread* is $0.01 per share. On the NYSE, the Home Depot specialist makes a market in the stock.

You then decide to buy 200 shares of Home Depot at the market price. The transaction should be close to the $34.91 price per share if you place the order immediately after receiving the quote and if the market price of Home Depot does not fluctuate widely.

Your broker fills out a buy order (or you fill out an online order), which is transmitted electronically to the floor of the exchange. Figure 7–1 provides an example of an online buy-sell order. There, the *floor broker* (member of an exchange who executes orders on the exchange floor) takes the order to the Home Depot trading post to execute the buy order, from either another floor broker who has a sell order for 200 Home Depot shares or the specialist. When your order is executed, the brokerage firm mails or e-mails you a confirmation that the order has been executed.

Specialists are allowed to trade the assigned stocks in their own accounts and to profit from those trades. However, specialists are required to maintain a fair and orderly market in stocks assigned to them. For example, specialists are not allowed to compete with customers' orders. If a customer places a market order to buy, the specialist cannot buy for his or her own account ahead of the unexecuted market order. Similarly, specialists cannot sell from their accounts ahead of unexecuted market orders to sell. The purpose of allowing specialists to act as traders is to minimize the effects of imbalances in the supply and demand of assigned stocks.

Specialists are prohibited by law from manipulating stock prices. Even though the SEC monitors the trading activities of specialists and ensures that they follow its numerous rules, maintaining an orderly market, along with the profit motivations of the specialist, means stepping into a gray area. The reputation of the NYSE was tarnished by trading abuses of specialists and floor brokers on the exchange floor who traded stocks ahead of investors' orders for their own profit in 2003. A useful Web site providing basic information on the markets and how those markets work is www.pathtoinvesting.org.

Dealer Market

In a dealer market, dealers make markets in stocks from their inventories by using a computerized system. Numerous dealers can provide both bid and ask prices for the same stock. This form of trading takes place in the Nasdaq system for OTC trades. The NASD implemented the Nasdaq, which allows subscribing brokerage firms to obtain price quotations on stocks in the system.

FIGURE 7-1

A Typical Online Order Ticket

Symbol/Name _____
Quantity _____ shares

Transaction Type: Select one
                 Buy/Sell/ Sell Short/ Buy to Cover
_____

Order Type: Select one
            Market/Limit/Stop
_____

Limit Price _____   Stop Price _____

Duration: Select one
            Day/Good -Till Canceled
_____

Account Type: Select One
             Cash/Margin
_____

When buying or selling an OTC stock, you place an order with a brokerage firm. That order is sent to the brokerage firm's trading department, which then shops among that stock's market makers for the best price. To serve the needs of different brokerage firms, the Nasdaq provides three levels of quotes:

Level 1. This basic level provides a single quote for each stock. The price is updated continuously.

Level 2. This level provides instantaneous quotes (bid and ask prices) for Nasdaq stocks from all the different market makers. A brokerage firm takes an investor's order for a particular stock to find the best price (the lowest ask price if the investor is buying and the highest bid price if the investor is selling) from those quotes. See Table 7–2 for an example.

Level 3. This level, for market makers and dealers, provides level 2 quotes and the capacity to change those quotes.

Many criticisms have been leveled at the potential conflict of interest between market makers and dealers regarding execution of trades on the OTC market. That brokerage firms can act simultaneously as agents for their customers and self-interested dealers might be a conflict of interest. Acting as an agent, a broker should find the best price for customers. This responsibility becomes blurred when the agent's brokerage firm is also looking to profit from the deals it makes. You have no need to look for more competitive prices if your brokerage firm can fill your order as a market maker and thereby fulfill its profit objective. Table 7–3 discusses the importance of spreads.

TYPES OF ORDERS

When you are buying and selling securities, you can place different types of orders to improve your execution prices. The incremental size of an order is also important. Using a *round lot* usually means that the number of shares traded is 100 or a multiple of 100. For very cheap stocks ("penny stocks"), a round lot may be 500 or 1,000 shares; for high-priced shares, a round lot could be considered 10 shares. These 10-share round lots are referred to as *cabinet stocks*. Berkshire Hathaway A stock is a good example of a cabinet stock. It was currently trading around $110,000 per share (May 11, 2007). This is the most expensive stock on the NYSE. An *odd lot* for most cabinet stocks consists of a trade of between 1 and 9 shares. On regular-priced shares, an odd lot consists of between 1 and 99 shares;

TABLE 7-2

Examples of Level 2 Quotes and What They Mean

Some online brokerage firms provide level 2 quotes for OTC stocks for their online clients. The following example illustrates the quotes offered by market makers and ECNs for a particular stock. Many actively traded stocks could have as many as 40 market makers. Microsoft, for example, might have 20 to 40 market makers.

Market Maker/ECN	Bid	Size	Ask	Size
1	19.25	20	19.26	20
2	19.24	5	19.27	5
3	19.25	7	19.27	5
4	19.24	20	19.26	20
5	19.22	5	19.28	5

With level 2 quotes, a market buy order for a particular stock receives each market maker's or ECN's best bid offer. In this example, the best offer (ask) price is $19.26 per share for this particular company from ECNs 1 and 4. A market order to sell transacts at the best bid price, which is from ECNs 1 and 3 at $19.25 per share.

When a market order is entered, it is executed at the best price and continues to be filled incrementally until the order is completed. For example, a market order to buy 5,000 shares of the stock listed above would be transacted as follows:

   2000 shares from dealer 1 at $19.26 per share
   2000 shares from dealer 4 at $19.26 per share
   500 shares from dealer 3 at $19.27 per share
   500 shares from dealer 2 at $19.27 per share

An investor also can place an all-or-none order to make sure that it fills at the same price. The identity of each market maker or ECN is available to the investor. The size indicates the inventory that is available.

---

for very cheap stocks, an odd lot consists of fewer than 500 shares. Investors trading in odd lots generally pay more to trade than investors trading in round lots. The commissions paid in order to execute odd-lot trades may be higher.

Orders for stocks in excess of 10,000 shares are called *block trades*. These orders, typically placed by institutional customers, are handled in a variety of ways. Commissions are much lower than for normal trades, and orders are executed instantaneously.

By knowing the types of orders to use and how they are executed, you might be able to lower your transaction costs and avoid any misunderstandings with your brokers.

TABLE 7-3

What Spreads Disclose

Stock spreads are determined by their bid and ask prices. Bid and ask prices are determined in some ways by supply and demand for the stocks but more specifically by the availability of the stock at particular prices. Bid and ask prices change rapidly in real time. Paying attention to the bid and ask sizes (the amount of stock available from each market maker) of each stock can provide more information about the supply and demand for the direction of the stock price. Spreads have narrowed because of the greater pricing transparency gained from access to real-time quotes through technology. The result of having narrower spreads is better execution prices. For example, the reduction in spreads from $0.03 to $0.02 per trade of 1,000 shares results in a $10 savings. If you make 100 trades per year, the total saving is $1,000. These savings can meaningfully increase returns on your portfolio. You can draw these inferences about spreads:

- A wide spread indicates an illiquid stock.
- A narrow spread indicates a liquid stock.

Use limit orders when buying and selling stocks to specify the exact purchase or sale price. With a market order, the purchase (or sale) price could be higher (or lower) than the ask (or bid) price.

The bid and ask size also indicates the relative strength or depth of the bid and ask prices. When the supply of a stock (the ask size) is larger than the demand for the stock (the bid size), the short-term price indication is that the stock price will fall. Conversely, if the ask size is smaller than the bid size, the short-term price of the stock is pressured upward. The following quote is used as an example to illustrate the price direction using the bid and ask size:

Ticker Symbol	Bid Price	Ask Price	Size (Bid/Ask)
GE	34.71	34.73	1,000 × 200

In this example, the bid size is larger than the ask size, indicating greater demand for the stock than the supply. In other words, the short-term price is headed upward. You can use the bid and ask size to assist in the determination of whether to use a market or limit order.

Market Order

A *market order,* the most frequently placed order type, is an instruction to buy or sell a stock at the best available price at the time that the order is executed. If you obtain a price quote for Intel stock, for example, and place an order to buy 100 shares without specifying the price, it is a market order. Market orders are given priority in the communications systems of brokerage firms, so the stock is purchased before the price changes much. Market orders generally are executed within seconds of being placed. In a few situations, a market order may not be executed—when curbs are in effect on the exchange floor, for example, or when the trading of that particular stock has been halted for some reason.

The good news is that market orders are filled soon after they are placed. The downside is that you do not know in advance the price at which the order will be executed. The order generally is executed at or close to the quoted price because of the order's prompt execution. However, if the stock is actively traded at the time the order is placed, some price deviation from the quoted price may take place. For example, a market order placed to buy a newly issued stock that begins trading for the first time on the secondary market might be executed at a much higher price than the offering price. When a fast-moving market occurs for a particular stock or stocks, a market order can be transacted at a significant price discrepancy from the quoted price.

These fast markets have a bearing on online trading. Even if investors receive real-time quotes, a market order might not keep pace with those real-time quotes. By the time an order is placed online, the market may have moved considerably, making the quote that is received only an approximation of what is happening. Because market orders are executed on a first-serve basis, if numerous orders are already ahead of the one that is placed, the execution price can be significantly different from the quoted price. In this type of market, you should use limit orders to protect against the risk of large price deviations.

A market order is usually a *day order*, which means mean that it expires at the end of the day if it is not executed by then.

Limit Order

A *limit order* is an instruction to buy or sell a stock at a specified price. The specified price can be different from the market price. A limit order specifies a maximum price for buying a stock or a minimum price for selling a stock. For example, if the price of a stock is anticipated to fall from its current price, you can place a limit order to buy that stock at a specified lower price. If you want to buy 100 shares of General Electric, for example, which has fluctuated between $31 and $35 per share, you can place a limit order to buy General Electric at $31 even though the market price is $34 per share at the time the order is placed. The length of time that the order stands before being executed depends on the instructions you give to your broker. Using a good-till-canceled (GTC) order, you can have the order remain active until it is either executed or canceled. If a time limit is not specified, the order is assumed to be a day order; in that case, if the stock price does not fall to the limit price, the order is canceled at the end of the day.

Similarly, a limit order to sell stock can be placed above the current market price. For example, if ExxonMobil Corporation's stock is trading at $68 per share and you think that the stock will continue on an upward trend, you might decide to place a limit order to sell at $75 per share or higher. This order is then executed if and when ExxonMobil's shares reach $75.

A limit order for an NYSE stock is sent from an investor's brokerage firm to the commission broker on the exchange floor, who sees whether the order can be filled from the crowd (other commission brokers). A *commission broker* is an employee of a member firm on the exchange who transacts the firm's orders on the exchange floor. If the limit order's price does not fall within the quotes of the current bid and ask prices, the order is given to the specialist (a member of the exchange who makes a market in one or more listed stocks on the exchange). If the specialist does not execute the order, the limit order is entered into the specialist's book for future execution. In this case the specialist is acting as a broker for the commission broker. If the price of ExxonMobil, for example, rises days or months later, the higher-priced limit orders in the specialist's book are executed in the order in which they were entered, known as the *first-in, first-out* (FIFO) basis. The specialist receives part of the customer's commission for executing this limit order.

The advantage of placing a limit order is that investors have an opportunity to buy (or sell) shares at a lower (or higher) price than the market price. The obvious disadvantage is that limit orders might never be executed if the limit prices are never reached. Placing a limit order does not guarantee that your order will be executed; with a market order, however, you are assured of execution but not the price of execution.

Stop Order

A *stop order* is an instruction to buy or sell a stock whenever the stock trades at or past a specified price, when it then becomes a market order. You can use a stop order to protect existing profits or reduce losses. Although a stop order might appear similar to a limit order, they have some differences.

A stop order differs from a limit order in that after the stock's price reaches the stop-order price, the stop order becomes a market order. Suppose that you buy some stock at $20 per share that is now trading at $30 per share. Selling those shares would result in a $10 per share profit. To protect this profit from a rapid price drop, you can place a stop order to sell at $28 per share. If the stock drops to $28, the stop order then becomes a market order and is executed at the prevailing market price. If the stock is sold at $27.75 per share, you have protected a profit of $7.75 per share. On the other hand, if the stock keeps increasing from $30 per share after the stop order is placed, the stop order lies dormant (if it has no time limit and is a GTC order) until the share price falls to $28.

Similarly, you can protect profits on a short sale by using a stop order to buy. (Short selling is explained in Chapter 8.)

In addition to protecting profits, stop orders can be used to reduce or prevent losses. Suppose that you buy a stock at $10 in anticipation of a price increase. Soon after your purchase, news from the company suggests that the price may go down rapidly. You can place a stop order to sell at $9, which limits your loss if the stock price declines below $9 per share. Limiting losses on a short sale is the other use for stop orders and is explained in Chapter 8.

Another danger awaits when you are setting a stop-order price. If you place the stop-order price too close to the current price, a temporary surge or fall in price of the stock can trigger execution of a market order. Then, although the stock price might move back in the direction you anticipate, you no longer have a position in that stock. On the other hand, if the stop-order price is set further away from the current market price, less profit is protected (or you risk a greater loss).

Of course, the use of stop orders does not increase profits if you do not correctly anticipate the direction of the market price.

STOCKBROKERS

Financial advisors provide investors with assistance in their financial planning. A financial advisor evaluates your financial situation and then formulates a financial and investment plan. Stockbrokers provide investment advice about individual securities and place investors' trade orders. To trade securities, you need access to the marketplace, and you attain access through a brokerage firm. The selection of a stockbroker is a personal decision. You can choose from three types of brokers:

- Full service
- Discount
- Online

The amount and level of services among these basic types of brokers differ, as do methods of compensation.

Stockbrokers charge commissions for executing trades. These commission costs vary considerably and can affect your profits and losses. Commission charges can be based on three factors: number of shares traded, the share price, and the total amount of the order.

Full-service and national brokerage firms generally charge the highest fees and commissions, followed by *regional* service brokerage firms, which tend to be marginally cheaper. Discount brokerage firms offer reduced commissions, and they charge either no fees or reduced fees for miscellaneous services. Commissions are discounted even more at deep-discount brokerage firms.

Electronic trading or *online brokers* allow you to place your own trades using a computer linked to the Internet. The costs of online trading can vary from $5 to $20 per trade. Research is widely available through these online trading services. Some brokerage firms charge nominal amounts for Standard & Poor's (S&P's) reports or Zack's research reports, and others provide them for free. Online investing can mean online research no matter which type of brokerage firm is used. The government's Web site Edgar Online (www.freeedgar.com) provides data derived from the thousands of SEC documents filed by publicly traded companies.

If you are comfortable using a computer and do not require information and research from a personal broker, you can benefit from the lower commissions charged by online brokerage firms. You also should ask about the broker's fee structure for custodial services, account management, and transactions before making a final choice.

TYPES OF ACCOUNTS AT BROKERAGE FIRMS

Opening an account at a brokerage firm is as easy as opening a bank account. Many brokerage firms require little more than a deposit. You are asked to supply basic information, such as your occupation and Social Security number, in addition to more specific information about your financial circumstances. Brokers are required to get to know their customers, to be able to use judgment with regard to sizable transactions, and to determine whether customers can use credit to finance their trades.

Brokerage firms must ask their customers how securities are to be registered. If you decide to leave your stock certificates, for example, in the custody of your brokerage firm, the securities are registered in street name. *Street name* refers to the registration of investor-owned securities in the name of the brokerage firm. Accrued dividends of street-named securities are mailed to the brokerage firms, where they are then credited to customer accounts. The main disadvantage of registering stocks in street name is that the brokerage firms may not forward to you all the mailings of company reports and news. The advantage of holding securities in street name is that when securities are sold, the customer has no need to deliver the signed stock certificates within the three days required before the settlement of the transaction.

Securities that are registered in your name can be kept either in your broker's vault or mailed to you. You should store these security certificates in a bank safe-deposit box because they are negotiable securities. If they are stolen, you might face losses.

Three types of accounts are used for buying and selling securities:

- Cash
- Margin
- Discretionary

Cash Account

A *cash account* with a brokerage firm requires that cash payments be made for the purchases of securities within three days of the transaction. With a cash account, you are required to pay in full for the purchase of securities on or before the settlement date. The *settlement date* is defined as three business days after an order is executed and the date on which the purchaser of the securities must pay cash to the brokerage firm and the seller of the securities must deliver the securities to the brokerage firm. If you buy stock on a Monday, for example, your payment is due on or before the Wednesday of that week, assuming that no public holidays take place during those three days. That Monday is referred to as the *trade date* (the date on which an order is executed). If you do not pay for the securities by the settlement date, the brokerage firm can liquidate them. In the event of a loss, the brokerage firm can require additional payments from you, to make up for the loss and to keep your account in good standing. For online accounts, the money generally needs to be in the account before the trade is made.

When stocks are sold, stock certificates must be delivered or sent to the brokerage firm (if securities are not held in street name) within three days to avoid any charges. After the settlement date, the proceeds of the sale, minus commissions, are either mailed to the investor or deposited into a cash account with the brokerage firm, depending on the arrangements made in advance. Determine whether any fees are charged for the management of cash in the account or for access to a money market account.

Margin Account

A *margin account* with a brokerage firm allows a brokerage client to purchase securities on credit and to borrow securities to sell short. In other words, a margin account with a brokerage firm allows you to buy securities without having to pay the full cash price. The balance is borrowed from the brokerage firm. The maximum percentage of the purchase price that a client can borrow is determined by the *margin requirement* set by the Federal Reserve Board. Brokers can set more strict requirements for their clients. For example, with a margin requirement of 50 percent, if you are buying stock worth $12,000, you would have to put up at least $6,000 in cash and borrow the other $6,000 from the brokerage firm. If the margin requirement is 60 percent, you would have to put up at least $7,200 and borrow the balance. The brokerage firm uses the stock as collateral on the loan. These securities are held in street name and also can be loaned to other clients of the brokerage firm who are selling short. Short selling is discussed in Chapter 8.

The brokerage firm charges interest on the amount borrowed by the margin investor. Risks are magnified in margin trading because losses represent a greater portion of the money invested. However, if the price of the stock goes up, the rate of return is greater for the margin investor than for the cash investor because the margin investor has invested less money. In both cases the investor must pay interest on the margin loan, increasing a loss and slightly reducing a profit. This concept is illustrated in Table 7–4.

TABLE 7-4

Rate of Return Using a Cash Account versus a Margin Account

An investor buys 100 shares of Johnson & Johnson (JNJ) at $60 per share and sells at $65 per share. The margin requirement is 50 percent. Commissions per trade are $50. Interest on the margin account is $45.

	Cash Account	Margin Account
Proceeds from sale of 100 shares of JNJ at $65	$6,500	$6,500
Less commissions	(50)	(50)
Net proceeds	6,450	6,450
Cost of 100 shares plus commission	(6,050)	(6,050)
Gross profit	400	400
Less interest expense		45
Net profit	$400	$355

$$\text{Rate of return} = \text{profit/invested funds}$$
$$= 400/6{,}050 = 6.6\% \text{ (cash account)}$$
$$= 355/3{,}025^* = 11.73\% \text{ (margin account)}$$

* Invested funds = $3,025 ($6,050 × 50%).

The proceeds and the gross profit are the same for both the cash and margin accounts. The differences are that the investor deposits the entire cost of the shares for the cash account ($6,050), whereas an investor in the margin account only puts up 50 percent ($3,025). The rate of return is greater for the margin investor because the amount invested is much less than that of the cash investor despite the lower net profit caused by the interest expense for the margin investor.

Determine the rate of return if the data above are the same except for Johnson & Johnson stock being sold at $50 per share.

	Cash Account	Margin Account
Proceeds from sale of 100 shares of JNJ at $50	$5,000	$5,000
Less commissions	(50)	(50)
Net proceeds	4,950	4,950
Cost of 100 shares plus commission	(6,050)	(6,050)
Gross loss	(1,100)	(1,100)
Less interest expense		45
Net loss	(1,100)	(1,145)
Investment	$6,050	$3,025*

$$\text{Rate of loss} = -1{,}100/6{,}050 = -18.18\% \text{ (cash account)}$$
$$= -1{,}145/3{,}025 = -37.85.\% \text{ (margin account)}$$

* Margin requirement $3,025 ($6,050 × 50%).

The rate of loss is magnified with a margin account because the net loss is greater and the amount invested is less than the figures in the cash account.

If stock prices decline in a margin account, the amount owed to the brokerage firm becomes proportionately larger. In order to protect their positions, brokerage firms set *maintenance margins*, which are minimum equity positions investors must have in their margin accounts. When funds fall below the maintenance margin, the broker sends the investor a margin call. A *margin call* is a notice requesting that the investor pay additional money to maintain the minimum margin requirement. If the investor does not deposit additional funds, the brokerage firm can liquidate the securities. The investor is then liable for any losses incurred by the brokerage firm. Table 7–5 shows an example of margin maintenance.

Two types of transactions can be performed with only a margin account: selling stocks short (described in Chapter 8) and writing uncovered stock options.

Discretionary Account

A *discretionary account* is a brokerage account in which the broker is permitted to buy and sell securities on behalf of the investor. If you have this type of account, you agree to allow your brokerage firm to decide which securities to buy and sell, as well as the amount and price to be paid and received. (For an unethical broker, a discretionary account is the answer to all prayers!)

TABLE 7-5

Margin Maintenance

Determine whether a margin call takes place in the following situation:

The margin requirement set by the Federal Reserve is 50 percent, and the brokerage firm's maintenance margin requirement is 40 percent. The investor buys 100 shares of Cisco at $15 per share. The share price drops to $13 per share. Commissions are ignored in this example.

Purchase price 100 shares Cisco $15 per share	$1,500
Investor's equity (50% × $1,500)	750
Borrowing in margin account	750
Value of Cisco at $13 per share	1,300
Less borrowed amount	(750)
Investor's equity	$550
Investor's equity percentage (550/1,300)	42.3%

Because this percentage exceeds the maintenance margin requirement of 40 percent, no margin call is placed.

You should monitor the activity in your discretionary account monthly to determine whether your broker has engaged in any excessive trading for the sole purpose of earning more commissions. In this process, called *churning*, stocks are turned over frequently even though they have only moved up or down a few points. Unless you know the broker and trust him or her implicitly, be careful with a discretionary account.

REFERENCES

Barker, Robert. "Just How Juicy Is That IPO?" *BusinessWeek*, October 6, 1997, pp. 168–169.

Craig, Susanne. "IPO Allotments: A Guide to the Game." *Wall Street Journal*, August 29, 2002, pp. C1, C10.

Faerber, Esmé. *All About Investing.* New York: McGraw-Hill, 2006.

McNamee, Mike. "A Magic Bullet for Nasdaq?" *BusinessWeek*, September 30, 2002, pp. 80–81.

Ritter, J. R. "The Long-Run Performance of IPOs." *Journal of Finance* 46 (March 1991), pp. 3–27.

Ritter, J. R. http://bear.cba.ufl.edu/ritter/ipos; accessed June 24, 2004.

Schroeder, Michael, and Anita Raghavan. "SEC to Fine Firms, Ending Nasdaq Probe." *Wall Street Journal*, January 6, 1999, p. C1.

Zweig, Philip L., Leah Nathans Spiro, and Michael Schroeder. "Beware the IPO Market." *BusinessWeek*, April 4, 1994, pp. 84–90.

CHAPTER 8

How Short Selling Works

KEY CONCEPTS

- How short selling works
- The risks of short selling
- Use of stop orders to protect profits
- Short interest
- NYSE circuit breakers

Investment Snapshot

- In 1992, George Soros profited by $2 billion from selling short the British pound.
- Short selling allows hedge funds to profit during bear markets.

HOW SHORT SELLING WORKS

Most investors invest in common stocks by buying them and then selling them later. Outright ownership of shares is referred to as a *long position*. The opposite is a *short position*, which is based on the expectation that the price of the security will decline. A short position indicates that a security is borrowed and then sold and bought back in the future when the price declines. When stock prices are expected to increase, you can benefit from buying stocks.

When stock prices are expected to decrease, you can benefit from selling short stocks before their prices decrease.

In a short sale, you borrow stocks to sell with the expectation that the prices of the stocks are going to decline. If the stock prices do decline, you can buy the stocks back at a lower price and then returned the borrowed shares to the lender. An example illustrates this process.

Ms. X thinks that the stock of Dell (the computer company), ticker symbol DELL, is overvalued and that its price will drop. She places an order with her broker to sell short 100 shares of Dell, which is transacted at $43 per share (the total proceeds are $4,300 without commissions). The brokerage firm has three business days to deliver 100 shares of Dell to the buyer and has several sources from which to borrow these securities. It might borrow the 100 shares of Dell from its own inventory of Dell stock, if it has any, or from another brokerage firm. The most likely source is from its own inventory of securities held in street name from its margin accounts. In this example, the brokerage firm locates 100 shares of Dell in a margin account belonging to Mr. Y. The brokerage firm sends these shares to the buyer, who bought the shares sold short by Ms. X, and Dell is notified of the new ownership.

All parties in this transaction are satisfied. The buyer has acquired the shares. The short seller, Ms. X, has $4,300, minus commissions, in her margin account, and the brokerage firm has received the commissions on the trade. The $4,300 (minus commissions) is held in the margin account (and cannot be withdrawn by Ms. X) as protection in case Ms. X defaults on the short sale.

Mr. Y, who more than likely signed a loan consent form when he opened his margin account, is indifferent to the process. He still has all his rights of the ownership of the 100 shares of Dell. This process is illustrated in Figure 8–1.

When the stock in question is a dividend-paying stock, who receives the dividend?

Before the short sale, the brokerage firm would have received the dividend on the 100 shares held in street name in Mr. Y's margin account, and this amount would then be paid into his account. However, those shares have been used in the short sale and forwarded to the new buyer, who receives the dividend from the company. Mr. Y is still entitled to his dividend. The short seller, Ms. X, who borrowed his securities, must pay to Mr. Y an equal dividend amount via the brokerage firm.

FIGURE 8-1

A Short Sale

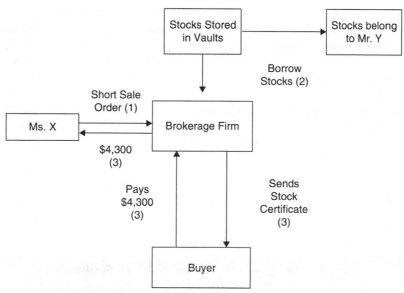

When Dell declines to $18 per share, Ms. X puts in a buy order to cover her short position. The securities are returned to the brokerage firm, and Ms. X has made a profit of $25 per share, not counting the commissions on the trades and the dividend.

Short sales are transacted in margin accounts. The possibility always exists that Ms. X could skip town, and then the brokerage firm would be short the 100 shares of Dell. By using a margin account, the short seller (Ms. X) has to leave the proceeds from the short sale in the account and is also required to pay in an additional amount of cash—that's the margin requirement discussed in Chapter 7. Assuming a margin requirement of 50 percent, Table 8–1 illustrates Ms. X's margin account.

Margin accounts provide greater leverage than cash accounts. Ms. X paid $2,125 and received a 111 percent return ($2,358/$2,125). Cash transactions require the entire investment in the stock to be put up in cash, which reduces the rate of return. *Leverage* is the creation of profit or loss proportionally greater than an underlying investment by using other people's money. The use of leverage has the effect of a double-edged sword. In the event of losses, the percentage loss is greater on margin trading than on cash trades.

TABLE 8-1

Margin Account Illustrating a Short Sale

Proceeds from short sale of 100 shares of DELL at $43	$4,300
Less commissions and fees	(50)
Net proceeds	4,250
Add total margin requirement (50%)	2,125
Balance	6,375
Minus interest expense on borrowed funds	(42)
Net proceeds	6,333
Cost to purchase 100 shares of DELL at $18	$1,800
Add commission	50
Total cost	1,850
Balance	4,433
Less margin deposit	2,125
Profit	$2,358

What Are the Risks of Short Selling?

Short selling allows you to sell a security without owning it. (Doing so for virtually everything other than stocks, can land a person in prison!) If a stock's price falls below its short-sale price, you make a profit.

If the stock price increases, however, you can lose money. The potential loss is limitless because if the stock keeps going up, the amount of the loss increases. Suppose that you thought that certain Internet stocks were overvalued during their period of "irrational exuberance" and decided to sell some of them short. Tremendous losses would have resulted during the wild inflation of prices. AOL stock (now part of Time Warner) went from $100 to about $400 per share on a presplit basis in a short period. If you had sold short at $100 and had not covered your position (bought back the stock), you would have faced the prospect of buying back the stock at an enormously high price, resulting in a large loss per share. With a long position, the most that you can lose is the amount of your investment (buy a stock at $12 per share, and it falls to $0), whereas short selling imposes no limits. The higher the price, the greater is the loss. Stocks generally appreciate over time, which means that by selling short, you are betting against the trend of the market.

Stocks that have a large number of short positions incur additional risk when the stocks rise in price. Short sellers rush to buy back the stocks to cover their positions, which drives prices up, further resulting in a *short squeeze* in the stock. Technically, it is risky to short a stock with large short positions (short interest).

You have to be aware of other risks. Stocks can be sold short only if the price of the stock on its preceding trade was traded on an uptick or a zero-tick. An *uptick* means that the price of the existing trade exceeds the price of the preceding trade. A *zero-tick* means that the price of the most recent trade is the same as the preceding trade. Thus, if the price of a stock declines precipitously, your short sale might not be executed.

The short seller is also required to pay any dividends that are declared by the company to the owner of the borrowed securities. In addition, the proceeds of the short sale are held as collateral for the securities borrowed by the brokerage firm. The short seller is also required to provide additional funds (the margin requirement of 50 percent set by the Federal Reserve). If the stock remains in a flat trading range, the short seller's funds and the margin requirement are tied up in the account.

Using Stop Orders to Protect Profits on a Short Sale

Stop orders can be used to protect profits on a short sale. If you sell short a stock at $40 and the stock declines to $32, you might be reluctant to buy back the short position, hoping that the stock will decline even further. To protect profits against an unanticipated price increase, you place a stop order at $34 to preserve your $6 profit per share.

Similarly, use of a stop order can reduce the losses in an unfavorable short sale. If you sell short a stock at $15, you might place a stop order to cover a short position at $16. This strategy limits the losses should there be a rise in the price of the stock. Without a stop order, the investor potentially could face a large loss if the stock keeps going up in price.

With a long position in stocks, the most that an investor could lose is the entire investment (if the company goes bankrupt, and the stock falls to zero with nothing left for the shareholders). However, with short selling, if the price of a stock keeps rising, the losses theoretically could be unlimited.

Selling short may be risky for investors who do not have the stomach to watch the price of the stock turn in an unanticipated direction.

There are rules governing short sales on the New York Stock Exchange (NYSE) and the American Stock Exchange (AMEX), as well as for stocks on the National Association of Securities Dealers Automated Quotations (Nasdaq). Short sales may not be made when stocks are falling in price because this will exacerbate the price declines. On the exchanges, short sales may be made for a higher price than that of the previous trade, on an *uptick,* or for a price that is equal to that of the previous trade but more than the trade prior to that, on a *zero-plus tick.*

WHAT IS SHORT INTEREST?

Short interest is the number of shares of a company's stock that have been sold short and have not been bought back. In other words, the shares borrowed have not been bought back and returned to the lenders. Both the NYSE and the AMEX, as well as the Nasdaq, publish monthly figures of the short sales of listed companies. These are published in the financial newspapers at the end of each month. Short interest can be expressed as a percentage, which is the number of shares shorted divided by the company's number of shares outstanding.

A large increase or decrease in a company's short interest is used as an indicator of investors' sentiment for that stock. For example, if Intel's short interest increases by 15 percent in one month, you know that 15 percent more investors believe that Intel will decrease in price. However, these investors also could be wrong, which leads to the contrarian point of view: If there are so many who believe that the stock is going to decline, this puts a floor under the stock price at a certain point where these short sellers are going to have to buy the stock back to cover their short positions, resulting in an increase in the stock price.

Contrarian investors use the short-interest ratio for more information about the stock. The *short-interest ratio* (also known as the *days-to-cover ratio*) is the number of shares sold short divided by the stock's average daily volume. For example, if Intel has a short-interest ratio of 1.5, it would take 1.5 days for short sellers to cover their positions. The higher the ratio, the longer it takes to buy back shares to cover short positions. Short-interest ratio also can be used as a barometer for the market. The higher the short-interest ratio for the NYSE, for example, the more bearish is the sentiment for that exchange.

NYSE CIRCUIT BREAKER SYSTEM

In an attempt to reduce volatility and maintain investor confidence when the market goes up or down significantly, the NYSE instituted a circuit breaker system of trading curbs. This was as a consequence of the market crash of October 1987, which was blamed on program trades. *Program trades* are defined as a basket of 15 or more stocks from the Standard & Poor's (S&P) 500 Index valued at $1 million or more that are bought or sold when they reach certain price limits and are triggered by computers. The NYSE resets the trading curbs on a quarterly basis based on the Dow Jones Industrial Average (DJIA). Following were the curbs for the third quarter of 2006:

> *160-point move on the DJIA.* A 160-point move up or down from the previous day's close on the DJIA will trigger the circuit breaker. This affects arbitrage or program trades on the component stocks of the S&P 500 Index. In an up market, arbitrage buy orders can be executed only on a minus or zero-minus tick. Similarly, in a down market, sell orders can be executed only on an up-tick or zero-plus tick.

> *1,100-point move.* If the DJIA goes down by 1,100 points or more from the previous day's close, trading halts are instituted. The point levels for the trading halts are adjusted four times a year (January 1, April 1, July 1, and October 1). The point levels are set at 10, 20, and 30 percent of the Dow's average closing values for the previous month rounded to the nearest 50 points. The current 1,100-point level is reflective at the time of this writing. The trading halts are one hour if the downside of 1,100 points or more occurs before 2 p.m. Eastern Daylight Time. If the downside occurs between 2 and 2.30 p.m., trading is halted for 30 minutes.

> *2,250-point move.* If the DJIA goes down by 2,250 points or more (20 percent decline) before 1 p.m., this will cause a trading halt of 2 hours. Such a drop between 1 and 2 p.m. will trigger a trading halt of one hour. After 2 p.m. it will cause the NYSE to close for the day.

> *3,350-point move.* A drop of 3,350 points or more (30 percent decline) from the previous day's close of the Dow will close the NYSE for the day.

CHAPTER 9

Valuing Common Stock

KEY CONCEPTS

- What is the value of common stock?
- Discounted cash flow method of valuing common stock
- Relative valuation methods

Investment Snapshot

- A buyer of Cisco stock at $20 per share is optimistic about the appreciation of the price, whereas the seller of Cisco stock at $20 thinks that the stock is fully valued.
- D. R. Horton, the home builder, traded at a valuation of four times its earnings, whereas Google traded at 54 times its earnings.
- Bank of America has a dividend yield of around 4 percent, whereas Apple Computer does not pay a dividend.

WHAT IS THE VALUE OF COMMON STOCK?

We all hate to pay too much when we buy something. Similarly, the same standard of valuation applies to stock investments. You need to determine the underlying or intrinsic value of a stock to determine whether that stock is undervalued, fairly priced, or overvalued. For stocks, this is not easy. The *intrinsic value* is the fair value of the stock based on the risk and the amount and timing of future cash flow, in other words, the present value of the stream of receipts from a stock.

Theoretically, the value of a stock is equal to the discounted future cash flow of both dividends and the sale price of the stock. Neither the receipt of nor the amount of the dividends is guaranteed for common stockholders, and uncertainty exists about the amount of the future sale price. There are a number of different metrics with which to find the intrinsic value of a stock that make various assumptions about the amount of future dividends and the growth rate of the company.

The amount of dividends paid to shareholders is based largely on two factors:

- The company's profitability
- The decision by the company's board of directors to declare and pay dividends rather than retain the profits of the company

Many profitable companies decide not to pay dividends even though they are profitable and can sustain the payment of dividends, for example, Cisco and Oracle. These companies have large amounts of cash on their balance sheets, but they have chosen to retain their profits and reinvest them to accumulate future profits. Consequently, companies fuel their own growth by retaining profits and reinvesting them in future business projects. Generally, when a company's earnings increase, the increase is reflected in a higher price for the company's stock.

Other sources of value to shareholders besides the payment of dividends and increasing retained earnings are the repurchase of stock by a company and the reduction of its debt. A repurchase of its own shares by a company reduces the number of its shares outstanding, and if earnings increase or stay the same, *earnings per share* increase. Many analysts base their buy, hold, and sell ratings of companies on the growth of earnings per share.

Not all stock buybacks by companies increase shareholder wealth. Amgen announced in February 2006 that it would sell $4 billion of convertible debt, with $3 billion of the proceeds to be used to fund the buyback of its stock. This action caused Amgen's stock price to fall from $71 to $66 per share because more debt results in greater interest expense, which decreases earnings. Consequently, when a company reduces its debt, interest payments are decreased, which increases earnings. The result is an increase in earnings per share. In reality, the decision to increase or reduce debt is not as clearcut with regard to earnings because earnings per share can be increased using debt financing as long as the company can earn a return that is greater than the cost of the debt.

Investors buy and value stocks based on their expectations of receiving dividends and/or capital appreciation. In other words, the total return for a stock is composed of the dividend received and the appreciation in the value of the stock price. If a company can increase its earnings, dividends can be increased over time, which produces greater total returns for investors. An investor's *expected rate of return* for a stock is the sum of the dividend yield plus the expected growth rate. For example, suppose that a stock pays a dividend yield of 3 percent and is expected to grow at 10 percent for the year; then its expected rate of return is 13 percent. If an investor's *required rate of return* for stock investments is less than 13 percent, the stock provides a superior return. On the other hand, a required rate of return of greater than 13 percent would make this stock an inferior investment. The required rate of return has two components: the risk-free rate you can earn on Treasury bills plus a risk premium associated with the stock and the market. A riskier stock would require a higher risk premium, and if the risk-free rate increases, an investor would require an appropriate increase in the rate of return.

Two basic approaches to stock valuation are discussed in this chapter:

- Discounted cash flow method
- Relative valuation methods

DISCOUNTED CASH FLOW METHOD

A company's earnings play a role in the valuation of its stock. However, in the discounted cash flow method it is dividends that play a key role and not earnings directly. Future estimated dividends are discounted to the present value at the investor's required rate of return to determine the intrinsic value of the stock. Suppose, for example, that a stock pays a dividend of $0.50 per year, indefinitely, and that your required rate of return is 10 percent; the stock's value is $5 (the perpetual dividend divided by the required rate of return). For a greater than 10 percent required rate of return, the purchase price of the stock must be less than $5 per share.

A stock price of greater than $5 per share will result in a lower than 10 percent required rate of return.

In reality, the amount of a common stock dividend is not fixed indefinitely. Dividends fluctuate over time depending on the company's earnings and the board of directors' decision to pay dividends or retain the profits for internal reinvestment by the company. Dividends can remain constant, grow at fixed rates, or grow or decline at variable rates. To get around these difficulties in the valuation of a stock, this model assumes that dividends grow at a constant rate.

The following formula illustrates the valuation model by discounting the constantly growing dividend by using an investor's required rate of return.

$$\text{Value of a stock} = \frac{\text{future dividend}}{(\text{investor's required rate of return} - \text{constant growth rate})}$$

Consider the following example using this formula to value a company's stock. Company X paid a dividend last year of $1 per share and is expected to continue paying dividends every year. The company is expected to grow at 8 percent. An investor interested in buying this stock has a required rate of return of 10 percent.

The dividend of $1 was paid last year, which means that you must compute the next or future dividend to be paid.

$$\text{Future dividend} = \text{current dividend} \times (1 + \text{growth rate})$$
$$= \$1(1 + 0.08)$$
$$= \$1.08$$

You can now substitute the figures into the equation.

$$\text{Value of the stock} = \$1.08/(0.10 - 0.08)$$
$$= \$50$$

A price greater than $50 results in a lower required rate of return of 10 percent, and a price below $50 results in a rate of return greater than 10 percent.

This valuation model depends on dividends paid by the company, and the investor's expected rate of return is the dividend yield plus the company's growth rate. Suppose that the dividend is $1.08 and that the stock price is $55:

$$\text{Expected rate of return} = (\$1.08/55) + 8\%$$
$$= 9.96\%$$

The dividend growth valuation model makes a number of assumptions:

- The required rate of return of the investor is greater than the rate of growth of the company. The purpose of the valuation process is to find stocks with intrinsic values that are less than their market values (which occurs only when the growth rate is less than the required rate of return).
- Dividends are expected to grow at a constant growth rate. This valuation model can be adapted to include variable dividend growth rates.

The implications of this model are

- The larger the dividend, the greater the stock price. Table 9-1 discusses whether a company should pay dividends or retain its earnings.
- The greater the growth rate of a company, the greater the stock price.
- The lower an investor's required rate of return, the greater the stock price.

TABLE 9-1

Should Companies Pay Dividends or Retain Their Earnings?

One implication of the dividend growth valuation model is that the larger the dividend payments to shareholders, the greater is the stock price. However, if a company can generate a rate of return on its investment higher than an investor's required rate of return, the stock price should see greater increases than if the earnings were paid to shareholders in dividends. For example, suppose that a company generates earnings per share of $2 and pays out the entire amount in dividends. If an investor's required rate of return is 8 percent, the stock is valued at $25 per share ($2 ÷ 0.08). No earnings growth takes place because the company has not retained any earnings.

If the company's dividend payout ratio (the percentage of net income paid to shareholders) is 40 percent, the dividend is $0.80 (0.40 × $2). The earnings retention ratio (percentage of net income that is not paid out in dividends) is 60 percent. If the company has a return on its investment (equity) of 12 percent, the growth rate for the company is 7.2 percent (0.12 × 0.60).

Value of the stock = dividend/(required rate of return – growth rate)

= $ 0.80/(0.08 – 072)

= $100

When the company retains and reinvests part of its earnings in new investments, its share price increases from $25 to $100 per share.

The degree of risk of a company is not measured directly in the dividend growth model but is instead adjusted through the investor's required rate of return. A company's risk is measured by its beta coefficient, which in itself is a problem. The beta coefficient has not been a consistent measure of risk. Beta coefficients for the same stock differ because different market measures are used. Use of the Standard & Poor's (S&P) 500 Index as a measure of the market versus the Value Line Stock Index results in two different beta coefficients for the same company. Similarly, the use of different time periods results in different beta coefficients for the same stock.

Another problem for the dividend growth valuation model is the growth rate. Should you use past earnings growth or estimate future growth rates for a company? If historical growth rates are chosen, what length of time should you choose? Table 9–2 illustrates how to determine the growth rate of a company.

Although the dividend growth valuation model is sound theoretically, these problems do have a bearing on the valuation of a company's stock. Consequently, other approaches to valuing common stock are less theoretical and more intuitive.

TABLE 9-2

Determining the Growth Rate of a Stock Using a Computer Spreadsheet

A company's sustained earnings are a major determinant of whether the company can afford to pay out dividends, maintain its dividend payments, or increase dividend payouts. If a company decides to retain earnings and reinvests the profits in its business rather than paying them out, it can accelerate its earnings growth. You can determine a company's growth rate by measuring the increase in a company's earnings over a certain period. This is just one way to measure a company's growth rate. Others are the growth of a company's assets or sales.

List the earnings per share (EPS) and dividends per share (DPS) for a company for the past five years. You can find this information on a company's website by clicking on financial statements or looking at its annual report. For example, the following EPS and DPS for Johnson & Johnson are on its website at www.johnsonandjohnson.com:

	2005	2004	2003	2002	2001	2000
Diluted EPS	$3.46	$2.84	$2.40	$2.16	$1.84	$1.61
DPS	$1.275	$1.095	$0.925	$0.795	$0.70	$0.62

Price per share: $60.10 (year-end close)

(*continued*)

•

Determine the growth rate. In 2000, earnings per share were $1.61 and grew to $3.46 in five years. Follow these steps using Excel:

Step 1: Click on f* in the tool bar.

Step 2: Highlight *financial*, and click on *rate*.

Step 3: Enter the data as shown below:

Nper	5
Pmt	0
PV	−1.61
FV	3.46
Type	0
Formula result	− 0.165332999

Johnson & Johnson's growth rate for the five-year period was 16.533 percent. Using this historical rate of growth, you can compute the expected return for this company:

Expected return = (future dividend/price of stock) + growth rate

Future dividend = present dividend × (1 + growth rate)

= $1.275(1 + 0.16533)

= $1.423

Expected rate of return = ($1.423/$60.10) + 0.16533

= 18.901%

The expected rate of return is 18.901 percent if the investor bought the stock at $60.10 per share.

RELATIVE VALUATION METHODS

The relative valuation methods for valuing a stock are to compare market values of the stock with the fundamentals (earnings, book value, growth multiples, cash flow, and other yardsticks) of the stock.

Price/Earnings (P/E) Ratio

The most commonly used guide to the relationship between stock prices and earnings is the price/earnings (P/E) ratio, computed by dividing the market price of the stock by its earnings per share. The P/E ratio indicates the multiple that an investor is willing to pay for a dollar of company's earnings.

There are two widely held assumptions regarding P/E ratios. The first is that stocks in the same industry have similar P/E ratios; the second is that stocks tend to trade within a range of P/E ratios. Pharmaceutical stocks, for example, have similar P/E ratios, and one of them, Merck, has P/E ratios that trade in a range of 13 to 32 times its earnings.

The P/E ratio shows the number of times that a stock's price is trading relative to its earnings, and because stock prices fluctuate, so do their ratios. Rising P/E ratios generally are linked to higher stock prices.

You can determine a company's stock price by multiplying the P/E ratio by the company's earnings per share. For example, if a P/E ratio for a stock is 8 and it is projected to earn $4 per share, the value of the stock is $32 (8 × $4 per share). If this stock is trading at a market price of less than $32 per share, it is undervalued. A market price of greater than $32 per share indicates that the stock is overvalued.

This method of valuation was used to determine that Google's stock was undervalued when it was trading in the low $300-per-share range. Google was expected to earn $8 per share and was trading at a 50 P/E multiple, prompting many analysts to raise their price targets for Google stock to $400 per share ($8 EPS × 50 P/E ratio).

Another use of the ratio is to divide a company's market price by its projected earnings per share. If the market price of a stock is $30 and its projected earnings per share are $4, the P/E ratio is 7.5. If analysts think that the appropriate ratio for companies in this industry is 9, then this stock is undervalued.

Using P/E ratios to value stocks has several weaknesses. Determining the appropriate P/E ratio is subjective, and P/E ratios can fluctuate considerably. Theoretically, if earnings per share increase, the stock price should rise so that the P/E ratio stays the same. In reality, this situation does not happen often. P/E ratios can be volatile and fluctuate considerably, making this a difficult indicator to read over short periods of time. Longer term, P/E ratios are more accurate in determining whether a company is over- or undervalued.

Another major weakness is the use of earnings per share (EPS). By definition, earnings per share include extraordinary gains and losses that are nonrecurring. The inclusion of a one-time gain overstates earnings per share and causes the P/E ratio to be lower. Consequently, the stock might appear to be undervalued.

Another stumbling block is the use of historical earnings versus future earnings, which is discussed further in Table 9–3. Because of these weaknesses in the use of the P/E ratio, short-term results as to the valuation of a stock could be misleading. Over longer time periods, these aberrations even out, and the P/E ratio becomes a more meaningful indicator of a company's stock value. When comparing the P/E ratios of stocks in different industries, you should be aware of these differences in computation so that your yardstick of comparison is the same.

Price/Earnings Growth (PEG) Ratio

The price/earnings growth ratio is the company's P/E ratio divided by the company's estimated future growth rate in earnings per share. The price/earnings growth (PEG) ratio indicates how much

TABLE 9-3

Which Price/Earnings Ratio to Use?

On November 20, 2002, the P/E ratio for the S&P 500 Index was 22, 16, and 49 (The Vanguard Group, 2003, p. 3). Which is the correct number? This situation might seem confusing, but all three numbers are correct. The different numbers were caused by the use of different earnings figures:

- Historical earnings are the actual earnings a company reports for the prior year.
- Forward earnings are the estimated earnings a company is expected to earn in the coming year.
- Operating ernings, or earnings before interest and taxes (EBIT), exclude gains and losses, interest expense and income, and taxes.

Which one should you use?

Historical earnings show a company's actual earnings, but the past is not always accurately projected into the future. The use of historical earnings results in higher P/E ratios than using forward earnings during periods of earnings growth. The opposite is also true: In periods of declining earnings growth, the use of historical earnings results in lower P/E ratios than use of forward earnings. Forward earnings are only estimates that are determined subjectively by financial analysts.

The use of net income versus operating income also reflects differences in the ratio outcome. The use of net income results in higher P/E ratios than does the use of operating earnings.

When you are comparing P/E ratios, be aware of the different definitions of earnings, and then consistently base your comparisons of stock valuations on the same category of earnings. Second, compare the P/E ratio for the stock with the ratios of stocks in the same industry, and look at the historical trading ranges for the P/E ratios. For example, in the years 1935 to 2002, the S&P 500 Index had a high P/E ratio of 46.5 and a low of 5.9, with an average of 15.3, based on historical earnings (The Vanguard Group, 2003, p. 3).

an investor pays for the growth of a company. For example, a company with an estimated growth rate of 16 percent and a P/E ratio of 20 has a PEG ratio of 1.25 (20 ÷ 16). For growth rates that are less than the P/E ratio, the value of the PEG ratio is greater than 1.0. A growth rate that exceeds the P/E ratio results in a value that is less than 1.0. The lower the ratio, the greater is the potential increase in stock price, assuming that the company can grow at its projected growth rate. A stock generally is perceived to be undervalued if the growth rate of the company exceeds its P/E ratio. A high PEG ratio implies that the stock is overvalued. Put another way, the lower the PEG ratio, the less an investor pays for estimated future earnings. Bear in mind that if the estimated earnings growth rate is inaccurate, the PEG ratio will be unreliable as an indicator of value.

Several questions might immediately come to mind. How high is high and how low is low for a PEG ratio? Is a PEG ratio of 3 acceptable, or is it on the high side? The answers to these questions depend on your interpretation of the data. A popular rule of thumb is that a stock with a PEG ratio below 1.0 is considered to be undervalued, and a stock with a PEG ratio of greater than 1.0 is considered to be overvalued. The PEG ratio should not be used in isolation in choosing stocks in which to invest but should be included with additional information about the company's fundamentals to determine value.

Table 9–4 compares the PEG ratios of companies in different industries.

TABLE 9-4

Comparison of PEG Ratios

Company	PEG Ratio
Microsoft Corporation	1.38
Cisco Systems, Inc.	1.04
PepsiCo	1.95
Johnson & Johnson	1.75
ExxonMobil	1.47
Citicorp	1.14
Google	1.25
Boeing	2.10
Diamond Offshore	0.47

Source: Yahoo.com, August 29, 2006.

Price–to–Book Value Ratio

Some investors look for stocks whose market prices are trading below their book values. The book value per share is computed by deducting the total liabilities from total assets and then dividing this number by the number of shares outstanding. The use of book value per share as a valuation tool is not compelling because many factors overstate or understate the book value of a stock. For example, buildings and real estate are recorded at historical costs (original purchase prices), although market prices can be significantly higher or lower, thereby distorting the book value per share.

A low value suggests that the stock is undervalued, and a high value indicates the opposite. As with the P/E and PEG ratios, what differentiates a stock from being overvalued and undervalued is determined subjectively.

Investors looking for value stocks would place more emphasis on finding stocks whose book values are greater than their market values. Value stocks tend to have lower P/E ratios, lower growth rates, and lower price–to–book value ratios than growth stocks do.

Price-to-Sales Ratio

The price-to-sales ratio indicates how much an investor is willing to pay for every dollar of sales for that company. The ratio is computed by dividing the market price of the stock by the sales per share. This ratio measures the valuation of a company on the basis of sales rather than earnings. You should compare the company's price-to-sales ratio with that of the industry to determine whether the company is trading at a compelling valuation to its sales base.

The price-to-sales ratio was used to value Internet-related companies that had no earnings during the stock market boom of the late 1990s. A low price-to-sales ratio indicates that the company has room to expand its sales and, therefore, its earnings.

Price–to–Cash Flow Ratio

Earnings are an important determinant of a company's value, but the company's cash position is another important way to assess value. A company's statement of changes in cash is a good starting point for assessing cash flow. Cash flow is computed by adding non-cash charges, such as depreciation and amortization, to net income (after-tax income). Cash flow per share is computed by dividing the cash flow by the number of common shares outstanding.

Cash flow per share is considered by many analysts to be a better yardstick of valuation than earnings per share. The amount of cash flow a company can generate indicates the company's capability to finance its own growth without having to resort to external funding sources.

The price–to–cash flow ratio is similar to the P/E ratio except that the cash flow per share is substituted for earnings per share. In other words, the market price of the stock is divided by the cash flow per share to equal the price–to–cash flow ratio. As with the P/E ratio, the lower the price–to–cash flow ratio, the more compelling is the value of the company. The advantage of using cash flow over earnings per share is that a company can have negative earnings per share but positive cash flow per share.

REFERENCE

The Vanguard Group. "Making Sense of P/Es." *In the Vanguard,* Winter 2003, p. 3.

CHAPTER 10

Financial Statement Analysis and Fundamental Analysis

KEY CONCEPTS

- Financial statement analysis
- Competitive analysis
- Assessing the financial strengths and weaknesses of a company

---

Investment Snapshot

- Leading companies in their industries are not immune from ending up in bankruptcy.
- One of Enron's goals was to become the biggest company in the world.
- Enron became the largest bankruptcy on record.
- Laws and regulations such as the Sarbanes-Oxley Act will not insulate investors from poor investments.

Why bother with financial statement analysis and number crunching to determine in which stocks to invest? It is easy for investors to follow the published buy, sell, and hold ratings of analysts with regard to which investments to make.

The process isn't quite that simple, though. The lesson you can learn from the bankruptcies of Enron, WorldCom, and others (in addition to the stock research abuses by analysts) is that investors must look out for themselves. State and federal regulators fined many investment banks and brokerage firms for their analysts' conflicts of interest between their investment banks and their stock research recommendations. Enron and WorldCom showed that investing in the leading companies in their industries also was not foolproof.

Consequently, politicians and regulators created laws and regulations in the hopes of making investors feel safe. But even if auditors are more thorough in their examinations of financial statements, greedy executives still will be hired, and boards of directors still will "rubber stamp" the wishes and deeds of management teams. Laws and regulations still will not insulate investors from poor investments and the misdeeds of strategists, analysts, and executives, so investors must scrutinize financial statements, including those of the largest companies. Finding a company with a strong financial position based on analysis of its financial statements goes a longer way than listening to the recommendations of those who have their own motives for generating their investment opinions.

FINANCIAL STATEMENT ANALYSIS

The basic premise of financial statement analysis is to examine a company's performance to either identify an investment opportunity or avoid an investment disaster. A company's stock price generally is influenced primarily by the company's performance. The benefits from financial statement analysis are numerous. You can

- Analyze a company's historical earnings to project future earnings.
- Compare a company's historical earnings with those of its peer companies in an industry to identify superior or inferior performance.
- Analyze a company's historical earnings over a certain period to identify weaknesses in performance or other problems.
- Use the company's historical data to project future rates of return.
- Assess the likelihood of a company's capability to meet its financial obligations.
- Analyze a company's financial statements to gather information needed for the stock valuation models discussed in Chapter 9.

Sources of Corporate Information

You can find much of the information you want to know about a company in its financial statements and filings with the Securities and Exchange Commission (SEC). Public companies with more than $10 million in assets and more than 500 shareholders must file their financial documents electronically with the SEC. You can obtain these filings for free from a company's Web site, by requesting them directly from a company's investor relations department or from the SEC's Edgar Web site at www.sec.gov/edgar.

The *Form 10-K* report provides the most comprehensive information about a company. The report includes a complete set of financial statements (audited three-year comparative income and cash flow statements and comparative year-end balance sheets), along with notes to the financial statements. A careful reading of the notes often provides crucial information that can affect the company's operations. The 10-K is more comprehensive than the annual report, which is sent to shareholders of record. Companies might emphasize *pro forma* financial results that exclude certain expenses. These "as if" financial results do not conform to *generally accepted accounting principles* (GAAP). GAAP are the rules and guidelines used by accountants in the preparation of financial statements.

You also can obtain information about a company by listening to the company's conference calls when they announce quarterly or annual earnings and make other announcements.

Financial Statements

Financial statements indicate the status of a company's operations and performance. After analyzing these statements, analysts render their investment recommendations for the company's stock. Any perceived long-term changes in a company's earnings have an effect on the company's dividends and its stock price. If earnings are projected to be greater than the expectations on Wall Street, more investors will want to buy the company's stock, pushing prices up. Similarly, if the company's earnings fall short of expectations, investors might sell those stocks if they perceive this trend to be a long-term one, putting downward pressure on the stock price. A steady increase in the company's earnings also raises the expectation of increases in dividends, which often contribute to rising stock prices. The opposite is true with decreased earnings.

Forecasting whether companies will meet their expected sales and earnings projections is not an easy task, and you should consider a number of other factors in addition to financial analysis.

Many investors do not have the time or the inclination to study a company's financial strengths and weaknesses. If you are one of these people, you can choose from many sources of published information, such as Standard & Poor's or Value Line's tear sheets, in addition to brokerage reports.

For many investors, however, the starting point for investing in a company is the company's financial statements, found in its annual report and 10-K report, both filed with the SEC. Annual financial statements are audited by independent certified public accountants (CPAs) and are distributed to shareholders and other interested parties. The annual report contains four financial statements: income statement, balance sheet, statement of changes in retained earnings, and statement of changes in cash.

Income Statement

An *income statement* provides a summary of a company's earnings during a specified period (a year for annual statements and three and six months for quarterly and semiannual income statements, respectively). The income statement begins with revenues (sales), from which various expenses are deducted: the cost of goods sold and selling, general, and administrative expenses. Interest expenses reflect the costs of a company's borrowing. After all expenses and taxes are deducted, the "bottom line" is what remains, which is the *net income.* The income statement shows profits, if revenues exceed costs, and losses, if expenses exceed revenues, during a specified period. You can compare these profits or losses with the profits or losses in previous periods. Table 10–1 summarizes the features of an income statement.

Analysts are always looking to see whether companies will meet their revenue expectations for each quarter, which puts pressure on companies to increase their revenues. This situation, unfortunately, opened the door for many unscrupulous executives to overstate their revenues to show growth when their revenues were declining. For example, some telecommunications companies used fiber-swap transactions to increase revenues through the sale of fiber-optic capacity and then capitalized the fiber rather than expensed it. This practice increased revenues and inflated earnings because the asset was written off over time rather than expensing it. You can be

TABLE 10-1

Features of an Income Statement

Summarizes revenues and expenses over a specified period
Measures revenues received from customers over a certain period
Measures the amounts spent on materials, labor, and overhead
Measures the amount of gross profit (sales minus cost of goods sold)
Measures the amount spent on selling, general, and administrative expenses
Measures operating profit (earnings before interest and taxes)
Measures the cost of borrowed funds
Summarizes the amount paid in taxes
Measures the profitability (net income) over a specified period

on the lookout for this type of practice by reading the revenue recognition policies in the footnotes to the financial statements and management's discussion and analysis section, which can provide additional information about the company's use of accounting principles.

The *gross margin* is of interest to investors and analysts because it shows a company's efficiency in managing its costs to produce its products. For example, Cisco System's gross margin (sales minus cost of goods sold divided by sales) was 64 percent in 2000, and it decreased to 49.7 percent in 2001 and then increased to 63.5 percent in 2002. The notes to the financial statement explain the reason for the increase in gross margin from 2001 to 2002. The company wrote off excess inventory in the third quarter of 2001. A drop in gross margin was a signal to many stock investors to sell the stock.

Deducting total operating expenses from the gross margin shows you the operating income (loss), also referred to as *earnings before interest and taxes* (EBIT). After the interest payments are deducted from (or interest income is added to) EBIT, the result is taxable income, or *earnings before taxes* (EBT). *Net income or loss* is EBT minus taxes, also referred to as the *bottom line*. Following the net income figures in an income statement are the earnings per share (EPS) figures (earnings minus preferred dividends divided by the number of shares outstanding).

Balance Sheet

A balance sheet is a statement that shows a company's financial position at a specified point in time. The balance sheet lists a company's *assets* (all resources that belong to a company), *liabilities* (the company's obligations), and *shareholders' equity* (the amount of the stockholders' capital).

Assets (resources) minus liabilities (obligations) equal shareholders' equity. From this equation, anyone reading a balance sheet can see how much the stockholders and creditors have contributed to the financing of the total assets.

On the assets side of the balance sheet are current assets and long-term assets. *Current assets* include cash, marketable securities, accounts receivable, inventories, and all other resources that are convertible into cash within one year. The cash generated from these assets generally provides for the day-to-day expenses of operations.

Long-term assets consist of resources with holding periods of greater than a year. These include long-term investments, property, plant and equipment, intangible assets (goodwill, patents, and leasehold improvements, for example), and any other assets that can be converted into cash in longer than one year. Property, plant, and equipment are recorded on the balance sheet at cost, and these tangible assets are depreciated (a systematic charge is recorded against income for wear and tear) over their useful lives. Intangible assets are amortized over their useful lives.

Analysts check to see whether any assets are significantly undervalued. The historical cost concept used to record assets does not recognize any increases in the market value of these assets until they are sold. Thus property on the balance sheet that might have been bought many years ago at low prices may be significantly understated (in terms of its market value).

The *liabilities* side of the balance sheet is also divided into two parts: current and long term. *Current liabilities,* or a company's obligations that fall due within one year or less, consist of account and trade payables, accrued (unrecorded) expenses, and other short-term debts. *Long-term liabilities* are a company's debts that have maturities beyond one year.

You should compare total current assets with total current liabilities. The cash generated from the turnover of current assets to cash generally is used to pay current obligations that fall due. If current assets are equal to or less than current liabilities, a company might have difficulty meeting its current obligations. This situation raises warning flags. In the same vein, if current assets are significantly lower than current liabilities, cash must come from selling off long-term assets or raising more debt to pay off the current liabilities. In this case, you should study the notes to the financial statements to determine whether the company has open lines of credit or other short- or long-term sources of credit.

The *shareholders' equity* section represents the claims of the shareholders against the company's assets. A company's total assets minus its total liabilities equal the shareholders' equity. The three main parts of the equity section are the capital stock accounts, the paid-in capital accounts, and the retained earnings or deficit.

- The capital stock accounts include both common stock and preferred stock issues. Multiplying the stated or par value of the stock by the number of shares issued determines the value of the stock accounts.

- The *paid-in-capital accounts* represent the amounts that shareholders paid in excess of the stated (par) value in the capital accounts when the company originally sold the shares.

- *Retained earnings* are the accumulated earnings that have been retained by the company, in other words, earnings that have not been paid out in dividends. Companies accumulate earnings for a number of reasons—namely, to acquire fixed assets, pay down liabilities, or accumulate reserves for contingencies. Retained earnings do not represent cash. Even though a company might have accumulated a large amount in retained earnings, it is still restricted by the amount held in cash in terms of spending for projects.

Table 10–2 summarizes the features of a balance sheet.

TABLE 10-2

Elements of a Balance Sheet

Shows a company's financial position at a particular point in time
Lists the types and amounts of assets that the company owns
Lists the current assets of a company (cash, accounts receivable, and inventory)
Shows the cost of a company's fixed assets (land, buildings, and equipment)
Shows the accumulated depreciation of these assets
Lists the current debts (liabilities) that the company owes to suppliers and others
Lists the long-term debts of the company
Shows the amount invested by the company's shareholders
Shows the earnings retained by the company

   With a balance sheet, you can compare a company's current assets with its current liabilities. You also can determine the amount of assets that are financed by debt as compared with the assets financed from equity.

Statement of Shareholders' Equity

The link between the income statement and the balance sheet is the company's net income (or loss) that is added to (or subtracted from) retained earnings shown in the statement of changes to shareholders' equity. Dividends on common and preferred stocks are paid out of net income, and the balance of the earnings is then added to the retained earnings in the equity section of the balance sheet. The *statement of shareholders' equity* is the third statement included in the financial statements of an annual report. From this statement you can see how the earnings retained are used by the company. For example, in 2002, Cisco Systems used its additional income largely to repurchase its own shares.

Statement of Changes in Cash

A *statement of changes in cash* analyzes the changes in a company's cash over a specified period by showing the sources of and uses of cash. The first of three sections in the statement, *cash from operations*, shows how much cash was provided or used by the company's operations. The changes in the *cash from investing* section show the uses and sources of cash from the purchases and sales of fixed assets and investments. The changes in *cash from financing* section summarize the uses and sources of cash from the changes in long-term liabilities and equity sections of the balance sheet. Table 10–3 summarizes the features in a statement of changes in cash.

TABLE 10-3

Features of the Statement of Changes in Cash

Summarizes the major categories of sources and uses of cash to show what has happened to the cash account during a period of time
Measures the noncash charges within the specified period
Shows the cash inflows and outflows from operations
Shows the cash amounts spent and received by buying and selling long-term assets
Shows the cash received from borrowing and cash used to repay debt
Shows the cash received from issuing common and preferred stocks and the cash amounts used to buy back stock
Shows the amount of dividends paid

Cash flow is the amount of net cash generated by a business over a certain period. To compute the cash flow, noncash expenses are added to (or noncash revenues are deducted from) net income. Noncash items are expenses (depreciation, amortization, and deferred charges) and income that are not paid out or realized in cash. This calculation explains why companies can have negative earnings and still have positive cash flows.

Another, more refined measure of cash flow is *free cash flow,* or cash flow minus capital spending (investments in net working capital and long-term assets). Companies that do not generate strong free cash flows have less flexibility, and this is recognized most often in their stock prices. Table 10–4 discusses the value of using cash flow to assess a company's financial position.

TABLE 10-4

Cash Is Not as Easy to Manipulate as Earnings

Many companies manipulated their earnings during the economic downturn of 2000–2003. Health South overstated its earnings by $1.4 billion during the period 1999–2002 according to a guilty plea from its former chief executive officer. WorldCom also overstated its profits by capitalizing expenses. These expenses were amortized over a period of time rather than deducted as expenses in the period in which they were incurred. The Dutch company Ahold also overstated its profits, even though you might think that the supermarket business is more simple and straightforward and would not lend itself to the manipulation of figures quite like more complex forms of business such as the telecommunications industry.

The analysis of cash is a better tool for determining a company's strengths and weaknesses because cash is harder to manipulate than earnings. The *cash flow adequacy ratio* (CFAR) gives a more accurate assessment of the profile of a company (Hoens and Foley, 1994).

CFAR (which consists of cash flow after taxes, interest, and capital expenditures) is net free cash flow, which is compared with the average annual principal debt maturities over the next five-year period. Thomas W. Hoens and Keith B. Foley (1994) used this CFAR analysis in the following example, which illustrated Enron's inability to generate positive cash flows in the years prior to its bankruptcy:

Enron Corporation
CFAR Analysis
1996 to 2000

	2000	1999	1998	1997	1996	Cumulative
Revenues	100,789	40,112	31,260	20,273	13,289	205,723
Costs	98.836	39,310	29,882	20,258	12,599	200,885
EBIT	1,953	802	1,378	15	690	4,838
Depr/Amor	855	870	827	600	474	3,626

(continued)

EBITDA	**2,808**	**1,672**	**2,205**	**615**	**1,164**	**8,464**
Cash Interest	834	678	585	420	290	2,807
Cash Taxes	62	51	73	68	89	343
Capital Expenses	2,381	2,363	1,905	1,392	864	8,905
NET FREE CASH FLOW	**(469)**	**(1,420)**	**(358)**	**(1,265)**	**(79)**	**(3,591)**
Equity Invest (1)	933	722	1,659	700	619	
	(1,402)	(2,142)	(2,017)	(1,965)	(698)	(8,224)

Depreciation and amortization, both noncash charges, were added back to earnings before interest and taxes to equal earnings before interest, taxes, depreciation, and amortization (EBITDA), which were positive for Enron for each year in the five-year period shown in the example. However, when interest, taxes, and capital expenses were deducted from EBITDA, Enron had negative free cash flows. This meant that Enron did not have the cash to cover its scheduled debt maturities during the five-year period, the payment of dividends, or the investments in its equity affiliates.* Enron had a large number of transactions with affiliate companies that siphoned off large amounts of cash. From this analysis, you can see why members of Enron upper management went to such great lengths to hide its debt from its balance sheet. Enron's debt and dividend payments are listed below (Hoens, 2003):

Dividend Analysis.

Common	368	355	312	243	212	
Pfd2	17	17	17	17	16	
Pfd A & B	66	49	0			
	451	421	329	260	228	1,689

Scheduled Debt Maturities.

Year 1	2,112	670	541		
Year 2	750	569	413		
Year 3	852	432	66		
Year 4	646	494	182		
Year 5	1,592	493	656		
Total	5,952	2,658	1,858		
Average	**1,190**	**532**	**372**	**NA**	**NA**

Because net free cash flows were consistently negative in each of the five years, a cash flow adequacy ratio for Enron would be meaningless (because the ratio would be negative). A company with a negative trend of CFARs certainly raises red flags for potential investors. Companies with CFARs between 0 and 1 indicate that they are not generating sufficient cash to fund their expenditures and would need access to outside sources of cash. A company with a CFAR higher than 1 generates sufficient cash to fund its major cash expenditures. You must look at the trend as opposed to one year's figures in isolation because companies with strong cash flows in some years might have negative CFARs in other years (Hoens, 2003).

*Equity investments are not common items in CFAR, but in Enron's case, these expenditures were large.

Financial statements provide the data for an analysis of a company's financial position and an assessment of its strengths and weaknesses. The relative financial position of the company in relation to its past data and in relation to other companies in the same industry provides a more meaningful picture than merely looking at one set of financial statements in isolation. The company's strengths and weaknesses can become more apparent through ratio analysis.

COMPETITIVE ANALYSIS

Whether a company can achieve its sales and earnings objectives depends in part on how it competes within its industry. Industry sales and earnings may be growing, but if the company is not competitive enough, it may not capture a large enough portion of the increasing sales in the industry.

How a company competes in an industry depends on many factors:

- The resources the company has in relation to its competitors
- The company's range of products versus its competitors' products
- The level of success of the company's existing range of products
- The company's level of innovation in its introduction of new products
- The company's ability to diversify into new markets
- The strength of the company's competitors

You should consider these factors when determining the relative strength of a company in an industry.

Quality of Management

Another factor to consider is the quality of management. Access to a company's management is often difficult for financial analysts and virtually impossible for the general investing public. The most you can do to determine the quality of management is to look at the company's history and read financial newspapers for stories about management. For example, a high turnover rate for top and middle management indicates that all is not well. A company with an effective management generally is assumed to be more successful in meeting its sales and earnings objectives than a poorly managed company.

ExxonMobil, for example, managed to consistently increase its earnings, even during periods of declining oil prices. In addition, ExxonMobil faced a negative climate in the early 1990s owing to the *Exxon Valdez* oil spill. ExxonMobil's management was not deterred and stuck to its original investment objectives, which were projects with high returns. This strategy supported the company's profits, in contrast to the frivolous investments made by many of the other oil companies during the same period.

How chief executive officers (CEOs) are paid in relation to the company's stock performance tells much about management. The stock price of Cisco Systems declined by 31 percent in 2002, but the CEO's compensation declined by 67 percent in that same year. These circumstances were certainly not the same at many other companies, such as K-mart, JDS Uniphase, Quest, and WorldCom. When their stock prices declined significantly, the CEOs and members of top management rewarded themselves with additional salaries and bonuses.

The Internet has made gaining access to information about companies and management a little easier for individual investors. If you want more information, the first stop is the company's home page on the Web. At the ExxonMobil Web site (www.exxonmobil.com), for example, you can read about the company's sales strategies and how it is positioning itself for the future. Investors also can read the company's annual and quarterly reports. Read the "Management Discussion" section to assess any future trends or investments.

You also can e-mail questions to the investor relations' staff of companies in which you are interested. The speed and quality of their replies will tell much about how management views its shareholders.

FUNDAMENTAL ANALYSIS

Fundamental analysis uses a company's financial statements to determine the value of the company with regard to its potential growth in earnings. Fundamental analysts use projected forecasts of the economy to focus on industries that are expected to generate increased sales and earnings. Companies within those industries are evaluated to determine which stocks to buy.

The financial statements provide the basis for ratio analysis, which assists in determining a company's strengths and weaknesses. Ratio analysis uses a company's financial information to predict whether it will meet its future projections of earnings. Although ratio analysis is simple to compute, its projections and extrapolations can become complex. Ratio analysis is a tool that can assist you in your selection of stocks. From financial ratio analysis, you can assess a company's past and present financial strengths. Then, armed with this information, you can project trends by using each of the five groups of ratios:

- Liquidity ratios illustrate the ease with which assets are converted into cash to cover short-term liabilities.
- Activity ratios show how quickly the assets flow through the company.
- Profitability ratios measure a company's performance.
- Leverage ratios indicate a company's level of debt.
- Common stock–related ratios relate share price information.

Table 10–5 provides a list of the different ratios in each of these groups to use to evaluate a company's strengths and weaknesses.

Liquidity

Liquidity is defined as assets that are easily convertible into cash or a large position in cash. Although liquidity is of greater concern to a company's creditors, this is a starting point for a potential investor in a company's common stock. Liquidity indicates the ease (or difficulty) with which a company can pay off its current obligations (debts) as they come due.

The *current ratio* is a measure of a company's ability to meet its current obligations. It is computed by dividing the current assets by current liabilities. The current ratio shows the coverage of the company's current liabilities by its current assets.

A company's current assets generally should exceed its current liabilities, so that if its current assets decline, it can still pay off its liabilities. A low current ratio might indicate weakness because the company might not be able to borrow additional funds or sell assets to raise enough cash to meet its current liabilities. Yet there are always exceptions to a low current ratio. ExxonMobil, one of the strongest companies in the oil industry, in some years has had its current ratio fall below 1. However, ExxonMobil has always had the

TABLE 10-5

Framework to Evaluate Common Stock

	Year	Year	Year	Year	Year	Year
Company name						
Current ratio = current assets/current liabilities						
Quick ratio = (current assets − inventory)/current liabilities						
Accounts receivable turnover = credit sales/accounts receivable						
Inventory turnover = cost of goods sold/inventory						
Gross profit = cost of goods sold/sales						
Operating profit = EBIT/sales						
Net profit = net income/sales						
Return on equity = net income/equity						
Return on common equity = (net income − preferred dividends)/ (equity − preferred stock)						
Debt ratio = total liabilities/total assets						
Coverage ratio = EBIT/interest expense						
P/E ratio = market price of stock/earnings per share						
Earnings per share = (net income − preferred stock)/number of shares outstanding						
Dividend yield = dividend/price of stock						
Dividend payout ratio = dividend per share/earnings per share						
Book value = shareholders' equity/number of shares outstanding						
Price/sales ratio = price per share/sales per share						
P/E to growth ratio = P/E ratio/growth rate						
Cash flow						

capacity to borrow on a short-term basis to pay off its current obligations. In those years, the notes to the ExxonMobil financial statements showed that Exxon had unused lines of short-term
financing with its banks and could issue commercial paper.
Potential investors should always read the *footnotes*, which contain
additional information that provides more insight into the figures
on the financial statements.

Moreover, you should not look at a ratio for one period in
isolation. By examining past current ratios, you can establish a
trend and see more easily whether the most recent current ratio has
deteriorated, stayed the same, or improved over this period. What
might be the norm for one industry might not hold for another.
Utility companies tend to have current ratios of less than 1, but the
quality of their accounts receivable is so good that virtually all the
accounts receivable are converted into cash. (Most people pay their
utility bills; otherwise, they find themselves without power.)
Creditors of utility companies are therefore not as concerned with
low current ratios. Similarly, ExxonMobil's liquidity was not
significantly different from that of the rest of the oil industry, which
suggests that the oil industry typically has current ratios of around
1 or less of current assets to current liabilities.

The *quick ratio* is a more refined measure of liquidity because
it excludes inventory, which is typically the slowest current asset
to be converted into cash, from the current assets in the calculation.
The quick ratio is always less than the current ratio unless the
company has no inventory. The quick ratio indicates the degree of
coverage of the current liabilities from cash and other, more liquid
assets. A low quick ratio indicates that the company might have
difficulty in paying off its current liabilities as they become due.
However, this statement might not always be true because many
other factors influence a company's ability to pay off current debts:

- Its capability to raise additional funds, long or short term
- The willingness of its creditors to roll over its debt
- The rate at which current assets such as accounts receivable
  and inventory turn over into cash

Activity Ratios

Activity ratios measure how quickly a company can convert some of
its accounts into cash. This type of ratio measures how effectively
management is using its assets.

Accounts receivable turnover indicates the number of times within a period that a company turns over its credit sales into cash. This ratio gives an indication of how successful a company is in collecting its accounts receivable. This ratio is computed by dividing accounts receivable into annual credit sales. The larger the accounts receivable turnover, the faster the company turns over its credit sales into cash. For example, an accounts receivable turnover of 17 indicates that sales turn over into cash every 21 days (365 days/17), or 0.7 times a month (12 months/17).

Inventory turnover measures the number of times a company's inventory is replaced within a period and indicates the relative liquidity of inventory. This ratio gives an indication of the effectiveness of the management of inventory. The higher the inventory turnover, the more rapidly the company is able to turn over its inventory into accounts receivable and cash. For example, an inventory turnover of 7.8 indicates that it takes the average inventory 47 days to turn over (365 days/7.8). If the inventory turnover for the same company increases to 9, the inventory turns over in roughly 41 days (365 days/9).

With both the accounts receivable turnover and inventory turnover you do not want to see extremely low values, indicating that the company's cash is tied up for long periods. Similarly, extremely high turnover figures indicate poor inventory management, which can lead to stock-outs (not having enough inventory to fill an order) and therefore customer dissatisfaction.

Accounts payable turnover indicates the promptness with which a company makes its payments to suppliers. This ratio is computed by dividing accounts payable into purchases. If information on purchases is not available, you can use the company's cost of goods sold minus (plus) any decreases (increases) in inventory. The accounts payable ratio indicates the relative ease or difficulty the company has in paying its bills on time. If the average terms in the industry are "net 30 days" and a company takes 50 days to pay its bills, you know that many of the bills are not being paid on time.

Table 10–6 discusses how a company can alter its balance sheet to make the company more liquid.

Profitability

A company's profits are important to investors because these earnings are either retained or paid out in dividends to shareholders, both of

TABLE 10-6

How a Company Can Improve Its Financial Position by
Sprucing Up Its Balance Sheet at Year-End

Some companies spruce up their balance sheets for their year-end financial statements. Many of the techniques that are used are within accounting and legal limits.
One such method is for a company to reduce its working capital through a reduction
of inventory levels, accounts receivable, and accounts payable. *Working capital* is
defined as an excess of current assets over current liabilities. If working capital is
high, it indicates inefficiency in that resources are tied up in inventory and accounts
receivable. Lower levels of working capital are a sign of a company's efficiency and
financial strength because less cash is tied up in inventory and accounts receivable.

REL, a London based consultancy group, looked at the balance sheets of 1,000
companies and found that companies could cut their inventories by shipping more
products at year-end. In the quarter following, inventories backed up as customers
either returned some of the inventory or cut back on their purchases because they
had too many goods in stock.

At the same time, companies worked hard at getting their customers to pay their
bills faster before year-end. REL found that companies could reduce their receivables by 2 percent at year-end only to have them increase by 5 percent in the
quarter following.

Companies paid their own bills, thereby reducing their accounts payable at year-
end. REL found that accounts payable fell by 7 percent at year-end only to increase by 12 percent in the next quarter. Assume that a company has $50,000 in
total current assets and $40,000 in total current liabilities, resulting in a current
ratio of 1.25. If the company pays its accounts payable of $10,000 before the end
of the accounting year, current assets will be $40,000 and current liabilities
$30,000, resulting in an improvement to the current ratio from 1.25 to 1.33.

Any significant reductions in inventory and accounts receivable at year-end should
be followed up in subsequent quarters. Answers often can be found in the footnotes and management discussion and analysis sections of the annual report.

Has the company been selling its accounts receivables? Although this practice is
common among various companies, it can signal that the company is experiencing
a cash crunch.

An increase in a company's inventory level is another red flag. Analyze where the
increases are. If they are in finished goods while raw materials have decreased,
this is a signal that the company is having trouble selling its goods. On the other
hand, if raw materials have increased while finished goods have decreased, this
indicates that sales are expanding and that the company is gearing up for an
increase in sales.

Source: Ken Brown, "How to Spot the Dirt in Rosy Annual Reports." *Wall Street Journal*, February 14, 2003, pp. C1, C3.

which affect the company's stock price. Many different measures of
profitability indicate how much the company is earning relative to
the base that is used, such as sales, assets, and shareholders' equity.
The different profitability ratios are relative measures of the success of
the company.

Using sales as a base, you would compare the different measures of earnings on the income statement. Compare the sales for the period with the sales figures for previous years to see whether sales have grown or declined. For example, sales might have increased from the preceding year, yet the company may report a net loss for the year. This situation indicates that expenses have risen significantly. You would then examine the income statement to see whether the additional expenses were nonrecurring (a one-time write-off) or whether increased operating costs were incurred in the normal course of business. In the latter case, you should question management's capability to contain these costs. Establishing a trend of these expenses over a period of time is useful in the evaluation process.

Several profitability ratios use sales as a base: gross profit, operating profit, and net profit.

Gross Profit Margin

The *gross profit margin* is the percentage earned on sales after deducting the cost of goods sold. The gross profit margin reflects not only the company's markup on its cost of goods sold but also management's ability to control these costs in relation to sales. The gross profit margin is computed as follows:

Gross profit margin = (sales − cost of goods sold)/net sales

Operating Profit Margin

The *operating profit margin* is the percentage in profit earned on sales from a company's operations. Operating profit is the income from operations [also known as *earnings before interest and taxes* (EBIT)] divided by sales. This profit includes the cost of goods sold and the selling, general, and administrative expenses. This ratio shows the profitability of a company in its normal course of operations and provides a measure of the company's operating efficiency.

Operating profit margin = operating profits/net sales

The operating profit or loss often provides the truest indicator of a company's earning capacity because it excludes nonoperating income and expenses.

Net Profit Margin

The *net profit margin* is the percentage profit earned on sales after all expenses and income taxes are deducted. The net profit margin includes nonoperating income and expenses such as taxes, interest expense, and extraordinary items. Net profit is calculated as follows:

$$\text{Net profit margin} = \text{net income/net sales}$$

You might not think that calculating all these profit ratios is important because of the main emphasis on the net profit margin alone. This belief could be misleading because if tax rates or interest expenses increase, or if some large, extraordinary items occur during the year, a significant change in net profit occurs, even though operating profits have not changed. A company could have a net profit at the same time that it posts an operating loss. This situation occurs when a company has tax credits or other one-time gains that convert the operating loss into net income. Similarly, if the net profit margin declines in any period, you would want to determine the reasons for the decline.

Other measures of profitability are the returns on equity, common equity, and the return on investment. These ratios are more specific to common shareholders because they measure the returns on shareholders' invested funds.

Return on Equity

The *return on equity* is a measure of the net income a company earns as a percentage of shareholders' equity. This ratio indicates how well management is performing for the stockholders and is calculated as follows:

$$\text{Return on equity} = \text{net income/shareholders' equity}$$

Return on Common Equity

The *return on common equity* is a measure of the return earned by a company on its common shareholders' investment. When a company has preferred stock, the common shareholders might be more concerned with the return attributable to the common equity than to the total equity. To determine this return, adjustments are made for the preferred dividends and preferred stock outstanding.

Return on common equity =
(net income − preferred dividends)/(equity − preferred stock)

Return on Investment

The *return on investment* is a measure of the return a company earns on its total assets. This return relates the profits earned by a company on its investment and is computed as follows:

Return on investment = net income/total assets

Leverage Ratios

Leverage is the use of borrowed funds to acquire assets. During periods of rising income, the use of borrowed funds can magnify the increases in returns of a company.

Leverage measures the use of debt to finance a company's assets. Although leverage is a major concern for bondholders, who use leverage ratios to determine the level of debt and the servicing of the contractual payments of interest and principal, leverage is also important for common stockholders.

By increasing the use of debt financing, a company can increase its returns to shareholders. Table 10–7 shows how returns for a company can increase through the use of leverage (debt financing). This example illustrates how both the return on equity and the earnings per share can be increased from 14 to 21 percent and from $1.40 to $2.10, respectively, by increasing the use of debt financing from 0 to 50 percent of its total assets.

This increase occurs for two reasons. First, the company can earn more than the 10 percent cost of borrowing. Second, the interest payments are a tax-deductible expense. The federal government bears 30 percent (the tax rate used in this example) of the cost of the interest payments (30 percent of $50, which is $15).

Because the use of debt increases the return to shareholders as well as the earnings per share, why should shareholders be so concerned about the level of debt that a company uses to finance its assets? The answer is that the more debt a company takes on, the greater is its financial risk and the cost of servicing its debt. If a downturn in sales takes place, the company might have difficulty making its interest payments. This situation can lead not only to defaulting on a loan and, ultimately, to declaration of bankruptcy but also to significantly reduced returns to shareholders and earnings per share. Whenever a company increases the amount of its debt, the costs of raising additional debt issues increase, which means that the company must earn more than the cost of its borrowing or it will not see the benefits of leverage. When the level of debt reaches the point where the earnings on the assets are less than the costs of the debt, the return on equity and the earnings per share will decline.

For common stock investors, a highly leveraged company often indicates that great risk occurs, which requires a greater rate

TABLE 10-7

Example of the Use of Financial Leverage and Earnings

Company with No Leverage

Balance Sheet		Income Statement	
Assets	**Liabilities**		
		Revenue	$1,000
		Cost of goods sold	600
$1,000	$0	Gross profit	400
		Expenses	200
	Equity	Earnings before taxes	200
		Taxes 30%	60
	$1,000*	Net income	140
$1,000	$1,000		

*100 shares outstanding
Return on equity = 140/1,000 = 14%
Earnings per share = 140/100 = $1.40

Company with 50% Leverage

Balance Sheet		Income Statement	
Assets	**Liabilities**		
		Revenue	$1,000
		Cost of goods sold	600
$1,000	$500	Gross profit	400
		Expenses	200
	Equity	Earnings before interest and taxes	200
	$500*	Interest (10% × $500)	50
$1,000	$1,000	Earnings before taxes	150
		Taxes 30%	45
		Net income	105

*50 shares outstanding
Return on equity = 105/500 = 21%
Earnings per share = 105/50= $2.10

of return to justify the risk. This increase in the required rate of return could have a negative effect on the share price. The use of leverage increases the value of the stock when the level of debt used is not perceived as adding a great amount of risk to the company.

What Is the Optimal Level of Leverage?

All companies use different amounts of leverage, and some industries typically use more than others. Industries that require large investments in fixed assets, such as oil companies, airlines, and utilities use a higher percentage of debt to finance their assets. Banks typically also use large amounts of debt because deposits finance their assets; this leverage results in large fluctuations in the banking industry's earnings whenever slight fluctuations in revenues occur.

When you are considering the leverage of one company, compare it with the typical leverage for the industry. Investors should look at a company's debt and coverage ratios to see the extent of its borrowing and its ability to service the debt.

Debt Ratio

The debt ratio measures a company's use of debt as a percentage of total assets. The debt ratio indicates how much of the financing of the total assets comes from debt.

Debt ratio = total current plus noncurrent liabilities/total assets

Compare the debt ratio with the average of the industry to get a better feeling for the degree and extent of the company's leverage. A company with a large debt ratio becomes increasingly vulnerable if a downturn in sales or the economy occurs, particularly in the latter case if it is a cyclical company.

When you examine a company's financial statements, you should always check the footnotes to see whether any debt has been excluded from the balance sheet. If a company does not consolidate its financial subsidiaries into its financial statements, any debt the parent company is responsible for is reported in the footnotes to the financial statements.

Debt-to-Equity Ratio

The *debt-to-equity ratio* measures a company's use of debt as a percentage of equity. The debt-to-equity ratio is computed by dividing the total debt by the company's shareholders' equity. The higher the ratio, the greater is the level of financing provided by debt, and the lower the ratio the greater is the level of financing provided by shareholders. This ratio is similar to the total debt ratio.

Coverage Ratio

The *coverage ratio* is a measure of a company's ability to service its debt commitments (cover its interest payments). The *times interest earned ratio* measures a company's coverage of its interest payments. It is calculated as follows:

Times interest earned ratio =   .
earnings before interest and taxes (EBIT)/annual interest expense

For example, if a company has a times interest earned ratio of 1.12, you would want to know how much leeway the company has with a downturn in its earnings before interest and taxes before it will not have sufficient earnings to cover its interest payments. You compute the margin of safety of the coverage ratio as follows:

Margin of safety of the coverage ratio = 1 − (1/coverage ratio)

A company with a coverage ratio of 1.12 would have a margin of safety of 10.71 percent:

$$1 − (1/1.12) = 10.71\%$$

The company's EBIT can fall by only 10.71 percent before the earnings coverage is insufficient to service its debt commitments.

Common Stock Price Ratios

Common stock price ratios provide information about a company's stock price.

The Price/Earnings (P/E) Ratio

The *price/earnings ratio* is a measure of how the market prices a company's stock. The most commonly used guide to the relationship between stock prices and earnings is the price/earnings (P/E) ratio, which is calculated as follows:

Price/earnings ratio = market price of the stock/earnings per share

The P/E ratio shows the number of times that a stock's price is trading relative to its earnings. The P/E ratios for listed common stocks are published daily in the financial newspapers and on financial Web sites. For example, the P/E ratio for Cisco Systems as of September 26, 2006, was 26.4 ($23.50/$0.89), with a market price of $23.50 per share and trailing earnings per share of $0.89 per share. This number indicates that shareholders were willing to pay 26.4 times Cisco's earnings for its stock. Put another way, it would take 26.4 years of these earnings to equal the invested amount ($23.50 per share). P/E ratios also can be computed on expected or future earnings. Cisco's forward earnings per share are projected to be $1.47, resulting in a forward P/E ratio of 15.99 ($23.50/$1.47).

A company's P/E ratio shows how expensive its stock is relative to its earnings. Companies with high P/E ratios (higher than 20 as a general rule) are characteristic of growth companies. Although with the average market multiple around 17 (in September 2006), a forward P/E ratio of 15 for Cisco makes it almost seem like a value stock. Investors might be optimistic about a company's potential growth, and hence the stock price is driven up in anticipation. This situation results in a high stock price relative to the company's current earnings. Some investors might be willing to pay a high price for a company's potential earnings; other investors might consider these types of stocks to be overpriced.

What becomes apparent is that high P/E ratios indicate high risk. If the future anticipated growth of high P/E ratio stocks is not achieved, their stock prices are punished, and their prices fall quickly. On the other hand, if they live up to their earnings expectations, investors benefit substantially. A low P/E ratio stock (<10) is characteristic of either a mature company with low growth potential or a company that is undervalued or in financial difficulty.

By comparing the P/E ratios of companies with the averages in the industries and the markets, you can get an idea of the relative value of the stock. For example, the average P/E ratio for companies on the U.S. stock markets was around 17 times earnings in September 2006. During bull markets, the average ratio goes up, and during bear markets, the average declines (perhaps as low as six times earnings, which happened in 1974).

P/E ratios fluctuate considerably, differing among companies as a result of many factors, such as growth rates, earnings, and other financial characteristics.

Earnings per Share

The *earnings per share* (EPS) figure for a company is the amount of reported income on a per-share basis. The earnings per share indicate the amount of earnings allocated to each share of common stock outstanding. EPS figures can be used to compare the growth (or lack of growth) in earnings from year to year and to project future growth in earnings.

Earnings per share = (net income − preferred dividends)/
                              number of common shares outstanding

The number of shares outstanding equals the number of shares issued minus the shares that the company has bought back, called *treasury stock*. In many cases, companies report two sets of earnings per share, regular earnings per share and fully diluted earnings per share.

When companies have convertible bonds and convertible preferred stock, rights, options, and/or warrants, their EPS figures may be diluted because of the increased number of common shares outstanding, if and when these securities are converted into common stocks. Companies are then required to disclose their fully diluted EPS figures and their basic earnings per share.

Earnings per share that are increasing steadily because of growth in sales should translate into increasing stock prices. However, earnings per share also can increase when companies buy back their own shares. The number of shares outstanding is then reduced, and if earnings stay the same, the earnings per share increase. Conceivably, earnings per share can increase when sales and earnings decrease if a significant number of shares are bought back. Astute investors examine a company's financial statements to determine whether the increase in earnings per share is caused by a growth in sales and earnings or by stock buybacks. If the latter is true, the result can be a loss of confidence in the stock, which can lead to a decline in the stock price.

Companies with poor fundamentals may try this tactic of buying back their shares to improve their earnings per share and ultimately their stock prices, but this strategy may not work over the long term.

The earnings per share also can be determined as follows:

Earnings per share = market price of the stock/P/E ratio

Dividends and Dividend Yields

Investors buy stocks for their potential capital gains and/or their dividend payments. Companies either share their profits with their shareholders by paying dividends or retain their earnings and reinvest them in different projects to boost their share prices. Look in the financial newspapers or use the Internet to find the dividend amounts that listed companies pay. Companies generally try to maintain their stated dividend payments even if they suffer declines in earnings. Similarly, an increase in earnings does not always translate into an increase in dividends. Certainly, many examples exist in which companies experience increases in earnings that result in increases in dividend payments, but this is not always the case. An imprecise relationship exists between dividends and earnings. Sometimes, increases in earnings exceed increases in dividends; at other times, increases in dividends exceed increases in earnings. Thus growth in dividends cannot be interpreted as a sign of a company's financial strength.

Dividends are important because they represent tangible returns. In contrast, investors in growth stocks that pay little or no dividends are betting on capital appreciation rather than on current returns.

The *dividend yield* is a measure of the annual dividends a company pays as a percentage of the market price of the stock. This ratio shows the percentage return that dividends represent relative to the market price of the common stock.

Dividend yield = annual dividend/market price of the stock

In an extended bull market, many investors are nervous about growth stocks that either pay no or low dividends and turn to stocks that yield high dividends. A strategy of buying this type of stock might offer some protection against the fall in stock market prices owing to rising interest rates. Dividend yields of many utility companies, real estate investment trusts (REITS), and energy companies might be as high as 4 to 7 percent. High dividend yields are characteristic of a few blue-chip companies and the utility companies.

Choosing stocks purely because of their high dividend yields, however, is risky. Dividends always can be reduced, which generally puts downward pressure on the stock price.

When you are choosing stocks with high dividend yields, you should look at the stocks' earnings to ensure that they are sufficient to support the dividend payments. As a general rule, earnings should be equal to at least 150 percent of the dividend payout.

The *dividend payout ratio* is the percentage of earnings a company pays out to its shareholders in dividends.

Dividend payout ratio = dividend per share/earnings per share

In addition to looking at earnings, you also should look at the statement of changes in cash to see the sources and uses of cash. For example, if the major sources of cash come from issuing debt and selling off assets, a company cannot maintain a policy of paying high dividend yields.

Dividends and dividend yields are not good indicators of the intrinsic value of a stock because dividend payments fluctuate considerably over time, creating an imprecise relationship between the growth in dividends and the growth in earnings.

PRO FORMA FINANCIAL STATEMENTS

Pro forma financial statements are constructed using projected figures based on assumptions about future sales, income, and cash flow. Pro forma financial statements focus on forecasts of future sales and earnings. These financial statements are not subject to generally accepted accounting principles (GAAP), even though companies are required to file the statements with the Securities and Exchange Commission (SEC).

Pro forma statements often exclude certain expenses and charges, sometimes making their projected earnings look more favorable than they truly are. Restructuring charges typically are excluded, and every type of projected gain is included. The lack of standards for earnings also adds to the confusion, making it difficult to compare the pro forma earnings of one company with those of another in the same industry.

Even though companies may not know the amounts of special restructuring charges that could occur in the future, they should provide more guidance with regard to these special charges and try to quantify them. You should be aware of these shortfalls in your analysis of a company's pro forma statements and not disregard the results of past financial statements as water under the bridge because past statements still may be more accurate than pro forma statements.

Table 10–8 discusses whether you can trust the numbers put out by management.

TABLE 10.8

Can You Trust the Numbers Put Out by Management?

After the Enron, WorldCom, and Global Crossing debacles of "cooking the books," the SEC spent a year reviewing annual reports from the 500 largest companies in the United States and found fault with 350 of the annual reports. The major problem areas were in accounting (the companies did not explain their use of accounting policies and how different interpretations might affect reported profits), revenues (companies did not spell out what they counted as revenue), pensions (companies did not disclose their assumptions on interest rates and how they used them to calculate liabilities on their pension funds), impairments (companies

(continued)

did not disclose how they wrote off their intangible assets), and management discussion (companies failed to analyze industry trends, risks, cash flow, and capital requirements) (McNamee, 2003, p. 74).

This corporate shortfall has been an invitation to lawmakers in Washington, D.C., to step in to regulate and limit the leeway with which corporations can report their numbers. New, tougher accounting rules were set. The SEC demanded that companies provide full explanations whenever they deviate from using GAAP.

The Financial Accounting Standards Board put limitations on how companies account for their restructuring costs and has requirements in the works to have companies expense their stock options (Henry and Berner, 2003, pp. 72–73).

Accounting scandals probably will continue to occur, so you should continue to look for warnings signs in industries and companies before you invest in their securities. An economy in recession, with declining sales and earnings, seems to provide the right atmosphere for unscrupulous corporate executives to overstate assets and revenues, understate expenses, and hide debt by keeping it off the balance sheet. Similarly, companies that had stellar growth records and were then confronted with slowing sales and earnings also "fudged" their numbers. Another situation was the Tyco story. Growth through aggressive acquisition practices gave the self-serving CEO a chance to pay himself enormous amounts, which were hidden in the numbers pertaining to the acquisition of other companies.

How seriously should you take pro forma earnings? Not very seriously, even though pro forma earnings form the basis of analysts' forward projections. Moreover, the track records of analysts were not very good for 2002. Analysts, watching projections for 2002, predicted a recovery in the latter half of the year. They forecasted 16 percent earnings increases in the third quarter and 21 percent in the fourth quarter that never came about.

REFERENCES

Brown, Ken. "How to Spot the Dirt in Rosy Annual Reports." *Wall Street Journal*, February 14, 2003, pp. C1, C3.

Enron Annual Reports.

Henry, David, and Robert Berner. "Ouch! Real Numbers." *BusinessWeek,* March 24, 2003, pp. 72–73.

Hoens, Thomas W. Personal conversation, March 26, 2003.

Hoens, Thomas W., and Keith B. Foley. "Cash Is King in Bond Analysis." Special report. Fitch Investor Service, January 10, 1994.

McNamee, Mike. "Annual Reports: Still Not Enough Candor." *BusinessWeek*, March 24, 2003, p. 74.

CHAPTER 11

Technical Analysis

KEY CONCEPTS

- What technical analysis is all about
- Constructing the different charts and their patterns
- The use of market indicators
- How to use moving averages
- Structural theories
- The implications of the use of technical analysis

Investment Snapshot: Using Technical Analysis to Determine Which Stocks to Buy and Sell

Would you make important decisions in your life based on answers provided by fortune-tellers or readers of tea leaves? Similarly, would you buy or sell stocks based on charts of stock price patterns and trading volumes? Technical analysts, who follow market and stock price movements, patterns, and trading volumes, say that technical analysis is the most reliable method for trading in the markets. Technical analysts even have names for all their chart patterns, for example, symmetrical triangles, ascending triangles, descending triangles, head and shoulders, double bottoms, and even flags and pennants. The charts also come in different varieties: line charts, bar

charts, point and figure charts, and candlestick charts, which
originated in Japan. The terminology used in technical analysis
is creative and different from standard business and financial
jargon. The terms *breakout* and *resistance* and *support levels* are
reminiscent of terms used in war games.

The use of technical analysis to select stocks is undoubtedly easier
than analyzing financial statements and crunching numbers. The
conclusions to be drawn about the use and benefits are yours.
However, after reading this chapter and looking at the results of
using technical analysis in stock selection, you might well find
some use for number crunching from fundamental and financial
statement analysis.

TECHNICAL ANALYSIS

Technical analysis is the study of market and stock variables, such as
the relationships between trading volumes and price movements, to
determine the supply and demand for securities and the markets.
Technical analysts are not all that concerned about fundamental
factors of companies and the economic environment. Rather, the
focus of technical analysis is on a company's historical stock price
movements and the trading volumes of the stock in relation to those
of the market. From this information, technical analysts predict
future stock price behavior. The technical analyst has a shorter time
horizon than the fundamental analyst. Even though many people
dispute the value of technical analysis, it is a widely used method
for selecting stocks. Most large brokerage firms have at least one
technical analyst on staff, and many rely on the information provided by their technical analysts in the selection of stocks. In academic
circles, however, technical analysis does not have very much credi-
bility. Despite the many shortcomings of technical analysis, you
should be aware of how it works.

Advocates of technical analysis feel that fundamental analysis
is of minimal value, whereas advocates of fundamental analysis
feel precisely the same way about technical analysis. In reality, these
two approaches do not work in isolation. Generally, technicians are
aware of the fundamentals of the stock they are interested in, and
fundamentalists are cognizant of the volume and trading range of

the stocks they are interested in. An awareness of the contradictions between these approaches will make it easier for you to recognize the philosophies your brokers and financial analysts follow in giving you advice.

Technical analysis focuses on past price movements of stocks, using them as a basis for predicting future stock prices. The assumption is that these price movements will be repeated. In other words, investor behavior always will be the same in similar situations, enabling technical analysts to predict future stock prices and whether stocks should be bought or sold. Technical analysts use several methods to predict future price movements, one of which is the use of charts. Charts show the patterns of stock price movements, which are the basis for interpreting future price movements. In other words, investors determine the markets for stocks, and when the same price conditions recur, investors react to them in the same way they did in the past. These repetitions of previous patterns in the stock prices then become the basis for technicians' buy and sell recommendations.

Technicians consider trading volume, together with price, to be an important indicator of the supply and demand for a stock. For technicians, the combination of price movements and trading volume indicates the mood of the market, as summarized in Table 11–1. When both volume and stock prices are increasing, investors are bullish because the increasing trading volume will continue to push prices up. However, the opposite situation occurs when trading volume is increasing and stock prices are decreasing. This situation indicates bearish sentiment because more people are selling than buying, which depresses stock prices.

Decreasing price and decreasing volume indicate a mixed mood in the market. Decreasing volume shows that the market for a stock is bottoming out. When the price reaches a low enough point, more investors will start buying, which pushes the price up.

TABLE 11-1

Volume and Price Movements That Indicate Market Mood

Volume	Price	Market Mood
Increasing	Increasing	Bullish
Increasing	Decreasing	Bearish
Decreasing	Decreasing	Somewhat bullish
Decreasing	Increasing	Somewhat bearish

Although decreasing volume and increasing price also describes a mixed market, this combination has a somewhat bearish tone because the increasing price will not be supported by the declining volume. The price will "top out" and start to fall.

You can easily see why technical analysis is so much more appealing than fundamental analysis: Price and volume data are easy to find (they are published daily in the financial newspapers) and to use.

You can classify technical analysis into four categories:

- Charts
- Market indicators
- Trends
- Structural theories

So many technical approaches exist within each of these broad categories that only a few of the more popular examples in each category are discussed in this chapter.

CHARTS AND THEIR PATTERNS

Technical analysts use charts to obtain historical information about individual stocks and markets. On these charts, analysts study the patterns to determine future trends, which will tell them when to buy and sell. These analysts don't have to know anything about a particular company or business. The charts reveal all! Past price movements and patterns are used to predict future price movements. The popular types of charts used are

- Line charts
- Bar charts
- Point and figure charts
- Candlestick charts

Line Charts

A *line chart* displays successive stock prices connected by a line over time. For example, this type of chart shows hourly changes to the Dow Jones Industrial Average (DJIA) in a day of trading and the closing prices of a stock or the market over time. Figure 11–1 shows an example of a line chart with the closing monthly prices of Amgen, Inc., for the months April 2005 through September 2006.

FIGURE 11-1

Line Chart for Amgen, Inc., Using Monthly Closing Prices
from April 2005 through February 2006

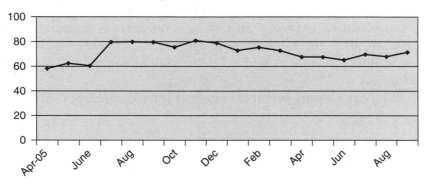

It shows the historical price patterns for the company and, according to technical analysts, shows trading opportunities in the stock.

Bar Charts

A *bar chart* displays successive high, low, and closing stock prices
over time. A bar chart is similar to a line chart, but it incorporates
more information. If charting daily stock prices, a bar chart includes
the stock's high, low, and closing prices. A vertical line shows the
high and low prices, and a horizontal line shows the closing price.
Figure 11–2 shows a bar chart for the following daily prices for
a stock:

Price	Mon	Tues	Wed	Thurs	Fri	Mon	Tues	Wed	Thurs	Fri
High	15	$15\frac{1}{2}$	$14\frac{3}{4}$	$15\frac{3}{4}$	$17\frac{3}{4}$	$18\frac{3}{4}$	$18\frac{3}{4}$	19	21	$20\frac{3}{4}$
Low	14	$14\frac{1}{2}$	14	$14\frac{1}{4}$	$15\frac{1}{2}$	$17\frac{3}{4}$	18	$18\frac{1}{2}$	19	$20\frac{1}{2}$
Close	$14\frac{1}{2}$	$14\frac{3}{4}$	$14\frac{3}{4}$	$15\frac{1}{2}$	$17\frac{3}{4}$	$18\frac{1}{4}$	$18\frac{1}{2}$	$18\frac{1}{2}$	21	$20\frac{3}{4}$
Volume	10,200	10,900	11,100	12,400	12,600	12,700	12,600	12,850	13,000	12,900

As more data are plotted, more of a pattern emerges, which
technical analysts study. From a chart, they can determine such
trends as the upward trend shown in Figure 11–2. Obviously, there
is an art as to the drawing of trend lines because no precise body of
data indicates how to draw them. The trend line is drawn from
the lowest points to the highest points. After a trend for a stock is
established, an analyst follows the stock price to look for any
changes in the trend. When the stock price falls below the upward

FIGURE 11-2

Bar Chart

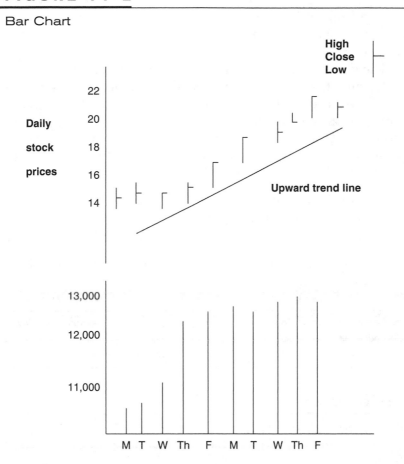

trend line, technical analysts recommend selling the stock because the trend has been broken. Similarly, the crossing of a downward trend indicates a buy signal for that particular stock. Trend lines form the basis for buy and sell signals.

Point and Figure Charts

Point and figure charts display predetermined price changes, which indicate the overall direction of prices. Point and figure charts, which differ from bar charts in a number of ways, record only significant changes in the stock price. *Significant* is defined by the analyst drawing up the chart. For higher-priced stocks (more than $50, for example), a 2-point difference might activate the recording of the price (see Figure 11–3). For lower-priced stocks, the difference might be 1 point. The second major difference between point and figure charts and other charts is that neither time nor trading volume is important. This type of chart is used to draw attention to emerging price patterns.

The first step in the construction of a point and figure chart is to determine the price movements you consider to be significant. For a high-priced stock in the hundreds of dollars, 3 to 5 points may be appropriate, whereas a stock in the $10 price range might have a 0.5 to 1 point differential. Assuming that the analyst has decided on 2 points for a stock in the $50 price range, the changes in price are plotted according to these guidelines:

- An X is inserted on the chart when the price of the stock advances by at least 2 points.

- An O is inserted when the stock declines by at least 2 points.

For example, the following prices result in the point and figure chart shown in Figure 11-3:

First week	50	51	51 1/2	52 1/4	52 3/4
Second week	50	47 3/4	46	47	47 1/2
Third week	48	49	50 1/4	51	53

FIGURE 11-3

Point and Figure Chart

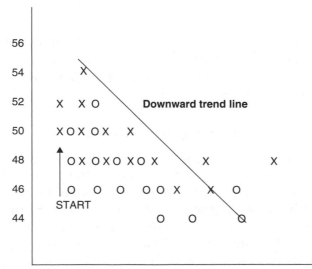

To begin drawing this chart, the first X at $50 is plotted. The next two entries in the first week (51 and $51\frac{1}{2}$) are ignored because they are less than the $2 stock price differential. The second X is placed at $52 to show the increase in the stock price to $52\frac{1}{4}$, whereas the next day's stock price of $52\frac{3}{4}$ is ignored.

In the second week, the stock price falls to $50, which necessitates putting the letter O (to signify a price decline) next to $50 in the second column. A second O is inserted at $48 to show the greater-than-2-point decline to $47\frac{3}{4}$, followed by a third O when the price falls to $46 per share. The third column shows the price increases to $48, $50, and higher than $52. Each time the stock advances by $2, an X is inserted, and when the stock price falls by $2, an O is inserted. Thus a point and figure chart shows, at a glance, price changes. Stock prices beyond the third week are plotted, and a downward trend line emerges. Technical analysts would view the penetration (the upward crossing) of the downward trend line as a buy signal.

Candlestick Charts

A *candlestick chart* displays high, low, open, and closing prices in addition to indicating whether the opening price for the day ends up higher than or lower than the closing price. The candlestick chart is the oldest type of charting method for determining stock prices. This method can be traced to Japan in the 1700s, where candlestick charts were used for predicting rice prices. As a consequence, the different candlestick shapes and patterns have Japanese names, which add some intrigue to the typical investment terminology. Candlestick charts present an alternative to the use of bar charts to identify price patterns and trends.

In addition to the high, low, and closing prices used by bar charts, candlestick charts use opening prices to show the direction of future stock prices. Each of these four types of information is included in the candlestick diagram, as shown in Figure 11–4.

The data conveyed by the candlestick chart include the following:

- The length of the body represents the range between the opening and closing prices. If the closing price is lower than the opening price (normally a bearish factor), the body of the candlestick is filled in (black). When the closing price is higher than the opening price, the body of the candlestick is open or white (normally a bullish sign).

FIGURE 11-4

Definitions of the Components of the Candelstick Chart

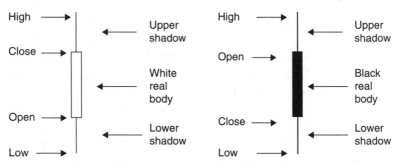

- The line above the candlestick body, called the *upper shadow,* represents the high price for the stock. The line below the candlestick body represents the low price of the stock. A candlestick with no upper shadow indicates that the stock closed (or opened) at the high price, and a candlestick with no lower shadow means that the stock closed (or opened) at the same price as the low price for the period.

The candlestick chart makes it easy to spot the changes in opening and closing prices. When you see a filled-in real body (black body), you know that the stock closed at a lower price than the opening price of the stock for that day (week, month, or whatever period you choose), indicating a weak close. Similarly, a long open body indicates that the stock closed at a higher price than the open for that day, which is a bullish indication for the stock.

Because the different candlestick patterns have many interpretations, a description of them all is beyond the scope of this chapter. Several books have been written on the topic in case you want to explore this charting technique further.

Chart Patterns

Chart patterns are a series of graphed stock prices forming recognizable patterns that can be used to forecast future stock prices. There are many well-known chart patterns, which are formations that technical analysts use to forecast the direction of future stock prices. Many technical analysts believe that by plotting prices over a period, they can predict how long a stock will advance or decline, as well as identify its support and resistance levels. After analysts

FIGURE 11-5

Chart Patterns

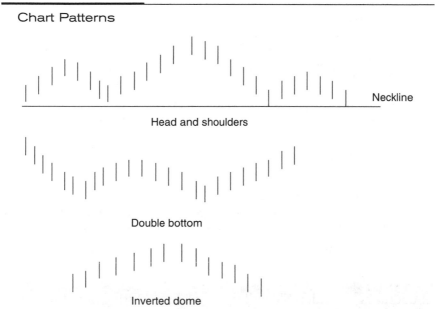

Head and shoulders

Double bottom

Inverted dome

choose the type of chart, they look for emerging price formations. See Figure 11–5 for a few examples of common formations. From volume and price chart patterns, trend lines, and support and resistance levels, technical analysts believe that they can predict the appropriate price at which to buy or sell a stock.

Interpreting the types of patterns can be difficult for beginning chartists. First, you have the nonemergence of common patterns (such as the example in Figure 11–5). Second, the buy and sell signals may not be obvious to the reader of the chart. Third, a technical analyst doesn't care whether a double-bottom formation chart belongs to Intel Corporation or a speculative company—the double bottom means the same for Intel and the speculative company, and their future stock prices are expected to perform in the same way. This statement implies that stock picking is a simplistic exercise that does not require any financial expertise other than obtaining price and volume information on stocks and the market.

A *trend* consists of relatively constant price movements of a security or market over time. Technical analysts plot their charts and then look for trends in their charts. A trend is the direction of the movement of the price of a stock or the market. The direction could be upward, downward, or sideways. Prices generally move in a jagged pattern. A succession of high and low points higher

FIGURE 11-6

Trend Lines

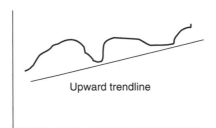
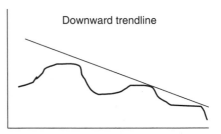

than the previous data signifies an upward trend. The opposite is true of a downward trend. These upward or downward trends are illustrated in Figure 11–6. Investors who follow technical analysis presume that the momentum in the markets will continue to perpetuate these trends.

A *resistance level* is the price at which a security or market encounters considerable selling pressure. During an upward or sideways trend, a pricing point to which the stock rises and then repeatedly falls below without breaking through is called a *resistance* level (see Figure 11–7). At this level of resistance, when the stock reaches the high side of its trading range, investors sell the stock in order to take profits. These sales prevent the stock from moving higher and breaking out of the resistance level.

A *support level* is the price at which a security or market encounters considerable buying pressure. Similarly, during a downward or sideways trend, a lower level of trading, called a *support level* might occur. At this level, the stock price bottoms out before increasing because investors are buying the stock. This concept also is illustrated in Figure 11–7, where the stock rises to around $30 per share only to fall back each time.

A *breakout* occurs when the price of a security or market moves above a resistance level or below a support level. Finally, the stock in Figure 11–7 surprises technical analysts by rising above the $30 level. For technical analysts, a *breakout* below a support level or above a resistance level is significant. Technical analysts believe that when stocks break out of their support or resistance levels, the stock prices will continue to move lower or higher, respectively, which establishes new levels of support or resistance. The analysts' explanations for this momentum appear to be twofold. When investors see that the price breaks through the resistance level,

FIGURE 1 1 - 7

Line Chart Showing Support and Resistance Levels

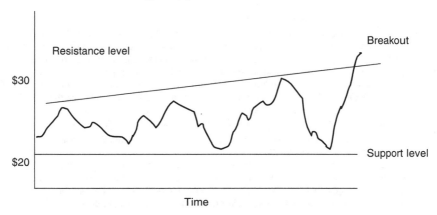

they will want to own this stock, which perpetuates additional enthusiastic buying of this stock. Second, some positive fundamental information might have accounted for the breakout, and when the public hears about this information, the stock price has already reacted. At that point, small investors jump on the bandwagon to buy. The opposite is true for breakouts in the support level, where selling momentum pushes the stock lower.

Technical analysts are not that concerned about fundamental information but rather about identifying trading patterns as a consequence of reactions to the release of information. Charting is much easier than fundamental analysis, and stock price information is easy to get at virtually no cost. However, the value of charting as a method for predicting future stock prices and profits has been questioned often by fundamental analysts and academicians. Table 11–2 discusses the views of fundamental versus technical analysts.

Many chartists attribute their successes to their charts, but the crux of the matter—when to buy and sell—may lie more in the chartist's judgment than in the charts themselves. If charting were that simple, investors all would have the stock market sewn up by now, and we could be sitting on the beaches of the French Riviera!

Many free sources on the Internet make charting information available, such as www.askresearch.com, www.stockcharts.com, and www.siliconinvestor.com. For the stocks of your choice, you can obtain line, bar, or candlestick charts along with moving-average trend lines.

TABLE 11-2

Should You Use Charts or Fundamentals to Choose Stocks

Technical analysis and fundamental analysis presented quite a different view of defense industry stocks. From a technical point of view, the prices of most of the defense stocks had fallen below their support levels, which indicated future negative trends. In contrast, the fundamentals for these stocks looked quite good, in that during the war with Iraq, the U.S. government would need to procure more weapons and develop new weapons systems. Figure 11–8 illustrates a five-year price chart of Boeing's stock price that shows the breakdown of Boeing's stock price below its support level. The chart pattern is a classic head and shoulders pattern (Zawadzinski-Edwards, 2003, p. 20).

Yola Zawadzinski-Edwards, an independent technical analyst, said that the drop in Boeing's stock, having broken down to $26.52, below the neckline, indicated that the stock would continue to fall toward 0 over the following 10 months. The head and shoulders pattern is indicative of a bearish outlook, especially when the stock price continues on a downward trend from the right shoulder. The other negative from a technical point of view is that the stock price had fallen below the support level of around $19 to $25 per share.

However, fundamental analysts were more bullish on Boeing's prospects. The threat of future terrorist incidents and the war in Iraq caused a drop in airline traffic that resulted in declining orders for airplanes from Boeing. However, the flip side of the coin is that only two major commercial airplane manufacturers exist: Boeing and Airbus. When world events settled down, Boeing would see its commercial aircraft business return to normal levels. Boeing's military business held the company's sales and earnings together. In fact, Boeing's low stock price was based on the valuation of the military business, whereas the commercial aircraft unit had no value. Consequently, an improvement in the commercial aircraft business caused Boeing's stock to rise significantly in the following years.

Source: Yola Zawadzinski-Edwards. "Under Fire: Charts Point to Woes for Defense Firms." *Barron's,*
March 31, 2003, p. 20.

FIGURE 11-8

Five-Year Stock Price Chart of Boeing

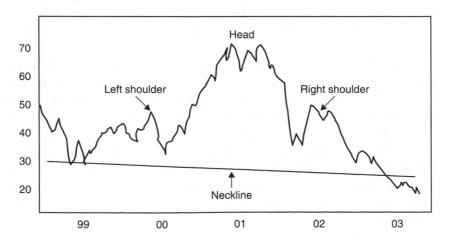

MARKET INDICATORS

Market indicators are used to determine the direction of the markets. Many technicians gauge the short- and intermediate-term directions of the market by looking at the following indicators:

- Daily volume
- Breadth of the market
- New highs and lows

Daily Volume

As mentioned at the beginning of this chapter, technicians consider volume and price movements to be indicators of supply and demand. When the daily volume on the New York Stock Exchange (NYSE) increases and stock prices rise, the market is considered to be in a bullish trend (it has more buyers than sellers). In a bear market, volume increases and prices decrease because of increased selling. Thus, in a weak market, prices might increase while volume declines. When both prices and volume decline, this is a somewhat optimistic sign that owners of stock are reluctant to sell.

Statisticians might differ considerably in their interpretations of price and volume combinations. Technicians can interpret even the more straightforward high volume differently. Some view this difference positively, and others see it negatively (Dorfman, 1993, p. C18). In practical terms, daily price and volume changes might be difficult to correlate to determine a trend in the market. Information about trading volume at the end of each trading day can be obtained using the Internet or in financial newspapers.

Breadth of the Market

The *breadth of the market* is a measure of the number of advancing and declining stocks to indicate the upward or downward direction of the market. By examining the numbers of stocks that have advanced, declined, and remained the same on a particular day of trading, analysts believe that they can determine the relative strength or weakness of the market. If the number of stocks advancing in price on any particular day exceeds the number of stocks declining in price, it is considered to be a strong market.

For example, of the 3,425 issues traded on the NYSE on October 6, 2006, 1,208 advanced, 2,058 declined, and 159 remain unchanged; these numbers presented a negative picture of the NYSE for that day. In other words, for every 20 stocks that declined in price, 12 stocks increased in price. A strong picture of the market is presented by a greater number of advancing stocks over declining stocks, which is a favorable sign indicating a rising market. The opposite is true when breadth is negative: A greater number of declining stocks over advancing stocks indicates a falling market.

The financial newspapers list these daily statistics for the markets, and many technicians use these data to calculate the advance/decline indicator. The *advance/decline indicator* is the cumulative total of the daily advancing stocks minus the total number of daily declining stocks. You calculate this indicator by subtracting the number of declining issues from the advancing issues and then dividing this difference by the total number of issues traded for the day. For example, assume the following trading information for the NYSE for the week:

	Advancing Stocks	Declining Stocks	Difference	Cumulative Difference
Monday	1,100	1,400	−300	−300
Tuesday	1,200	1,550	−350	−650
Wednesday	1,300	1,400	−100	−750
Thursday	1,250	1,300	−50	−800
Fruday	1,300	1,250	50	−750

Plotting the cumulative difference on a daily basis results in the *advance/decline line,* which is used to indicate the trend of the market. A declining advance/decline line indicates a falling market, and an increasing advance/decline line indicates a bullish market. When the advance/decline line is going up and the market is falling, this is a bullish short-term signal for the market; when the advance/decline line is falling and the market is going up, this is a bearish signal. No research consistently shows the predictive capabilities of the advance/decline line. Two more complex indexes are based on the advance/decline indicator: the ARMS index and the trading index.

New Highs and Lows

Many technicians monitor the daily new highs and new lows on the NYSE. When a sizable number of stocks reach their 52-week highs and they outnumber the stocks that reach their 52-week lows, and this pattern is maintained over time, technical analysts are bullish on the market.

Many technical analysts place importance on the signals given by volume, market breadth, and the new highs and lows. However, these signals are not foolproof, and possibly technical analysts place too much importance on their predictive capability for future market activity.

Short-Interest Theory

Short interest is a measure of the number of stocks sold short in the market over time, indicating future market demand. Technical analysts use the information about short interest as a sign of weakness or strength in the market. For instance, when stocks are sold short, it is with the anticipation that their prices will go lower so that they can then be bought back at lower prices. Analysts monitor short-interest figures, and they contend that short-interest positions that are large are bullish indicators. The reason is that when large short positions are open, short sellers eventually have to buy back the stocks, which drives the prices up. Small amounts of short interest are considered of no consequence to future market activity. The short-interest theory may not be a reliable indicator of future market sentiment because the number of stocks sold short is a small percentage of the shares outstanding on the NYSE. In addition, short selling also may take place for tax purposes rather than in anticipation of a lower price.

The *short-interest ratio* is the short interest divided by the average daily volume, which is used to determine the direction of the market. The short-interest ratio shows the relationship of short sales to the total number of shares traded. The short-interest ratio for the NYSE is calculated by dividing the short interest of the NYSE by the average daily volume on the NYSE for the same period. This ratio also can be calculated for other markets and for individual stocks.

$$\text{Short-interest ratio} = \text{short interest/average daily trading volume}$$

Short-interest figures are released in the middle of every month by each of the exchanges. If the short interest on the NYSE is 22 million for one month and the average daily trading volume for the NYSE in the same month is 20 million shares, the short-interest ratio for that month is 1.1 (22 million ÷ 20 million).

The ratio is greater than 1 when the average daily volume is less than the short interest. A short-interest ratio of between 1 and 1.6 is considered neutral. Technical analysts regard a ratio greater than 1.6 to be a bullish signal because short sellers will have to cover their positions and buy back the stocks. A ratio of less than 1 is considered bearish. This indicator invites some ambiguity because technical analysts believe that with a large short-interest ratio, short sellers will have to buy back the stocks eventually, which sends stock prices up. However, short sellers have shorted the stocks because they think that the stocks are overvalued and that their prices will decline.

Although this indicator is popular among technical analysts, it too is not infallible in predicting market direction, and no research appears to support the use of this technique as an accurate indicator of price movements.

Barron's Confidence Index

The *Barron's Confidence Index* is designed to measure investors' confidence in the stock market. The Barron's Confidence Index compares the yield of high-grade bonds (usually AAA rated, the highest rating) to the yield of lower-grade bonds (usually BBB rated). This relationship is used to predict price movements in the stock market. The assumption behind this theory is that bond traders are more sophisticated than stock investors, so their actions are assumed to have more insight into future market activity.

The Barron's Confidence Index is determined by dividing the yield of 10 top-grade corporate bonds by the yield of 10 intermediate-grade bonds.

Barron's Confidence Index = (yield on 10 top-grade bonds/yield on 10 intermediate-grade bonds) × 100

Yields on top-grade bonds are always lower than yields on lesser-grade bonds, so this index is always less than 100 percent. The trading range is generally between 80 and 95 percent. Advocates of this ratio watch to see how close the ratio can get to 1, its theoretical maximum value. For instance, if the average yield of the 10 high-grade bonds is 4.5 percent and the average of the intermediate-grade bonds is 5 percent, the Barron's Confidence Index is 90 percent (4.5%/5% × 100). When investors are confident about the future, they are willing to take more risk and buy more speculative bonds.

The price of higher-quality debt is then depressed, which increases the yield, indicating investors' optimism in the stock market.

When the Barron's Confidence Index falls to around 80 percent, the outlook for the stock market is bearish. Confidence in the economy is low, prompting investors to buy good-quality debt, which increases prices and lowers yields. The selling of lower-grade bonds decreases their prices and increases their yields. This situation results in an increase in the rate differential between high-quality and lower-quality bonds and a lower Barron's Confidence Index.

Like many other technical indicators, the Barron's Confidence Index has not been accurate in predicting stock price movements. Time lags may occur between the indicator and the results; when companies in the Barron's Confidence Index issue a large supply of bonds, the yields are distorted, which then distorts the indicator.

Insider Trading

Insider trading is the purchase and sale of shares held by corporate officers, directors, and owners of 10 percent or more of a company's securities. Corporate directors, officers, and large shareholders— referred to as *insiders*—have access to privileged information about their companies and therefore are required by the Securities and Exchange Commission (SEC) to report their purchases and sales of stocks. Insiders know first-hand how their companies are doing; if they are purchasing their company's stocks, it is a bullish signal for those stocks. Conversely, if insiders sell their stocks, it is a bearish signal.

You can follow insider transactions in the financial newspapers and on various Web sites. Many technicians follow insider activity as a method for selecting stocks. Academic studies tend to lend more support to insider transactions than to other technical approaches as a means of correlating changes in stock prices (Jaffe, 1974, pp. 410–428; Zweig, 1976, p. 5).

Odd-Lot Theory

The *odd-lot theory* states that investors should make investments contrary to those made by individual investors who invest in odd-lot orders of stocks. The odd-lot theory is concerned with the purchase and sale of securities by small investors. An odd-lot trade consists of fewer than 100 shares and is generally placed by individual investors who are considered to be unsophisticated. When "odd-lotters" are purchasing stocks, it is a sign to sell stocks. Similarly, when "odd-lotters" are selling stocks, you should buy stocks according to the odd-lot theory. Small investors are frequently wrong in their investment decisions. This type of investor is viewed as uninformed about the workings of the market. According to the theory, these small investors typically buy stocks at the peak of a bull market, which is when astute investors (advocates of this theory) start selling. Similarly, after a stock market decline, the time to buy is when small investors are bailing out of their stock positions.

The *Wall Street Journal* reports odd-lot trading on a daily basis, and *Barron's* reports it on a weekly basis. Technical analysts calculate the ratio of odd-lot purchases to odd-lot sales, which has a typical range from 0.6 to 1.4.

Odd-lot ratio = odd-lot purchases/odd-lot sales

A ratio that is approaching its upper limits (1.4) means that small investors are buying more than they are selling. This situation indicates that the stock market is about to turn and become a bear market. In other words, small investors become enthusiastic about the stock market when the market has reached its highs and become disillusioned after a crash in the market, which gives a low reading on the ratio. This is a contrarian indicator (going against the crowd; buying when the majority of investors are selling and selling when the majority of individual investors are buying).

Investment Advisory Opinions

Investment advisory opinions indicate whether investment advisors are bullish or bearish about the future of stock prices. Technical analysts who follow the predictions of investment advisors take a contrarian (opposite) view. When most of the advisors are bullish, technical analysts become bearish. Similarly, if the majority of advisors become bearish, technical analysts see it as is a signal to buy.

It is strange to think that investment advisors who spend most of their working hours studying the market should be given equal weight with the "odd-lotters," who are considered to be unsophisticated investors, in their assessments of the market. However, the investing public may never be sure about the underlying reasons for recommendations from stock analysts' and investment advisors because they might have conflicts of interest in recommending stocks to buy and sell.

Mutual Fund Cash Position

Mutual fund cash position in relation to the amount of total investments is used as an indicator of the direction of the markets. The amount of cash a mutual fund has in relation to the amount of its total investments is an indicator of the direction of the markets. By monitoring the cash positions of mutual funds, technical analysts can assess the potential purchasing power of mutual funds. Equity mutual funds hold between 5 and 25 percent of their assets in cash. When mutual funds are fully invested or hold little of their assets in cash, they have little purchasing power in the markets. However, when the funds hold larger percentages of their assets in cash (15 percent or higher), their potential purchasing power in the market is significant, which could trigger an upturn in the market when the cash is invested.

Relative Strength Ratio

The *relative strength ratio* is the price of a stock compared with another stock, index, or the market. The relative strength ratio allows you to compare the performance of one stock or market index relative to another. For example, to compare the performance of Coca-Cola Company with the performance of PepsiCo and determine which is the better performer, you construct the ratio of relative strength. The chart is constructed by plotting daily stock prices for a specified period. What matters in determining the relative strength is that the original investment is the same for both stocks. The process is illustrated in Table 11-3.

The relative strength shows the appreciation or depreciation of stock X to stock Y with an initial investment of $75 in each stock on the first Monday. In the first week, stock X declined relative to stock Y, but this situation reversed in the second week, where stock X appreciated more than stock Y.

TREND METHODS

Some technical analysts believe that it is important to identify a trend that is more likely to persevere over a period of time. In other words, once a trend has been identified, you should move with it:

TABLE 11-3

Relative Strength Ratio Between Stock X and Stock Y

	(1)	(2)	(3)	(4)	(5)
			(1) × 1	(2) × 3	(3)/(4)
	Price Stock X	Price Stock Y	1 Share X	3 Shares Y	Relative Strength
Monday	$75	$25	$75	$75	1.00
Tuesday	$70	$26	$70	$78	0.90
Wednesday	$69	$27	$69	$81	0.85
Thursday	$71	$26	$71	$78	0.91
Friday	$72	$27	$72	$81	0.89
Monday	$74	$25	$74	$75	0.99
Tuesday	$75	$25	$75	$75	1.00
Wednesday	$77	$24	$77	$72	1.07
Thursday	$78	$25	$78	$75	1.04
Friday	$79	$25	$79	$75	1.05

In an up market, you should be buying, and in a down market, you should be selling, until the trend is broken.

Moving Average

The *moving average* includes the most recent price and eliminates the earliest price from the figures in the distribution before computing the average. The moving average is one of the more popular methods for determining a trend. An average is the sum of a collection of figures divided by the number of figures used in the numerator; a moving average is an average over time. Table 11–4 illustrates the computation of an average for a stock using for a 10-day period.

A 10-day moving average adds the stock price for the eleventh day and drops the stock price for the first day. For instance, if the closing price on the eleventh day is $18 per share, the new 10-day moving average will be

$$\text{10-day moving average} = (\text{10-day average} + \text{eleventh-day price} - \text{first day's price})/10$$
$$= (165 + 18 - 15\tfrac{3}{4})/10$$
$$= \$16.725$$

By continuing this method of adding the next day's price and dropping the oldest day's price, the moving average is calculated

TABLE 1 1 - 4

Moving Average

Day	Closing Price
1	$15 3/4
2	16 1/4
3	17 1/2
4	15
5	16
6	15
7	16 1/4
8	17
9	17 1/4
10	18
Total	165
Average price	165/10 = 16 1/2

over time. You can plot this moving average to show the graphic trend over time and show how the moving average compares with daily stock prices. When the moving-average line crosses the line of actual prices, this indicates a change in trend. The moving-average line tends to smooth out any volatility in actual daily stock prices.

You can choose any length of time for a moving average: 10, 15, 30, or 200 days, for example. The 200-day moving average is frequently used, but calculating 200 days of stock prices can be tedious, particularly if you are interested in a large number of stocks.

The length of time chosen for the moving average has an effect on the trend line. A shorter-duration moving average results in greater sensitivity to price changes than a longer-duration moving average. With the former, an investor who religiously follows the signals given with the frequent crossing of the trend line and the price line will be encouraged to trade stocks after small changes in price, as illustrated in Figure 11–9. Technical analysts pay particular attention to the crossovers of the price line with the moving average, which indicates a buy or sell signal. The crossing and rising of the price line above the moving-average line indicates a buy signal. The opposite situation occurs when the moving average crosses and rises above the price line, which indicates a sell signal. A shorter-duration moving average encourages frequent trading with a volatile stock price, which results in both greater transaction costs and capital gains taxes paid, thereby reducing or eliminating any profits. With a

FIGURE 11-9

Buy and Sell Signals Using a Stock's Price and Moving Average

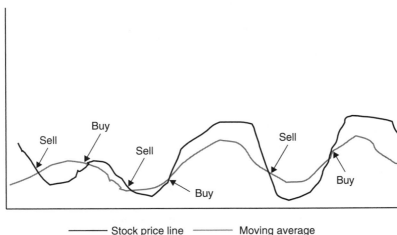

———— Stock price line   ———— Moving average

longer moving average, the trend line exhibits a greater lag behind the actual price line of these stocks. Technicians use the moving average of the DJIA to determine the trend for the market.

A study done by James C. Van Horne and G. G. C. Parker (1967) suggests that use of the moving average as a tool for buying and selling stocks does not produce superior results. Another study done by James (1968, pp. 315–326) indicates that buying and selling strategies based on moving averages produced lower returns than a buy and hold strategy.

The fact that investors need to decide on the time period to use for the moving average and whether they should buy or sell when the lines cross suggests a somewhat arbitrary and simplistic approach to the complexities of buying and selling stocks. If a major upward trend in a stock takes place, an investor profits from it by buying early. Of course, the opposite is also true. If an investor recognizes a major downward trend early and sells before the stock decreases in price, that investor is ahead of the game. However, for stocks that exhibit volatility, this method may give equivocal signs and encourage frequent trading, which is costly when transaction costs are involved.

STRUCTURAL THEORIES

The structural theories of technical analysis are based on repetitions of previous price patterns. Price patterns are believed to be regular over long periods. Many structural theories exist, some of which are esoteric, such as lunar phases or hemlines on dresses to predict the direction of the stock market. These types are not discussed in this book.

Seasonal Patterns

The *January effect* is a theory that small-cap stocks post large returns in January. Technical analysts monitoring the DJIA monthly have found seasonal patterns occurring in December, January, July, and August. Some attribute the seasonal pattern in December and January to tax planning. In December, many investors sell stocks whose values are depressed to produce capital losses that can then be offset against other capital gains. This action of selling further depresses the prices of these stocks, which presents opportunities for investors to buy them back in January, which results in a surge in their stock prices. This is known as the *January effect*. Historically, the prices of small-cap stocks have risen slightly in January. Gottschalk reported that during the period 1982–1987 small stocks increased by 4.2 percent annually as compared with 3.8 percent for larger stocks in January (Gottschalk, 1988, pp. C1, C16).

The following questions give some perspective on the gravity of the January effect: Which stocks will increase in January? Will they include the stocks in your portfolio? Maybe, maybe not! What about a bear market? During the bear markets of 1978 and 1982, the prices of small-cap stocks lost ground in January. Will the small percentage increases cover the transaction costs of buying and selling?

The same questions can be asked about *summer rallies* in the markets. The theory of a *summer rally* says that the stock market rises during the summer months.

Research by Hugh Johnson, chief investment officer at First Albany, showed net gains from May 31 to August 31 in the DJIA for 21 of the past 33 years, during the period 1961–1994 (Kansas, C1). Birinyi Associates also found support for the summer rally premise with a longer study going back to 1915. In only four periods from 1915 to 1993 did the Dow Jones Industrial Average report losses in all three summer months—June, July and August. The gains on the industrial average were reported to be 0.41 percent, 1.31 percent and 1.06 percent on average per year for June, July and August, respectively over the period from 1915. Surprisingly, even in 1929 a summer rally took place, where the Dow Jones Industrial Average surged 11.5 percent in June, 4.8 percent in July and 9.4 percent in August (Kansas, 1994, p. C2).

In the *weekend effect,* stock prices peak on Fridays and decline on Mondays. According to this theory, investors should sell their stocks at the end of the week rather than at the beginning.

Elliott Wave Theory

The *Elliott wave theory* is based on the premise that stock prices move in a five-wave sequence when they are following a major trend and in a three-wave sequence when they are moving against a major trend. Long waves can last longer than 100 years, and subwaves have short durations.

The Elliott wave theory gained a following after technicians used it to correctly forecast the bull market of the 1980s. However, the theory lost much of its following when the theory predicted a bearish market in the late 1980s and early 1990s, missing out on the continuing bull market.

The problem with this structural theory is that what is considered to be a wave by some analysts is considered a subwave by others. The Elliott wave theory may be too broadly defined to be conclusive, and many of its followers often include their successes while discounting their failures.

IMPLICATIONS OF TECHNICAL ANALYSIS FOR INVESTORS

The methods used by technical analysts attempt to predict future prices in the markets and individual stocks and to determining when to buy and sell. The number of new methods touted by technical analysts keeps growing.

What is the rationale for the success of technical analysis in identifying future prices of stocks and the markets? First, technical analysts believe that the crowd of investors will always react in the same way. When a pattern of rising prices occurs, investors will want to jump into the market (buy stocks). This action then pushes prices higher as more investors join in, causing a self-perpetuating increase in prices. As prices rise, so do the enthusiasm and fervor with which the buy recommendations of the technical analysts are touted. Technical analysts recommend stocks only when there is a price trend. In essence, they are encouraging you to buy stocks when prices have already gone up, after an established breakout or an upward trend has taken place. In other words, investors are encouraged to buy stocks when the prices have already risen. If these stocks do not continue their upward trend, investors find that they have bought stocks at high prices when the stocks have turned around to fall to prices below their purchase prices. On the downward trend, technical analysts then initiate their sell recommendations. You are then encouraged to buy at high prices and sell at low prices. (This situation does not sound like a winning formula to make money, let alone get rich.) The other problem is that stocks may take sudden turns in price, which could mean that technical analysts could "miss the boat" in their timed buys and sells.

Academic research has shown that technical analysts have not been able to outperform the results from a buy and hold strategy in the market. An astute reader will question this conclusion because most brokerage firms employ at least one technical analyst. What about that? Some good reasons exist for having technical analysts on staff. They read their charts and issue many buy and sell recommendations within short periods on the same stock, advocating active trading of stocks. This situation generates commissions for brokers and their brokerage firms. A buy and hold strategy, on the other hand, generates only one commission per stock when it is bought and held.

From the investor's point of view, a buy and hold strategy may not be exciting, but it does economize on paying taxes. The perpetual trader, who is in and out of stocks in periods of less than a year, pays taxes on capital gains at ordinary income tax rates. The investor whose holding period is longer than one year pays taxes on gains at the lower long-term capital gains rates. The buy and hold investor does not pay taxes on the gains until the stock is sold. By following the advice of technical analysts, you are bound to generate more commission costs and greater amounts of income taxes.

Take a look at some of the holes in technical analysis. The argument put forward by technical analysts is that if an established upward trend in a stock takes place, the momentum from buyers in the market will continue to fuel the stock upward, to even more dizzying heights. No attention is paid to the fundamentals of the stock or to other reasons that the stock is rising in price and whether it is overvalued. It does not matter, in fact, what the name of the stock is or what type of business the company is in. For example, if the stock prices of two different companies in two different industries have the same chart patterns with upward trends, there would be no differentiation in their buy recommendations. Yet most people know that the oil industry and the health care industry, for example, generally do not perform in the same way and that some fundamental factors could affect different companies in the same industry. What about company management? One management team might be more efficient and effective than another. The charts and chart patterns do not differentiate these factors, and neither do they take into account the possibilities of change. People might react differently in the future from how they reacted in the past, and events can change. If randomness exists in the market, past patterns have no effect on future prices.

Technical analysis encourages timing of buying and selling stocks and the markets. To do so profitably requires a high degree of accuracy. Although many famous technical analysts have predicted many bull and bear markets successfully, they have not been able to do so consistently. Elaine Garzarelli successfully called the "Black Monday" crash of 1987 but remained bearish thereafter while the markets went up. To get back into stocks and the market, the reentry points were much higher than if investors had merely stayed in the market and held their positions during the crash. To time the buying and selling of stocks and the markets successfully, you have to be accurate in your decisions, and you almost need clairvoyance.

REFERENCES

Dorfman, John R. "Technical Analysts Get a Chill as Winter Approaches." *Wall Street Journal*, December 14, 1993, pp. C1, C18.

Gottschalk, Earl C. "It's the 'January Effect' But Will It Occur in January?" *Wall Street Journal*, December 14, 1988, pp. C1, C16.

Jaffe, Jeffrey F. "Special Information and Insider Trading." *Journal of Business*, July 1974, pp. 410–428.

James, F. E., Jr. "Monthly Moving Averages—An Effective Investment Tool?" *Journal of Financial and Quantitative Analysis*, September 1968, pp. 315–326.

Kansas, Dave. "Analysts Expect Summer Rally, But Nothing Special." *Wall Street Journal*, June 6, 1994, pp. C1, C2.

Van Horne, James C., and G. G. C. Parker. "The Random Walk Theory: An Empirical Test." *Financial Analysts Journal*, November/December 1967.

Wright, Leonard T. *Principles of Investments*, 2d ed. Columbus, OH: Grid, Inc., 1977.

Zawadzinski-Edwards, Yola. "Under Fire: Charts Point to Woes for Defense Firms." *Barron's*, March 31, 2003, p. 20.

Zweig, Martin E. "Canny Insiders." *Barron's*, June 21, 1976, p. 5.

Theories of the Stock Market

KEY CONCEPTS

- Theories of stock prices
- Random walk theory
- The implications of the efficient market hypothesis
- The capital asset pricing model
- Other theories on returns
- Active and passive investment strategies
- Implications of the theories of the stock markets for investors

---

Investment Snapshot: How Easy Is It to Beat the Market?

You undoubtedly have heard many conversations in which investors have spoken about earning exorbitant returns from the stock market. "I bought eBay or Amazon.com at issue and made a 600 percent return in a short period of time," or "I missed buying Yahoo!, but I bought some other Internet stock, which doubled in value within hours after purchase."

Conversations such as these were prevalent during the "Internet bubble" of the bull market in 2000. The type of business the Internet companies were in or whether they ever would be profitable didn't matter. In fact, many Internet companies never managed to earn any profits during their short

(continued)

lifetimes. One of the few Internet companies that is still around today, Amazon.com increased its sales year over year but only years later was able to chalk up operating profits. Investors with no financial acumen invested in these newly issued stocks and were able to "beat" the returns of the market, which were weighed down by stocks that were profitable but did not have meteoric price rises.

With your investment knowledge to date you are correct if you are asking, "How is this possible?" You are especially astute if your thoughts are that the returns earned by these novice investors were not sustainable over extended periods of time. Similarly, you might question the aspect of risk in investing in high-flying companies based on ideas with questionable business models. Is it wise to invest large sums of money in a company whose future viability is uncertain?

These queries are all valid. Yes, some lay investors did beat the market averages during the Internet bubble, but did they continue to outperform the markets in the period after the downturn of Internet stocks? Probably not, or else their names would be in lights, and they would be hailed as the new investment gurus. Should you compare risky startup venture companies with the established companies held in the Dow Jones Industrial Average, for example? No, that would be equating the Wal-Marts and Coca-Colas of the world with the Globe.coms, which were in business briefly during the Internet bubble.

This chapter focuses on the theories behind the rise and fall of stock prices and whether investors can "beat" the stock market on a risk-adjusted basis over extended periods. The preceding two chapters outlined how stocks are chosen using fundamental and technical analysis. Fundamentalists are interested in what stocks are worth, whereas technicians look only at historical prices and volume records. A fundamentalist looks for stocks that are valued below their intrinsic value and is not concerned with the reactions of the crowds of investors, like technicians. This chapter explores the different theories behind stock prices and examines, in greater detail, the fundamental and technical approaches to buying stocks with regard to earning higher risk-adjusted returns than the market.

The trader's lament:

> *Buy and you'll be sorry.*
> *Sell and you'll regret.*
> *Hold and you'll worry.*
> *Do nothing and you'll fret.*

Many investors believe that they can successfully "time the markets" by buying stocks when the markets are moving up and then selling their stocks before the markets start to decline from their peaks. Many investment advisory newsletters are aimed at these investors, who are known as *market timers*. These newsletters advise their readers when to buy and when to sell their stocks.

Correctly anticipating a correction or a crash certainly can improve your rate of return. For instance, some newsletters correctly advised their readers to sell their stocks before the stock market crash in 1987 and to buy stocks after the Dow Jones Industrial Average (DJIA) had fallen to its low of the year. Following this type of strategy would have increased your returns over those who had stayed invested during and after the market crash. However, the trouble with market timing is that if you exit the market at the wrong time, you miss out on stock market gains and it greatly reduces your rate of return. History has shown that over extended periods, investors who stay fully invested in the stock market reduce their risk of mistiming the market.

THEORIES OF STOCK PRICES

Chapter 10 discussed *fundamental analysis,* which relates the movement of stock prices to earnings. Anticipating changes in earnings precipitates a change in stock prices. According to the theory, an astute investor analyzes the fundamentals of a company regarding its effects on future earnings. When future earnings are expected to rise, the stock price increases in advance of the actual changes in earnings. The belief is that by buying and selling stocks in advance of their changes in earnings, investors will increase their returns. In other words, it would be too late to buy stocks after earnings increases are announced or to sell them after decreases in earnings are announced because the stock price would have already reacted to this news. However, if earnings were expected to continue their growth, investors would continue to buy these stocks.

A fundamental analyst is concerned with the financial characteristics of different stocks in order to find stocks that are undervalued. When the market price of a stock is less than its intrinsic value (a reflection of estimated earnings multiplied by a price/earnings ratio), the stock is undervalued. If the market price is above the intrinsic value, the stock is overvalued. This theory then implies that stock markets are inefficient, allowing for large profits to be made from undervalued securities.

What are some possible reasons that fundamental analysis may not work? Burton G. Malkiel, an economics professor at Princeton University, suggests three reasons in his book, *A Random Walk Down Wall Street* (1990, p. 124):

1. The information collected by the analyst may be based on assumptions and bad information. The analyst may be overly optimistic about assumptions on future sales, cost containment, and earnings that may not materialize, causing earnings disappointments.
2. An analyst may be missing the mark on value. Analysts may agree that a stock is growing at a certain percentage, but they may be incorrect in their perception of value. For example, some analysts agree that Pfizer is growing its sales into the future because of its pipeline of new drugs still to be released to the market, but their assumptions on the future value of Pfizer's stock may be incorrect.
3. The market may not value the stock in the same way as the analyst does. For example, Cisco stock is currently trading at a P/E multiple of 26 times (its earnings) with a growth rate of around 11 percent. The market might have viewed the stock as overvalued even though analysts still tout the value of Cisco. Rather than increase in price, Cisco's stock price decreased, which brought its P/E multiple down from its lofty levels.

Fundamental analysis may not always work and has been refuted by the efficient market hypothesis (discussed later in this section).

Because you have no assurances that stock prices will always move in the same direction as earnings over short periods of time, you might not be able to count on correctly forecasting stock price movements. Moreover, a multiplicity of conditions and factors over and above the fundamentals affects stock prices.

Chapter 11 discussed *technical factors*, which, unlike fundamental factors, affect stock prices because of conditions within the market. Technical analysis ignores the company's earnings, dividends, and factors in the economy such as interest rates as the cause of stock price changes. Instead, the focus is on past stock prices, their patterns, and trading volume. By charting these past price movements and volume, technical analysts forecast future price movements. Their belief is that past price patterns will be repeated, which is the basis for their recommendations about when to buy and sell stocks. Technical analysis has little support from the academic investment literature. The academic world not only has not been kind to technical analysis, but technical analysis also has been disdained by supporters of the efficient market hypothesis.

The Wall Street investment community's two methods for choosing stocks, fundamental analysis and technical analysis, have their limitations, as has been pointed out. Academicians, on the other hand, have their own theories, which they have advanced to explain the movement of stock prices. To recap, the Wall Street fundamental analysts believe that individual investors are totally lost without their recommendations and that investors will always underperform analysts. Academicians, on the other hand, have come up with a number of theories related to the dissemination of information that affects stock prices:

- If information were random, a randomly selected portfolio chosen by throwing darts at the names of stock companies would do as well as a portfolio carefully selected by analysts.
- If information about stocks is disseminated efficiently, stock prices will always be fairly valued.
- The capital asset pricing model (CAPM) states that a security's expected return is directly related to its beta coefficient (which is its rate of return relationship to the market index).
- Market information is disseminated inefficiently in the stock market, and stocks with low price-to-book ratios show greater returns than high price-to-book ratios.

These theories are discussed in detail in this chapter. By under-standing the different theories of stock prices in the market, you will be better prepared to formulate your own investment style in the construction of your portfolio.

RANDOM WALK THEORY

The *random walk theory* states that stock price movements are unpre-dictable, making it impossible to know where prices are headed. The random walk theory asserts that stock prices cannot be predicted from prior prices because no relationship exists between the two sets of prices. Events occur randomly, which then affect stock prices. An illustration of this theory is the flipping of a coin. The outcomes are not affected by previous throws.

Burton G. Malkiel, in his book, *A Random Walk Down Wall Street* (1990), argues that investors would do no better or worse than the market averages if they chose their investments by throwing darts at stock tables. The reason is that information about stocks occurs randomly, and then the stocks will react to the news. Bad news causes a stock's price to go down immediately, and good news has an immediate positive effect on a stock's price. The news about a stock cannot be anticipated accurately, which results in a random occurrence, meaning that stock prices move randomly. According to Dremen (1991), analysts were only accurate 40 percent of the time in forecasting the next quarter's earnings for companies they followed. Thus stocks react in advance of anticipated good or bad news, and by the time the news is announced, it is already reflected in the stock price. The random walk theory implies that technical analysis is a waste of time in that prices cannot be predicted from historical data.

EFFICIENT MARKET HYPOTHESIS

The *efficient market hypothesis* states that security prices reflect all available information and adjust instantly to any new information. Stocks are always correctly priced, making it impossible for investors to outperform the stock market averages except by buy-ing more risky securities. The basic premise of the efficient market hypothesis is that stock markets are efficient in the pricing of stocks because information about the stocks is rapidly disseminated throughout the investment community. Thus, if investors and analysts use the same public information about stocks, generating superior returns is difficult because the rest of the investment community has the same information. The stock's price then reflects all available information, which implies that few stocks are mispriced. If a stock is undervalued, investors quickly buy it, which drives up the price to its fair value and reduces returns for subsequent investors. Similarly, overvalued stocks are sold, which reduces the price to its fair value. In other words, stocks are not mispriced for long. Stocks settle at their intrinsic values, which reflect the investment community's consensus about their earnings, returns and risks.

The implication of efficient markets is that investors cannot expect to consistently outperform the markets or consistently underperform the markets on a risk-adjusted basis. On average, investors will do no better or no worse than the market averages over an extended period of time with a diversified portfolio of stocks. This statement does not mean that investors cannot find securities that earn abnormally high returns. For example, if you had bought Oracle Corporation's stock at $12 per share in October 2005 and held it for a year, you would have earned a 58 percent return as compared with a 17 percent return for the DJIA and a 16 percent return for the Standard & Poor's (S&P) 500 Index. The theory of efficient markets implies that investors cannot consistently buy stocks such as Oracle, for example, to earn abnormally high returns over long periods.

The question that is asked most often about the efficient market hypothesis is, "What is the degree of efficiency in the markets?" Obviously, investors who believe that the markets are inefficient will continue using different techniques and analyses to select stocks that produce superior returns. However, if markets are efficient, the value of these techniques and analyses is diminished. The implication from both fundamental analysis and technical analysis theories is that the markets are inefficient. By investing in stocks with low price/earnings (P/E) ratios or high earnings yields or by purchasing stocks at the low end of their trading ranges, investors expect to receive higher returns. This situation may occur; but according to the efficient market hypothesis, investors cannot consistently outperform the markets by earning abnormally large returns on a risk-adjusted basis.

Considerable debate takes place in academic circles about the degree of efficiency in the markets, centered on three forms of the efficient market hypothesis:

- Weak form
- Semistrong form
- Strong form

The degree of market efficiency has important ramifications for investors and the strategies chosen for the selection of their stocks.

Weak Form

The *weak form of the efficient market hypothesis* contends that successive changes in stock price movements are independent of one another. Consequently, no relationship exists between past and future stock price movements. The weak form of the efficient market hypothesis holds that historical information about stock prices has no bearing on future stock prices. In other words, the stock prices of today and tomorrow are unrelated to past stock prices. Thus a comparison of two stocks, as illustrated in Figure 12–1, would be meaningless in predicting future price behavior. Both stocks have a current price of $20 per share, but the stock of Company X rose from a low of $2 per share to $20, whereas the stock of Company Y fell from a high of $40 to $20. The weak form of the efficient market hypothesis maintains that past stock prices are independent of future stock prices. In other words, no relationship exists between past and future stock prices. This hypothesis would make futile the use of past prices, as shown in Figure 12–1, to determine which stock to buy. Technical analysts would argue that you would not want to buy a stock that has declined from $40 to $20 per share because of its downward trend. Technical analysts would advocate buying Company X over Company Y because of its upward trend going from $2 to $20 per share. In other words, the weak form suggests that the use of charts and past prices in technical analysis in the selection of stocks is inconsequential and does not produce superior returns.

According to the weak form of market efficiency, stock prices reflect all historical market data. The stock price already includes the price history of the stock, the trading volume, and all other information that forms the basis for technical analysis.

FIGURE 12-1

Evaluation of Past Stock Price Information in the Weak Form
of the Efficient Market Hypothesis

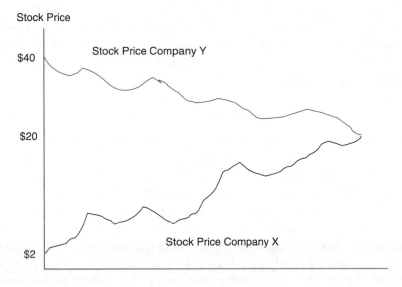

Studies testing the weak form of the efficient market hypothesis
show that stock prices appear to move independently or in a random
fashion because of the dissemination of information (Fama, 1965,
pp. 34–105). This statement refutes the view of technical analysts,
who assert that stocks move up or down in runs (trends). By spotting
the trend early, you can profit by sticking with the stock during its
uptrend or selling at the top of a downtrend.

For a number of years, the *Wall Street Journal* published results
that compared stocks picked by dart throwers with those chosen by
financial analysts. The stock picks of the analysts more often outperformed those of the dart throwers. Does this experiment mean
that the weak form of the efficient market hypothesis has no validity?
No, argue academicians. According to Burton Malkiel and Gilbert
Metcalf, analysts picked stocks that were riskier than the market (40
percent more volatile) as opposed to the dart picks, which were only
6 percent more volatile. The second reason that the results are slated
toward the analysts is the favorable publicity from the competition,
which ran up the prices of the stocks picked by analysts (Dorfman,
1993, p. C1). If the advantages of the analysts had been taken away,
then the competition would have been on an even footing.

Technical analysts and many others on Wall Street dispute the findings of the studies that support the weak form of the efficient market hypothesis. After all, if the weak form is not valid, technical analysts would be able to consistently earn superior returns by charting and analyzing past stock price information to predict future stock prices. The weak form, however, does not directly refute the use of fundamental analysis in selecting stocks that may produce superior returns.

Semistrong Form

The *semistrong form of the efficient market hypothesis* states that stock prices adjust quickly to publicly available information that is relevant to the valuation of the stocks. Public information includes all published reports (financial statements); analysts' reports; analysts' and brokerage firms' recommendations; press, radio, and television reports; and historical information. When a company announces new information, it is reflected quickly into its stock price. Therefore, analysis of this information may not produce superior returns because stock prices will have already incorporated the information. For example, when a company announces that it will exceed the estimates of analysts for a quarter, its stock price generally does not rise after the news announcement. The reason is that the stock price probably rose in anticipation of the news of the earnings expectations. Thus, when you read that Intel, for example, has released a new, faster chip, it is too late to earn superior returns from buying Intel stock. This information is already reflected in the price of the stock.

The semistrong theory asserts that investors can achieve superior returns through an analysis of this information, but over time this technique does not consistently produce superior returns when transaction costs are taken into account. This conclusion may be quite rational when you consider that analysts and investors are exposed to the same public information. In their competition with each other over changes in information, analysts and investors make the pricing of stocks much more efficient. If a perceived change occurs in a stock's value, investors buy it, thereby moving the price up to its equilibrium value.

Many studies support the validity of the semistrong form of the efficient market hypothesis, which asserts that stock prices change quite rapidly to reflect new public information and in many cases anticipate the announcements of information to the public. One study questioned whether investors could earn higher profits from buying stocks that were about to split (Fama et al., 1969, pp. 1–21). The authors found that even though stocks went up in the weeks before the split, when the split was announced, the stocks did not increase any more. To profit from a split, investors would have to buy the stock months before the stock split was announced. This theory implies that investors can earn superior returns by anticipating any new information before it becomes public and is reflected in the stock price. This strategy may be a clairvoyant's dream!

If any institution could outperform the market averages, it would seem to be the brokerage firms, which usually have many analysts on their payrolls. Dorfman (1993, p. C1) reported that only 6 of the 16 major brokerage firms outperformed the 38 percent earned by the S&P 500 Index in 1995.

However, research done on the semistrong form shows that some anomalies occur, which suggests that some inefficiency in the market can produce superior returns. These anomalies are discussed in the next section.

Strong Form

The *strong form of the efficient market hypothesis* holds that stock prices reflect all public and private information. Consequently, this information cannot be used to beat the market. Private information includes information known only to the insiders in management, boards of directors, and others who may be privy to this information such as investment bankers. This hypothesis assumes that the market is highly efficient and that stock prices react very quickly to insider information. If this is so, even corporate insiders will not have information that will benefit them because stock prices will have already reacted to the information. According to this form, no investors or groups of investors who are privy to monopolistic information (insider information) will benefit by earning superior returns because the markets are virtually perfect.

Research does not support the strong form of the efficient market hypothesis. This form of the efficient market hypothesis has been studied and tested with regard to returns earned by specialists and by insiders using insider information. A specialist on the stock exchange has a book of orders that are waiting to be executed at different prices. Specialists buy and sell stocks from their own inventories in order to provide a liquid market for stocks. The specialist thus has some valuable information about the direction of stock prices. For example, if a specialist has many unfilled limit orders to buy a stock at $9 per share and the stock is trading at $12, the specialist knows the price will not fall below $9 per share. A study sponsored by the Securities and Exchange Commission (SEC) reported that specialists earned, on average, a return of over 100 percent on their capital (SEC, 1971). Table 12–1 discusses how specialists and insiders affect the stock market.

TABLE 12-1

Specialists and Insiders and How They Affect the Stock Market

Specialists on the NYSE act on behalf of investors to bring buyers and sellers together. In other words, specialists are the "middlemen" on the floor of the exchange carrying out trading orders. These people are required to keep an orderly market, which means that if more selling than buying takes place, specialists will need to buy and sell from their own inventories of stock to provide liquidity in the stock. Thus the line between trading for self-interest and keeping an orderly market in the stock can be blurred easily. Specialists are not supposed to trade ahead of their clients' orders so that they can profit from the trades. This practice, known as *front-running*, occurs when specialists know that they can profit from buying shares ahead of clients. An NYSE investigation of the trading of some specialists has raised investors' concerns about the pricing of shares and left them clamoring for increased transparency of pricing. Proceeding in this direction does not please institutional clients, who do not want their orders disclosed. It is this knowledge of unfilled limit orders that give specialists the monopolistic information that allows them to earn excessive returns on their invested capital. One way to take this type of self-interest out of the equation is to do away with the specialist system by changing to automated trading, in addition to making prices more transparent.

Corporate insiders are the other group that earns excessive returns by using nonpublic information. Three arguments take place in defense of insider trading (Manne, 2003, p. A14). The first is that insider trading does not have an adverse impact on individual trading in the market. The second is that insider trading moves share prices to their "correct" prices, resulting in efficient markets. The third is that insider trading acts as a successful form of incentive compensation for hiring innovative and successful management.

Critics of insider trading have not been silent. They argue that if investors think that insider trading results in an "unfair" market, they will not invest, resulting in a market that is not liquid. The second argument is that if specialists and market makers are faced with insider trading, they will increase their bid and ask pricing spreads, resulting in higher prices for individual investors in the market.

There has been no overwhelming support to eliminate insider trading. Although the SEC requires periodic disclosure by insiders, the most powerful argument for insider trading is still the efficient pricing mechanism, which has prevailed. Corporate insiders trade their stocks until the "correct" price is reached.

Source: "Specialist Help Needed," *The Economist,* April 26, 2003, pp. 64–65.

Corporate insiders are privy to special information that brings about superior returns. Studies show that insiders achieve greater returns than those expected of a perfect market (Lorie and Niederhoffer, 1966, pp. 35–53). Insiders are defined as officers and directors of a company and those shareholders who own at least 10 percent of a company's stock.

Insiders are privy to information that has not been made available to the public. Hence there is a fine line that distinguishes between legal and illegal use of this information. Corporate insiders have access to privileged information but are not allowed to use that information to earn short-term profits or to engage in short-term trading (six months or less). They are allowed to trade and make profits on the stock on a long-term basis, and their trades must be reported to the SEC.

Despite the fact that specialists and insiders are able to earn superior returns, which rejects the strong form of the efficient market hypothesis, some support exists for the strong form based on the performance of mutual fund managers. Mutual fund managers receive information faster than the investing public, yet they have not been able to consistently outperform the market averages.

The different outcomes can be summarized this way: The use of privileged (monopolistic) information may help generate superior returns, and the use of publicly available information may not be able to assist in consistently earning superior returns.

Implications of the Efficient Market Hypothesis for Investors

The question for investors is, "How efficient is the market?" If the market is truly efficient, no information will be of any use to you, not even monopolistic information. In this case, the only way you can beat the markets is to become clairvoyant! However, the studies cited herein show that the market is not absolutely efficient because investors have in some cases beaten the market averages.

If investment strategies can beat the market averages consistently over long periods, the markets are inefficient. The next question is, "What is the degree of the market's inefficiency?" If you start with the extremes of the theory as shown in Figure 12–2, you can then move back to the center of the argument with the more debatable aspects of the degrees of inefficiency.

FIGURE 1 2 - 2

Degrees of Efficiency of Information in the Stock Market

Inefficient Market	Weakly Efficient	Semistrongly Efficient	Strongly Efficient	Totally Efficient
All Information Is Useful	Historical Information Is Not Useful	Historical and Public Information is Not Useful	Historical, Public, and Private Information is Not Useful	No Information is Useful

If the market is totally inefficient, all information is useful. You know that the market is not totally inefficient because none of the analysts and investors who analyze information has been able to consistently earn returns in excess of the market averages. Thus the question remains about how efficient the market is in processing information between the extremes of all and none, namely, historical, public, and private information.

If you are averse to number crunching, you can heave a sigh of relief from saving all those hours spent analyzing financial statements to determine numbers on sales, earnings, and growth figures of a company. Similarly, you do not have to waste the gas in your car to go out to buy graph paper in order to plot stock charts. According to the weak and semistrong forms of the efficient market hypothesis, the use of technical and fundamental analysis does not consistently produce superior returns. This statement may be disconcerting to you, but what about the technical and fundamental analysts whose occupations have been deemed to be worthless? It is no wonder that Wall Street has not embraced the efficient market hypothesis.

The two seemingly sure ways to earn returns in excess of the market returns are to obtain insider information and to become a specialist. This statement is not by any means a suggestion to prompt you to gain access to corporate privileged information, and neither should you change your existing professional occupational plans to become a New York Stock Exchange (NYSE) stock specialist.

The efficient market hypothesis suggests that all information (public and private) is incorporated into the price of the stock and that the prices of stocks with good fundamentals will be bid up to reflect this situation. Similarly, stocks that are in trouble will be sold to bring their stock prices in line with their intrinsic value. In other words, no undervalued or overvalued stocks exist.

If an even chance exists of stock prices rising or falling because of new information, it doesn't matter which stocks you choose or which stocks anyone else chooses for that matter. The random walk theory implies pure luck in picking stocks.

The efficient market hypothesis is hotly debated, and the jury of academicians is still undecided about the degree of efficiency of the market. Even though the efficient market hypothesis has not aroused the enthusiasm of most investors, the implications are important because they shatter any illusions of creating overnight wealth in the stock market. The efficient market hypothesis suggests that few investors will beat the market averages consistently over a long period. If the market increases by 10 percent over a one-year period, most investors will not earn more than an average of 10 percent. In fact, most investors earn less than the market average because of transaction costs and fees charged. However, this does not mean that some investors will not do much worse than 10 percent or will not earn abnormally high returns.

The following are some anomalies to the efficient market hypothesis whereby investors have been able to generate superior returns to beat the market:

- *Small-cap stocks.* A study by Avner Arbel and Paul Strebel (1982) suggests that undervalued stocks of small companies that have been neglected by the investment community may provide greater returns than the market averages. Analysts do not cover many of the small firms owing to their larger perceived risk. This lack of attention to these neglected small companies means that investors can find stocks that are trading below their intrinsic value. When such stocks are discovered by analysts, their prices are bid up and tend to outperform the larger company stocks. The result from this study suggests that the securities markets may not be equally efficient.
- *Low P/E ratio stocks.* Studies done by S. Basu (1975, 1977) show that portfolios of stocks with low P/E ratios outperformed portfolios of stocks with high P/E ratios on a risk-adjusted and non-risk-adjusted basis. This outcome refutes the semistrong form of the efficient market hypothesis because P/E ratios of stocks can be obtained from publicly available information.

  Benjamin Graham, who did the pioneering work that forms the basis of fundamental analysis, realized that markets were becoming more efficient, thus making it more difficult to find undervalued stocks. One of his guidelines was to select low P/E ratio stocks. Table 12–2 lists Graham's guidelines for selecting stocks. The greater the number of yes answers, the more ideal is the stock choice, according to Graham's model.

- *Other possible market anomalies that suggest inefficiencies in the market that result in superior returns.* One of these is the *January effect,* which finds that stocks that have done poorly in December may produce superior returns in January owing to tax selling.

These anomalies should not lead investors to think that the markets are inefficient. Rather, the anomalies should be viewed as exceptions. Academic studies lend support for the weak and semistrong forms of the efficient market hypothesis, which lends support to the conclusion that very few investors outperform the markets over extended periods. For investors who feel that the efficient market hypothesis is not equally efficient with regard to the pricing of the smaller, lesser-known stocks, fundamental analysis has a role.

TABLE 12-2

Benjamin Graham's Guidelines of Stocks to Buy

Stocks that conform to the following criteria would be bought.

Rewards

1. Is the stock's P/E ratio less than half the reciprocal of the AAA corporate bond yield? For example, if the current AAA yield was 5.7* percent, it would make the reciprocal 17.054 percent (1/0.057), The P/E ratio of the stock would have to be less than 8.77 percent (1/2 × the reciprocal, or 1/2 × 0.1705) to be bought.
2. Is the stock's P/E ratio less than 40 percent of the average P/E ratio of the stock over the past five years?
3. Is the stock's dividend yield equal to or more than two-thirds the AAA corporate bond yield? If two-thirds of the current AAA corporate bond yield of 5.7 percent was 3.8 percent, for the stock to be rated a buy, its dividend yield should equal to or be greater than 3.8 percent.
4. Is the stock price less than two-thirds of the stock's book value?
5. Is the stock's price less than two-thirds of its net current asset value per share?

---

*As of October 2006.

(continued)

Risks

1. Is the stock's debt-to-equity ratio less than 1? The total debt of the company should be less than its total equity.
2. Is the stock's current ratio equal to 2 or more? The total current assets divided by the total current liabilities should equal 2 or more.
3. Is the total debt less than twice its net current assets?
4. Is the company's 10-year average earnings per share (EPS) growth rate greater than 7 percent?
5. Did the company experience earnings declines of greater than 5 percent in no more than 2 years out of the past 10 years?

Source: Paul Sturm, "What If Benjamin Graham Had a P.C.?" *Smart Money,* March 1994, p. 32.

CAPITAL ASSET PRICING MODEL (CAPM)

The 1990 Nobel Prize laureates for economics, Harry Markowitz and William Sharpe, developed theories about the financial markets that have had a profound effect on investors. Harry Markowitz's work pioneered what is now known as the *modern portfolio theory.* Concerned with the composition of investments that investors would select for their portfolios, Markowitz determined that the major properties of an investment that should be of concern to investors are risk and return. By choosing a range of different investments for a portfolio, investors can determine and control the total risk in that portfolio through variance analysis of each investment. In other words, in plain English, investors can assemble portfolios of risky stocks in which the risk of the whole portfolio would be less than any of the individual stocks in the portfolio. By determining the given amount of risk, investors select the portfolio that offers the highest expected return.

A simple example illustrates this concept. Suppose that you have a portfolio with equal amounts invested in two stocks: a computer-related technology stock and a food stock. In good economic times, when computer sales are growing, the price of technology stocks is expected to increase by more than 50 percent, and food stocks have an expected return of 6 percent (including the dividends). During a recession, when computer sales are in the doldrums, the price of the technology stock is expected to decline by 20 percent. The food stock, however, because it is in a defensive industry, is expected to increase by 40 percent. Thus, in a good economy, the investors will earn an average return of 28 percent [(50% + 6%)/2]. In a recession, the portfolio will earn an average return of 10% [(40% − 20%)/2].

Although the technology stock is more risky than the food stock, by diversifying into the two different industries, the average returns are greater than if all the funds were invested in one stock. In addition to reducing your risk by increasing the number of stocks, you can reduce your risk by choosing stocks that react to economic conditions differently.

William Sharpe and John Lintner further developed Markowitz's approach into the capital asset pricing model (CAPM). The *capital asset pricing model* links the relationship between risk and the expected return of a stock. The stock's expected rate of return is the risk-free rate plus a risk premium based on the systematic risk of the stock. In this model, the risk of a stock or portfolio is broken down into two parts: systematic and unsystematic risk. The risk pertaining to the security itself (such as business and financial risks) can be reduced and eliminated through diversification. What remains is systematic risk, which becomes important in the relationship between risk and return. In other words, by combining several different stocks in a portfolio, the *unsystematic* or *diversifiable* risk is reduced, and all that is left is systematic risk. *Systematic risk*, also known as *market risk,* is the relationship of a security's price to changes in security prices in the general market. Some stocks go up and down more than the market, and other stocks fluctuate less than the market as a whole. Systematic risk is measured by the Greek letter *beta.* The *beta coefficient,* a measure of the systematic risk of a stock, links the sensitivity of the stock's rate of return to the rate of return of the market and is determined as follows:

$$\beta = \text{(standard deviation of the return of a stock/}$$
$$\text{standard deviation of the return of the market)}$$
$$\times \text{correlation coefficient between return of the}$$
$$\text{stock and the market}$$

The larger the standard deviation of the return of a stock relative to the return of the market, the greater is the risk associated with that stock. The *correlation coefficient* indicates the relative importance of variability. The range of the correlation coefficient is from $+1$ to -1. If the correlation coefficient is $+1$, the stock return and the market return move together in a strong correlation. Thus, if the standard deviation of the stock is 15 percent and the standard deviation of the market is 10 percent with a correlation coefficient of 1, the beta coefficient is 1.5

β = (standard deviation of the return of a stock/
     standard deviation of the return of the market)
     $\times$ correlation coefficient between return of the stock
     and the market
    = (0.15/0.10) $\times$ 1
    = 1.5

A correlation coefficient of -1 with a standard deviation of a stock equal to 8 percent and a standard deviation of 10 percent for the market results in a beta of -0.8:

$$\beta = (0.08/0.10) \times -1$$
$$= -0.8$$

A negative correlation coefficient results in the stock and the market moving in opposite directions. If no relationship exists between the return on the stock and the return on the market, then the correlation coefficient is zero, which results in a beta coefficient of 0, or no market risk.

For a stock with a beta coefficient of 1, if the market rises by 20 percent, the stock price will increase by 20 percent. If the market falls by 20 percent, the stock price also will see a 20 percent decline. The market is assumed to have a beta coefficient of 1, which means that this stock is perfectly correlated with the market.

Figure 12–3 illustrates the relationship between a stock with a beta coefficient of 1.5 and the market with a beta of 1. The stock has a return of 15 percent when the market increases by 10 percent. A stock with a return that is less than the market is drawn below the market line in the positive quadrant and it is drawn above the market line in the negative quadrant. Thus a stock with a beta coefficient greater than 1 should produce above-average returns in a bull market and below-average returns in a bear market. A stock with a beta coefficient of less than 1 is less responsive to market changes. Investors who seek higher returns are willing to assume more risk.

Increased diversification into many different stocks in a portfolio does not eliminate the systematic risk. In other words, these stocks are not immune to a downturn in the market. However, diversification into at least 20 different stocks can eliminate the *unsystematic risk*, which is the risk that pertains to the company. This includes financial, business, and purchasing-power risks, which affect a company's stock price.

FIGURE 12-3

Stock with a Beta Coefficient of 1.5

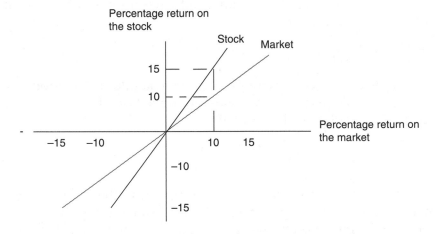

Calculating the beta coefficient is tedious. You can obtain beta coefficients for individual stocks from several sources, such as Value Line and Standard & Poor's, which are subscription services, and financial Web sites such as www.yahoo.com. You should not be alarmed if you find different beta coefficients for the same stock because beta coefficients can be derived using different market measures, such as the S&P 500 Index versus the Value Line Index. Similarly, discrepancies occur when the periods for the calculations differ, using, for example, three years versus five years of price data. Thus no correct beta coefficient exists. Table 12–3 compares different beta coefficients.

TABLE 12-3

Comparison of Beta Coefficients*

Company	Beta from moneycentral.com	Beta from Yahoo.com
Alcoa, Inc.	1.90	2.09
Johnson & Johnson	0.29	0.12
Boeing	0.74	0.93
ExxonMobil	0.65	1.03
Starbucks Corp.	0.52	1.14
Yahoo!	2.15	1.22

* As of October 18, 2006.

Application of the Beta Coefficient

The purpose of the beta coefficient is to explain the relationship between a stock's risk and return and that of the market. The formula illustrates that the required rate of return on a stock equals the risk-free rate of interest plus the stock's beta coefficient multiplied by the amount by which the market return exceeds the risk-free interest rate.

$$\text{Required rate of return} = \text{risk-free rate} + \beta(\text{market rate of return} - \text{risk-free rate})$$

Using this equation, an investor seeks a return from a stock that exceeds the risk-free rate of interest (the rate of return on a Treasury bill) and the risk premium of the stock (beta coefficient of the stock multiplied by the market rate of return minus the risk-free rate).

For example, if the risk-free rate is 3.5 percent and the market is expected to rise by 8 percent, the returns for two stocks with beta coefficients of 1.2 and 2, respectively are

Stock with a beta of 1.2:

$$\text{Required rate of return} = 3.5\% + 1.2(8\% - 3.5\%)$$
$$= 8.9\%$$

Stock with a beta of 2:

$$\text{Required rate of return} = 3.5\% + 2(8\% - 3.5\%)$$
$$= 12.5\%$$

Because the stock with a beta of 2 is riskier than the stock with a beta of 1.2, the required or expected rate of return is greater (12.5 versus 8.9 percent). The returns of both stocks are greater than those of the market (8 percent) because their betas are greater than 1, indicating greater risk (volatility) than that of the market.

Security Market Line

The *security market line* is a graphic illustration of the capital asset pricing model that depicts the risk/return relationship of a security. Figure 12–4 plots the security market line for the stock with a beta coefficient of 2 used in the example in the preceding section. With a beta coefficient of 0, the required rate of return is the risk-free rate

FIGURE 12-4

Security Market Line for Stock with a Beta Coefficient of 2

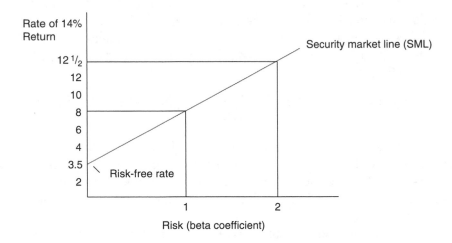

of 3.5 percent. With a beta coefficient of 1, the required rate of return is 8 percent (the same as the market rate of return), and a beta coefficient of 2 for this security results in a required rate of return of 12.5 percent. The security market line for this stock shows that as the beta (risk) increases, so does the required rate of return.

The key to this model is that in a rising market, people investing in stocks with higher beta coefficients than those of the market should increase their potential returns; in a down market, to minimize their potential losses, investors should invest in stocks with beta coefficient, that are lower than those of the market.

Use of the beta coefficient provides insight into the relationship between the nondiversifiable risk of stocks and their returns. However, beta coefficients are derived from past price movements, which often have no bearing on future price movements. Despite its enthusiastic adoption by Wall Street when the CAPM was introduced in 1964, the model has been under attack by academicians. Studies done to test the validity of the CAPM were not supportive. A study done by two professors, Eugene Fama and Kenneth French (1992), which also turned upside down the axiom "The greater the risk, the greater the return," taught in finance classes, showed that the beta coefficient did not explain the differences in returns on stocks. In their study, these authors grouped stocks into portfolios based on market capitalization (size), and there was a relationship between the size of the companies and their beta coefficients, even though there was a wide range of the latter. However, when stocks were grouped on the basis of size and beta coefficients, a good relationship to returns was not found.

According to Malkiel (1990, pp. 243–255), studies done to test the validity of the CAPM showed the following:

- There was some unsystematic risk that caused zero-beta securities to have higher returns. In other words, the security market line (SML) was too flat compared with the prediction from the CAPM.

- The risk/return relationship turned out to be different from that of the CAPM. Low-risk stocks earned returns higher than expected, and high-risk stocks earned returns lower than expected.

- For shorter-term periods, there were deviations from the relationships predicted by the CAPM.

- There was a problem estimating beta coefficients based on past sensitivity to the market. These relationships change, and there are other factors that need to be considered in determining the beta coefficient.

There is no perfect measure of risk, but the CAPM provides a framework to assess the relationship between the risk and return of a security.

OTHER THEORIES OF RETURN

A study done by Eugene Fama and Kenneth French (1992) showed that low-risk stocks, namely, value stocks, as measured with high book values relative to their market values, which were expected to perform poorly because of their low expectations, outperformed high-risk stocks over the 27-year period 1963–1990. High-risk or growth stocks with low book values relative to their market values underperformed low-risk stocks over the same 27-year period. The authors classified the stocks into 10 deciles based on their book-to-market ratios. Stocks with the highest book-to-market ratios averaged monthly returns of 1.65 percent, and stocks with the lowest book-to-market ratios averaged monthly returns of only 0.72 percent. This situation is similar to the competition between value and growth stocks. Wall Street analysts expect growth stocks to outperform value stocks, but this study negates that finding.

Looking at the performance of stocks over the three-year period 1996–1998, large-cap growth stocks in the S&P 500 Index outperformed value stocks. Growth stocks had strong records of performance, and stock investors bid them up to high price levels. For example, the stocks of two companies, Dell Computer and Cisco Systems, traded at lofty multiples of earnings, reflecting investor's high future price expectations. Value stocks have low expectations with regard to return on sales, return on equity, asset growth, equity growth, and book-to-market value. Clayman (1987, p. 58) identified growth stocks and value stocks in 1980 and tracked their performance in the years 1981–1985. She found that the rate of growth and book value fell in half for growth stocks, whereas value stocks showed substantial improvement. If investors had invested $100 in each of the value and growth portfolios, they would have earned $297.50 in the value portfolio versus $181.60 in the growth portfolio for the period 1981–1985.

The Fama and French study provides investors with an alternative to chasing overvalued growth stocks with their lofty multiples, although the jury is still out on the validity of their theory.

COMPARISON OF RISK-ASJUSTED RETURNS

To be able to compare returns on your portfolio with a benchmark index, you need to equalize the differences in risk and return. For example, a 5 percent return on a portfolio of Treasury securities is not the same as a 5 percent return on a portfolio of small-cap growth stocks because of the greater risk in the latter portfolio. Investors would prefer the 5 percent return from the low-risk Treasury security portfolio.

Three different measures adjust returns for the risk associated with a portfolio:

- Sharpe index
- Treynor index
- Jensen index

These measures allow you to compare different returns on a risk-adjusted basis.

The Sharpe Index

The *Sharpe index* is a risk-adjusted measure of performance that standardizes the risk premium of a portfolio using the standard deviation of the portfolio return.

Sharpe index = (portfolio return − risk-free rate)/
standard deviation of portfolio returns

The risk-adjusted return of a portfolio is the risk premium for a portfolio (portfolio return − risk-free return) divided by the standard deviation of the portfolio's returns. For example, suppose that a portfolio has an annual return of 7 percent and an annual standard deviation of 20 percent. The average Treasury bill rate during the year was 3.5 percent. What is the Sharpe index?

$$\text{Sharpe index} = (r_p - r_f)/\sigma_p$$
$$= (0.07 - 0.035)/0.2$$
$$= 0.175$$

The result is put in perspective when it is compared with another portfolio or the market. Assume that during the same year the market return is 6 percent, with a standard deviation of 18 percent and a risk-free rate of 3.5 percent. The Sharpe index for the market is 0.1389:

$$\text{Sharpe index} = (0.06 - 0.035)/\, 0.18$$
$$= 0.1389$$

The performance of the portfolio is superior to the return of the market because of the higher result (0.175 compared with 0.1389). The higher return of the portfolio more than balances the higher standard deviation or risk (20 percent for the portfolio versus 18 percent for the market).

Treynor Index

The *Treynor index* is a risk-adjusted measure of performance that standardizes the risk premium of a portfolio with the portfolio's systematic risk or beta coefficient. The Treynor index is similar to the Sharpe index except that Treynor uses the beta coefficient rather than the standard deviation of the portfolio to measure risk. The Treynor index uses only nondiversifiable risk, whereas the

Sharpe index includes the total risk of the portfolio. Treynor's index is determined as follows:

Treynor index = (portfolio return − risk-free rate)/ portfolio beta coefficient

The Treynor index is useful when it is compared with the market, or with other portfolios to determine superior performance. For example, if a portfolio has a total return of 9 percent and the risk-free rate is 3.5 percent with a portfolio beta of 1.1, the Treynor index is 0.05:

$$\text{Treynor index } p = (r_p - r_f)/\beta_p$$
$$= (0.09 - 0.035)/1.1$$
$$= 0.05$$

Comparing this portfolio with the market during the same period, in which the market return is 8.7 percent and has a beta coefficient of 1, the Treynor index for the market is

$$\text{Treynor index } m = (r_p - r_f)/\beta_p$$
$$= (0.087 - 0.035)/1$$
$$= 0.052$$

Thus the portfolio return is inferior to that of the market (0.05 versus 0.052). The portfolio return per unit of diversifiable risk is less than that of the market.

Jensen Index

The *Jensen index* is a risk-adjusted measure of performance that compares realized returns with returns that should have been earned per unit of nondiversifiable risk. Michael Jensen's performance index is based on the capital asset pricing model and differs from the Sharpe and Treynor measures. The Jensen index compares excess return with returns that should have been earned in the market based on the nondiversifiable risk of the portfolio. The result can be positive, negative, or zero. A positive result indicates that performance of the portfolio was superior to that of the market. A negative result indicates that the portfolio underperformed the market, and a zero indicates identical performance to that of the market. The Jensen index is determined as follows:

Jensen index = (total portfolio return − risk-free rate)
                 − [portfolio β × (market return − risk-free rate)]

For example, a portfolio with a return of 12 percent and a 1.3 beta coefficient when the market return is 9 percent and the risk-free rate is 4 percent results in a Jensen index of

$$\text{Jensen index} = (R_p - r_f) - [\beta_p \times (r_m - r_f)]$$
$$= (0.12 - 0.04) - [1.3(0.09 - 0.04)]$$
$$= 0.015$$

This portfolio outperformed the market on a risk-adjusted basis. Unlike the Sharpe and Treynor indexes, the Jensen index adjusts for the market return, which allows you to compare the portfolio return with that of the market in one computation. Because the Sharpe index uses the standard deviation as a measure of total risk, it reveals a poorly diversified portfolio, which will have a large standard deviation. A poorly diversified portfolio may not be uncovered by the beta coefficient, which is used in the Treynor and Jensen indexes.

A problem that occurs in comparing the performance of a portfolio to that of the market is determining which market index is the most appropriate to use. If a portfolio has small-cap, large-cap, and foreign stocks, then the use of the S&P 500 Index is problematic because it does not have the same composition as the portfolio for comparison purposes. This problem is compounded by the fact that beta coefficients based on different market indexes differ and may produce biased beta coefficients that distort the performance evaluations. A solution to the benchmark index is to determine a weighted-average return of the portfolio and compare it with the weighted-average returns of the corresponding bench- mark indexes, as illustrated in Table 12–4.

Using the weighted-average returns of the corresponding benchmark indexes for comparison with the portfolio returns makes the result more meaningful. The portfolio underperformed the corresponding weighted average of the benchmark indexes by 0.22 percent (3.92% − 3.7%) on a non-risk-adjusted basis.

The efficient market hypothesis assumes that even if your portfolio obtains returns that are superior on a risk-adjusted basis to those of the market, you cannot expect to consistently repeat the superior returns.

TABLE 1 2 - 4

Weighted-Average Returns

	(1)	(2)	(1) × (2)
Portfolio Assets	**Portfolio Weight**	**Portfolio Returns**	**Weighted-Average Returns**
Small-cap stocks	30%	9%	2.7%
Large-cap stocks	40%	4%	1.6%
Foreign stocks	30%	−2%	−0.6%
Weighted-average return			3.7%
Benchmark Indexes	**Portfolio Weight**	**Benchmark Returns**	**Weighted-Average Returns**
Russell 2000 (small-caps)	30%	10%	3.0%
S&P 500 (large-caps)	40%	3.5%	1.4%
EAFE Index* (foreign)	30%	−1.6%	−0.48%
Weighted-average return			3.92%

* Morgan Stanley Index of European, Australasian, and Far East stocks.

As can be expected, security analysts have not really embraced these academic theories, especially the efficient market hypothesis. Their view is that academicians are so immersed in their own research that they would not be able to recognize an undervalued stock even if it was brought to their attention. The ongoing battle between the analysts and the academicians is of little importance. What is important for investors is an awareness of these theories from several practical points of view.

The degree of efficiency of the market determines your investment strategy with regard to the selection of stocks and the length of time to hold those stocks. If you believe that the market is efficient and that all information is reflected in the price of the stock, your strategy might be to select quality stocks with good future earnings and hold them for long periods (the buy-and-hold strategy). On the other hand, if you believe that the markets are inefficient, you can use technical analysis to determine which stocks to buy and sell over shorter periods and fundamental analysis to select undervalued stocks to buy and hold for longer periods. The degree of efficiency is debatable.

The CAPM suggests that investors diversify their investments to eliminate unsystematic risk. The returns earned by most investments will be consistent with the returns of the market and the related amount of risk. Bearing this in mind, the investment strategy you choose should be consistent with your objectives.

No known method consistently beats the markets over long periods. Anomalies in the efficient market theory exist, but because of the competitive nature of the markets, they have not consistently earned abnormal returns for long periods. Yet, at the other extreme, overwhelming support of the efficient market hypothesis paralyzes investors into thinking that no research is valuable.

ACTIVE VERSUS PASSIVE INVESTMENT STRATEGIES

The debate over the degree of efficiency of the markets has resulted in the following investment strategies:

- *Passive* investment strategies suggested by efficient markets
- *Active* investment strategies suggested by inefficient markets

As an investor, you must decide on the degree of efficiency of the markets to determine whether you should pursue a passive or active investment strategy.

Passive Investment Strategy

A *passive investment strategy* involves the selection of diversified securities in a portfolio that will not change over a long period and is held over a long period. The securities in the portfolio are changed only when a market variable, such as an index, changes because passive investors believe that the markets are efficient and that they cannot beat the markets over extended periods. By investing in a mix of diversified securities, this type of investor hopes to do as well as the market averages over long periods. Passive investment strategies are achieved through buy-and-hold investing and/or indexing.

Buy and Hold Strategy
A buy-and-hold investment strategy is a passive strategy based on the premise of doing as well as the market by minimizing transaction

costs. No attempt is made to beat the market. By holding a broadly diversified portfolio, which reduces the unsystematic risks (the risks pertaining to the companies or the industries), investors should be able to approximate the returns of the market. Stocks in the portfolio are selected and held for the long term. Investors make few revisions and make no attempt to time the markets. The success of this type of strategy depends on the state of the market.

During an upward trend in the market, such as during the decade of the 1990s, a buy-and-hold strategy would have benefited most investors. Of course, in a market correction or crash, prices of most stocks decline. Historically, however, after most stock market declines, the markets typically have recovered and moved on to greater heights.

In many conversations about the stock market, investors recount how they were able to time the markets, selling their portfolios days before the stock market crash and then moving back into the market at a lower level. However, few investors like to tell the story of how they exited the market in anticipation of the crash that never materialized. This approach meant sitting on the sidelines during a bull market and reentering the market at a higher level.

The buy-and-hold strategy avoids the need to time the markets or read the financial stock tables in the newspapers daily. With a long time horizon, you have no need to time the markets because you remain fully invested in stocks.

The second advantage of a buy-and-hold strategy is that investors minimize their transaction costs. Similarly, they also avoid the cost of acquiring information. This strategy does not mean that they forget about the stocks they buy. In a buy-and-hold strategy, investors still should review the performance of their stocks with regard to growth in sales and earnings from time to time (year to year) and get rid of stocks that do not present future potential growth and earnings.

Indexing

The concept of indexing embodies the buy-and-hold strategy, thereby minimizing the transaction costs inherent in a passive investment strategy. By choosing a market index such as the S&P 500 or the DJIA and picking the same stocks as in that index for the portfolio, an investor replicates the performance of the market index. Individual investors may have difficulty replicating these indexes because of the large numbers of stocks in the indexes (500 for the S&P 500) and hence the enormous dollar cost. Index mutual funds and exchange-traded funds (ETFs), discussed in Chapters 14 and 15, make it easier to invest in all the stocks of the specific indexes. In fact, index mutual funds have outperformed the many actively managed mutual funds over the four-year period 1995–1999. Longer periods show a more compelling result:

	Amount Invested 1982	Amount January 1999
Vanguard S&P Index Fund	$10,000	$193,550
Actively managed equity fund	$10,000	$114,300

Source: Anne Tergesen and Peter Coy, "Who Needs a Money Manager?" BusinessWeek, February 22, 1999, p. 127.

Although the buy-and-hold strategy minimizes timing decisions of when to buy and sell, investors still need to decide which stocks to select. By approximating an index, the types of stocks to choose become an easy matter. Deciding which index to follow would depend on the investor's overall objectives. A conservative investor who is looking for income and capital preservation would consider blue-chip stocks, utility stocks, and some of the more established growth stocks. A more aggressive investor would include growth stocks and the small-cap company stocks.

Investors who believe the market to be efficient would choose stocks from various industries to form a diversified portfolio and hope to replicate the performance of the market. According to the efficient market hypothesis, investors could randomly select these stocks because if the markets are efficient, these stocks are correctly valued (at their intrinsic value). Efficient markets support passive investment strategies; inefficient markets suggest actively managed investment strategies.

Active Investment Strategy

An *active investment strategy* involves active trading of securities in a portfolio in an attempt to produce superior risk-adjusted returns to that of the market. Timing the market accurately always will produce superior returns. *Market timing* is buying and selling securities over short periods of time based on prices (patterns) and value. This strategy involves buying stocks before their prices increase. In other words, you would be fully invested in stocks in an increasing market and out of stocks in a decreasing market. Many newsletters advocate timing the markets. In timing the markets, you have to be accurate in calling not only the top of the market but also the bottom, and when to get back into the market.

The greatest disadvantage to timing is that little margin for error exists in the accuracy of the timing of your calls on the market. If you are correct 50 percent of the time, you earn less than if you had a buy-and-hold strategy, according to a study done by T. Rowe Price and Associates in 1987, as reported in Cheyney and Moses (19). During the period from 1926 to 1983, investors who were 100 percent accurate in their timing decisions would have earned an average of 18.2 percent per year versus an 11.8 percent average yearly return for a buy-and-hold strategy. With a 50 percent accuracy rate in calling the market, the return was 8.1 percent. Thus, to earn returns in excess of the market, investors would have had to be more accurate than 70 percent of the time in calling the market during this period (T. Rowe Price Associates, Inc., 1987, in Cheyney and Moses, 1992). Table 12–5 highlights the lessons learned from market timing.

TABLE 12-5

Lessons Learned from Market Timing

The falling stock market for the three-year period 2000–2002 showed disastrous results for buy-and-hold investors. This situation prompted many brokerage firms and institutional investors to advocate second-guessing the market through market timing. These actions involved selling stocks for bonds and then, over short periods, moving back into stocks from bonds. The condition for success for this type of market-timing strategy is a volatile stock market that moves on a flat, sideways trend. In a momentum-driven market where stocks are constantly going up (1998–1999), a market timer would have underperformed a buy-and-hold investor (Mattich, 2003). For example, the S&P 500 Index was up by 26.7 percent in 1998 and 19.5 percent in 1999, whereas one of the top market timers in 2000, Howard Winell, lost 34 percent in 1998 and an additional 18 percent in 1999. In 2000, which was the beginning of the bear market, investors following Winell's advice in his newsletter, *Winell Report,* would have earned a 46 percent return versus a loss of 10.1 percent for the S&P 500 Index (Cropper, 2001).

Yet the results for market timers were not compelling for the year 2000. According to Jim Schmidt of the *Timer Digest,* which follows the investment actions of 100 market-timer newsletters, only 65 percent beat the S&P average that year. This number was less than the performance of mutual funds that beat the market that year (Cropper, 2001).

(continued)

Market timing is a high-risk strategy that is also expensive to maintain. According to Mattich, William Sharpe, originator of the Sharpe index and the CAPM, found that to break even in a portfolio that switched between stocks and bonds, you had to be 70 percent accurate in your market-timing decisions to break even. Also, increased transaction costs and higher taxes are involved with short-term capital gains, which further erode any positive returns.

What are the lessons that can be learned with regard to market timing?

- Historically, stocks have risen over long periods, which means that every time you exit the markets, you go against this long-term upward trend, indicating that a buy-and-hold investment strategy will do better than market timing over long periods.
- When you exit the stock market, you have to time the market correctly to get back in at lower stock prices. If you do not time the market well, you go back in at higher prices. Consequently, you should not exit the stock markets completely. Keep some of your money in stocks, even if you lighten up on your stock portfolio holdings.
- Diversify your stock portfolio holdings. Concentrating on one sector of the market (technology, for example) has been a disaster. Recall the burst of the technology bubble in 2000 and the astronomic rise and then precipitous fall of initial public offerings (IPOs) during the period 1998–2000.

To paraphrase Professor Elroy Dimson of the London School of Economics, "Market timing is a real mug's game" (Mattich, 2003).

Technical analysis charts the past price movements of stocks to time when to buy and sell stocks and advocates timing the overall market and individual stocks. Fundamental analysis also advocates timing but with a longer time horizon and a more critical eye as to which stocks to buy and sell. Inefficient or weakly efficient markets suggest that investors may be able to earn returns in excess of the markets by pursuing active investment strategies. The downside to timing the markets is that you may be on the sidelines during an increasing market if you make a wrong call.

THE IMPLICATIONS OF THE THEORIES OF THE STOCK MARKETS ON INVESTORS

Many investors use formula plans such as dollar-cost averaging to avoid having to time the markets. These plans eliminate the need for timing the markets, although investors still need to choose the stocks to buy and sell using these plans. By buying shares of stocks over a specified period at different prices, investors lessen the effect of price fluctuations. Bear in mind that if the markets plummet, these methods do not result in investors not losing money. These methods keep investors in the markets whether the market is going up or down.

You can find formula plans and investment strategies for buying and selling stocks, but no "magic" plan for beating the market exists. Some investment strategies have produced returns superior to those earned by the stock market as a whole over various periods. However, over long periods, consistently beating the market becomes exceedingly difficult.

Investors still need to decide which stocks to invest in and when to buy and sell. Fundamental analysis provides insight into the makeup of a company and its industry, which may be helpful in the selection of stocks for the long term. Technical analysis uses past price and volume information as well as charting to determine when to buy and sell stocks. The efficient market hypothesis renders technical analysis a waste of time because, according to the hypothesis, past stock prices reflect all available information. Therefore, the movements of past stock prices have no relationships to future prices. The relationship between past and future stock prices reflects the weak form of the efficient market hypothesis. The semistrong form suggests that no undervalued or overvalued stocks exist because all public information is reflected in the stock prices, which is a kick in the teeth to fundamental analysts. The strong form implies that the markets are perfect. They have digested all information pertaining to a stock's value.

Little evidence exists to support the strong form. But some contradictions of the semistrong form suggest that the market has inefficiencies, particularly with regard to small stocks that have been ignored by fundamental analysts. After all, it is the fundamental analysts, in competition with one another, who make the markets more efficient, which lends support for the semistrong form.

The CAPM differentiates the risk in the portfolio into two parts: systematic and unsystematic risk. A diversified portfolio of stocks eliminates only unsystematic risk, which leaves the portfolio exposed to systematic risk. Thus, to earn higher returns in the market, you have to invest in stocks with higher beta factors (a coefficient measuring the systematic or market risk) than the market has.

The theories of stock prices and the market are important for three reasons:

- Investors will not consistently earn superior returns over those of the stock market for long periods.

- Diversification of a portfolio can reduce the overall risk of the portfolio.
- The way to increase returns is to invest in riskier securities. However, if the market "heads south," the riskier securities decline by more than the averages of the market. Other studies, such as the one by Fama and French (1992), show the opposite effect. The lowest-risk securities outperform the highest-risk securities.

These theories and reasons emphasize the importance of the construction of a portfolio of investments that is compatible with an investor's overall risk comfort level. Diversification can accomplish this goal and eliminate some risk. Furthermore, investors can improve returns by holding securities for at least a year to qualify for the lower capital gains taxes and the reduction of investment fees and commissions.

Tax planning can reduce taxes and increase returns to some extent. Long-term capital gains (securities held for longer than one year that are sold at more than their original purchase price) are taxed at lower rates than the higher marginal tax rates for ordinary income and short-term gains (investments held for less than one year). Capital gains become much more important than ordinary income for high-tax-bracket investors. Dividends also receive favorable tax treatment. In the years 2003 through 2008, dividends will be taxed at lower rates than the marginal-tax-bracket rates.

Reducing or eliminating fees and sales commissions can increase returns significantly. Because many brokers make their money by buying and selling securities, they have an incentive to advise their clients to trade more than they should. This process, called *churning*, involves the buying and selling of stocks at a rate that is not justified by their returns.

REFERENCES

Arbel, Avner, and Paul Strebel. "The Neglected and Small Firm Effects." *Financial Review*, November 1982, pp. 201–218.

Basu, S. "The Information Content of Price/Earnings Ratios." *Financial Management*, Summer 1975, pp. 53–64.

Basu, S. "Investment Performance of Common Stocks in Relation to their Price/Earnings Ratios: A Test of the Efficient Market Hypothesis." *Journal of Finance*, June 1977, pp. 663–682.

Cheney, John M., and Edward A. Moses. *Fundamentals of Investments*. St. Paul, MN: West, 1992, p. 19.

Clayman, M. "In Search of Excellence: The Investor's Viewpoint." *Financial Analysts' Journal*, May/June 1987.

Cropper, Carol Marie. "It's Not All in the Timing." *BusinessWeek Online*, March 5, 2001.

Dorfman, John R. "Luck or Logic." *Wall Street Journal*, November 4, 1993, p. C1.

Dremen, David. "Flawed Forecasts." *Forbes*, December 9, 1991, p. 342.

Fama, Eugene F. "The Behavior of Stock Prices." *Journal of Business*, January 1965, pp. 34–105.

Fama, Eugene F., and Kenneth French. "The Cross-Section of Expected Stock Returns." *Journal of Finance* 47(June 1992): 427–466.

Fama, Eugene F., Lawrence Fisher, Michael G. Jensen, and Richard Roll. "The Adjustment of Stock Prices to New Information." *International Economic Review*, February 1969, pp. 1–21.

Lorie, James H., and Victor Niederhoffer. "Predictive Statistical Properties of Insider Trading." *Journal of Law and Economics*, April 1966, pp. 35–53.

Malkiel, Burton G. *A Random Walk Down Wall Street*. New York: W.W. Norton, 1990.

Manne, Henry G. "The Case for Insider Trading." *Wall Street Journal*, March 17, 2003, p. A14.

Mattich, Alen. "Asset Class: Market Timing Makes a Comeback." *Wall Street Journal Online*, March 14, 2003.

Securities and Exchange Commission (SEC). *Institutional Investor Study Report*. Washington: U.S. Government Printing Office, 1971.

Sturm, Paul. "What If Ben Graham Had a PC?" *Smart Money*, March 1994, p. 32.

Tergesen, Anne, and Peter Coy. "Who Needs a Money Manager?" *BusinessWeek*, February 22, 1999, pp. 127–132.

Growth, Value, and Momentum Investing Styles

KEY CONCEPTS

- Investment style
- Selection of stocks using a value equity style
- Selection of stocks using a growth equity style
- Selection of stocks using a blend of growth and value styles
- Momentum investing style

Investment Snapshot

- At the time that the Dow Jones Industrial Average (DJIA) reached a record high, individual investors are turning away from foreign stocks and investing in U.S. stocks.
- The average price/earnings ratio of the DJIA was 22 and that of the Nasdaq composite was 35 as of October 2006.
- For the first eight months of 2006, value stocks outperformed growth stocks.
- In overnight trading on November 3, 2006, Whole Foods Market's stock price fell by more than 20 percent and Electronic Arts' stock price increased by 11 percent.
- In 2005, growth stocks outperformed value stocks.
- One investment style is usually dominant at any given time.

The preceding three chapters covered fundamental and technical analysis methods for selecting stocks and an evaluation of the different investment strategies, respectively. Armed with this information, you are now ready to construct a portfolio using an investment style that is suitable for your particular needs and circumstances.

CHOOSING AN INVESTMENT STYLE

The question that is often asked by investors is, "What types of stocks should I buy?" Should you rush to buy the small-cap growth stocks that have outperformed large-cap growth stocks or should you look for value stocks? The question relates not only to the investment type but also to the size of the company stocks. Some investors feel comfortable going after the winning categories, whereas the more patient investor is content to invest in the lagging categories, which will rise over time.

Studies have shown that stocks can be classified into categories that have similar patterns of performance and characteristics. In other words, the returns of the stocks within the categories were similar, whereas the returns of the stocks between the categories were not correlated (Farrell, 1975, pp. 50–62). Farrell found four categories for stocks, namely, growth, cyclical, stable, and energy. Other studies measured stocks by their market capitalization or size, which was then translated into small-cap, mid-cap, and large-cap stocks. What portfolio managers found was that they could enhance their performance by moving their money into the different categories of stocks from time to time.

From these categories of stocks, two investment styles have emerged, namely, value and growth investing. Figure 13–1 illustrates the common styles of equity investing as developed by Morningstar Mutual Funds for mutual fund investing, but they also can be used to determine individual equity portfolio holdings.

Investors can use this style box to determine if the bulk of their equity investments suits their investment style, as determined by their investment objectives. Value stocks have different financial characteristics and returns than growth stocks. Value stocks generally have low P/E ratios that are less than their expected growth rates. Growth stocks generally have high P/E ratios and are expected to experience high sales growth for a period of time. A blend includes a mixture of growth and value stocks. The size of the company is measured by market capitalization, which is the market value of its stock multiplied by the number of shares outstanding. Small-cap

FIGURE 13-1

Types of Equity Investing Styles. (*Morningstar Mutual Funds.*)

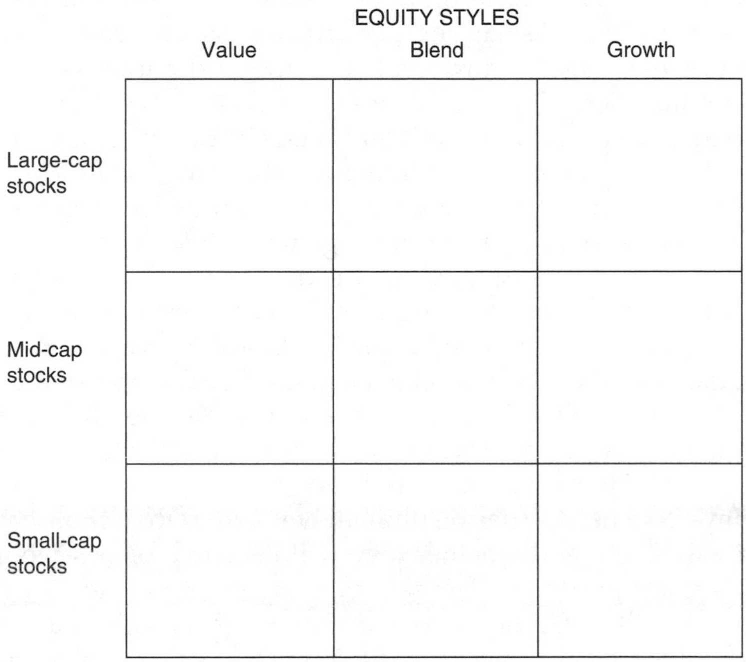

EQUITY STYLES

	Value	Blend	Growth
Large-cap stocks			
Mid-cap stocks			
Small-cap stocks			

companies are riskier than mid-cap or large-cap companies, but as the Ibbotson study showed, the returns over longer periods for small-cap stocks generally have exceeded the returns of large-cap stocks. Small-cap value stocks have outperformed large-cap growth stocks quite handily over the $2\frac{1}{2}$-year period 2003–2005. Consequently, stock picking becomes extremely important for individual portfolios, particularly when the investment style is to time the markets.

The style box in Figure 13–1 illustrates the choices in terms of investment styles and sizes of companies. Investors can choose the current winners (2006), which happen to be small-cap value stocks, in which to invest more money. Alternatively, some investors might not want to pay high prices for these types of stocks and instead would look for the quadrants of stocks that have not participated in the recent rally (large-cap growth stocks, for example). Some investors might want to have a combination of growth and value stocks in the different size categories. This style box also can be used with international stocks.

Research has shown that value and growth stocks do not perform in the same manner within the same time periods. This is evidenced recently by the spectacular performance of large-cap growth stocks in the late 1990s, during which time large-, mid-, and small-cap value stocks underperformed the market. Since 2000, small-cap value stocks have outperformed large-cap growth stocks. One investment style (growth versus value) is dominant at a given point in time. Some investors choose to invest all their funds in the stocks that are performing well and then shift to other investment styles when they perceive that things are about to change. This style of investing would be more conducive to an active management style, as opposed to a passive management style, where investors would allocate their stocks among the different categories and then hold them for long periods. Active managers are more likely to be market timers and are more inclined to be fully invested in stocks when they perceive the market to be going up. The opposite occurs when they think that the market is about to decline; they exit the market. Passive investors tend to stay fully invested in stocks irrespective of the state of the markets.

Investors need to decide ultimately whether they choose value or growth stocks and whether they will be active or passive managers of their portfolios. The selection of individual stocks can be made easier if direction is provided through an asset allocation model, which breaks down the different style categories of investment by the asset class. Table 13–1 lists a few examples of the different portfolio possibilities. Investors might invest in a mixture of value and growth stocks, which could be allocated among domestic U.S. stocks and international stocks. Investors then would decide on the amounts to allocate to the different stock sizes, large-, mid-, and small-cap (Example 1 in Table 13–1).

Example 2 illustrates a value stock portfolio and Example 3 a growth stock portfolio. Diversification within the stock sector of an investor's portfolio offers protection against the downside risk of being fully invested in only one sector, such as large-cap value or growth stocks, for example. If the tide turns against stocks in one sector, investors would be protected by being able to participate in any price improvement in other sectors should the stock market rally become more broad-based.

Active versus Passive Investment

Investors who believe in the efficient market hypothesis, discussed in Chapter 12, would argue on behalf of the passive investment

TABLE 13-1

Asset Allocation of Stocks by Style

Example 1	Example 2	Example 3
Value-growth blend	**Value**	**Growth**
Value stocks	**Value stocks**	**Growth stocks**
Large-cap U.S. stocks 20%	Large-cap U.S. stocks 25%	Large-cap U.S. stocks 25%
Mid-cap U.S. stocks 10%	Mid-cap U.S. stocks 15%	Mid-cap U.S. stocks 15%
Small-cap U.S. stocks 10%	Small-Cap U.S. stocks 10%	Small-cap U.S. stocks 10%
International stocks 10%	International large-cap stocks 20%	International large-cap stocks 20%
Growth stocks	International mid-cap stocks 20%	International mid-cap stocks 20%
Large-cap U.S. stocks 20%	International small-cap stocks 10%	International small-cap stocks 10%
Mid-cap U.S stocks 10%		
Small-cap U.S. stocks 10%		
International stocks 10%		
Total portfolio 100%	Total portfolio 100%	Total portfolio 100%

style. If stock prices reflect all relevant information and stocks are always priced at their intrinsic values, it would be difficult for investors to beat the markets over long periods. Consequently, if investors cannot profit from insider information and there are no undervalued stocks, they have two alternatives: (1) invest in market indexes or (2) choose individual stocks and hold them for long periods. These are known as *buy-and-hold strategies*.

Indexing

Those who subscribe to index investing believe that events affecting companies occur randomly. Therefore, investors have a 50–50 chance of being correct in picking stocks that will go up; hence their odds of beating the market become more muted. Consequently, these investors are satisfied with the returns of the market and would invest in the stocks that make up the market indexes. This strategy can be achieved in the following ways:

- Investing in the individual stocks in the index, for example, the 30 stocks in the DJIA. However, investing in the 500 stocks of the Standard & Poor's (S&P) 500 Index is not practical for most individual portfolios. Investors could invest more easily in sectors of the S&P 500 Index, such as the technology sector or the financial sector, or the "nifty fifty" stocks, or the Dogs of the Dow.
- Investing in index-tracking stocks (exchange-traded funds), which underlie the indexes. Examples of these are the SPDRs, which track the S&P 500 Index and the sector SPDRs of the S&P 500 Index; the DIAMONDs, which track the DJIA; and the Nasdaq 100 tracking stock, which invests in the largest 100 companies in the Nasdaq. These exchange-traded funds (ETFs) are discussed in Chapter 15.
- Investing in index mutual funds, also discussed in Chapter 14.

An examination of the results of index mutual funds versus the actively managed mutual funds, as a proxy of passive versus active investing, makes the case for indexing more compelling. Tergesen (1999, p. 110) reported that the average S&P 500 Index mutual fund earned around 18 percent annually over the 10-year period 1989–1999 as compared with 16 percent annually for the actively managed equity mutual funds. This 2 percent annual difference may not seem all that significant, but when this difference is compounded over time, the results point overwhelmingly toward indexing. Over a 10-year period, the compounded returns of index funds exceeded those of actively managed equity funds by about 80 percent (Tergesen, 1999, p. 110). More recently, according to Burton Malkiel, a finance professor at Princeton University, the S&P 500 benchmark index fund outperformed 84 percent of actively managed large-cap funds during the 10-year period 1993–2003 (Farrell, 2003).

There are a number of reasons to explain the advantages of indexing over actively managed mutual funds:

1. Actively managed mutual funds may keep some money in cash, anticipating a downturn in the market. If this does not materialize, then index funds will earn more from their holdings because they are always fully invested.
2. The annual expense ratios of index funds are considerably lower than those of their actively managed equity mutual

fund counterparts. Index funds do not change their holdings unless the stocks in the indexes are changed. Actively managed funds can experience high turnovers of their holdings, which means higher transaction costs.

3. Large-cap stocks, which are followed by many analysts, are probably efficiently priced, which gives index funds an advantage over the stock picker.

The opportunities for active managers and stock pickers are in the small-cap and international stocks, which may be under-followed by the analysts. Similarly, in a market downturn, active managers can put limits on the decrease in their funds' stock prices by raising cash or investing in defensive stocks, which may not go down as much as the fixed portfolios of the index funds. This is not to say that actively managed portfolios will not go down in a bear market. These portfolios will go down just like the index funds, but steps can be taken to reduce the amount of the decline in their value. This can be seen where small-cap equity managers have out-paced the Russell 2000 Index by including some large-cap stocks in their holdings. Other studies confirm that active managers do not consistently outperform indexing (Martin, 1993, pp. 17–20).

Buy-and-Hold Investing

Besides indexing, the other passive investment strategy for stock pickers is to buy stocks for the long term and hold them. In other words, investors would hold these stocks, making minimal changes over time. Performance between active and passive strategies is more difficult to evaluate because this depends on the composition of the stocks in both active and passive portfolios. However, using index funds as the basis for buy-and-hold investing, the results confirm that active portfolio managers do not outperform the buy-and-hold strategy. Jensen (1968, pp. 389–416) surveyed 115 mutual fund managers during the period 1945–1964 and found that the average returns of these funds were less than investments in a portfolio of Treasury bills and the market index would have returned.

Market timers often tout how they were able to exit the market successfully before a crash and then reenter the market at a lower point to increase their overall returns. This may be easier said than done. Research done by T Rowe Price showed that in order to do better than a buy-and-hold investor, market timers would need to be accurate in more than 70 percent of their calls to enter and exit the market. A study done by Nejat Seyhun covering the period 1963–1993 found that an investor who exited the market for just 1.2 percent of the market's best-performing days would have lost out on 95 percent of the total returns (Strong, 1998, p. 363).

There certainly appears to be a disconnect between the research results as reported from the ivory towers of academia and the communications and hype as reported from many people on Wall Street. The growth of newsletters forecasting the precise future movements of the markets and how to time them is on the rise as more investors enter the stock markets hoping to double or treble their money over a short period. As of this writing, the clairvoyant with 100 percent accuracy in calling the markets has yet to emerge. Until such time, the odds are stacked against timing the markets; they favor the buy-and-hold investor.

What becomes apparent is that it is difficult to beat the markets consistently over long periods regardless of the method. This theory certainly lends support for buy-and-hold strategies over market timers. In addition to those reasons already discussed, several reasons put forth for the underperformance of active investing over passive investing include

- Active trading means higher transaction (commission) costs.
- If the holding period for stocks is less than one year, the gains incurred are taxed at higher Federal tax rates than those of the longer-term holding periods of the buy-and-hold investors.

Value versus Growth Investing

Although growth stocks have outperformed value stocks over certain time periods, this trend has not always prevailed over longer periods. For the two-year period 2003–2005, value stocks outperformed growth stocks, giving value stocks the appearance of being overvalued. Consequently, an investor looking for value might consider buying growth stocks because he or she would pay a small premium for them. Therefore, should investors continue to choose the leadership in the sector that is doing well and ignore the other lagging sectors of the market? It is easier to answer this question for a long investment period, but over the short term, it becomes more of a guessing game. The *momentum investing* style is to jump into those stocks that have been going up in price. The major problem with momentum investing is that the turning point can never be predicted accurately. These leadership stocks eventually will become laggards, and the rotation will shift into the other sectors of stocks. If one is investing in these leadership stocks at the top of their price cycles, the returns may be not be positive for some time before they come back into favor. Over the long term, investors who have diversified portfolios of stocks among the different sectors (small-, mid-, and large-cap value and growth stocks) will see steadier returns.

An analysis of the stock market substantiates this premise. Over the 26-year period 1979–2005, there were times where value stocks outperformed growth stocks and where the opposite occurred (growth stocks outperformed value stocks), as summarized in Table 13–2.

Which stocks over a long-term period would have returned more to investors? The answer may be surprising. A study done by David Leineweber and colleagues reported that $1 invested in both value and growth stocks, as followed by the price-to-book value of S&P 500 Index stocks during the period 1975–1995, would have resulted in $23 for value stocks versus $14 for growth stocks (Coggin, Fabozzi, and Arnott, 1997, p. 188). These results also have been confirmed by studies done on foreign stocks. A study done by Capaul, Rowley, and Sharpe (1993, p. 34) determined that value stocks outperformed growth stocks abroad

TABLE 13-2

Performance of U.S. Stocks Over the Period 1979–2005

Value Stocks Outperform Growth Stocks	Growth Stocks Outperform Value Stocks
1981	1980
1983–1984	1982
1986	1985
1987–1988	1987
1992–1993	1989–1991
1995	1993–1994
	1996–1999
2000–2005	

(France, Germany, Switzerland, Japan, and the United Kingdom) during the period January 1981–June 1992. Jeremy Siegel, a professor at the University of Pennsylvania, found that value stocks outperformed growth stocks over the 35-year period between July 1963 and December 1998. Value stocks earned 13.4 percent annually, whereas growth stocks earned 12 percent annually (Tam and McGeeham, 1999, pp. C1, C19).

In short, this phenomenon—value stocks outperforming growth stocks over long periods—should have some significance in the choice of stocks for investment portfolios. The evidence shows that winning stocks do not keep their positions over time; they revert to the mean. Similarly, losing stocks do not remain losers over long periods of time because they too rise to the average. In other words, the high-flying value stocks of today will not be able to sustain their abnormally high returns, and they will turn into stocks with lower returns, and the low returns of the growth stocks of today eventually will surprise investors with higher returns.

This phenomenon of returns reverting to the mean over time can be applied to small- and large-cap stocks as well. However, small-cap stocks outperformed large-cap stocks during the periods 1974–1983 and 1991–1992. Investing in small- and mid-cap stocks from 1996 to 2000 would have resulted in either below-market or negative returns. Inevitably, though, small-cap stocks outperform large-cap stocks on a risk-adjusted basis over long periods. The second reason to include small-cap stocks in a diversified portfolio is that small-cap stocks have relatively low correlations with large-cap stocks, thereby improving the risk/return statistics in a portfolio.

Adding mid-cap stocks to small- and large-cap stocks in a portfolio reduces the volatility risks and optimizes the stability of returns. Many market timers consider that this style of investing across different sectors weakens the potential returns they could have achieved by moving with the top-performing sectors. Obviously, a diversified portfolio will not gain as much as the strongest-performing sector or fall as much as the weakest-performing sector. The results for market timers depend on their accuracy in timing their calls to move in and out of the different sectors. Your overall choice of whether to be an active or a passive investor and your motivation for the choice of equity style ultimately will depend on your outlook on the market and your specific makeup with regard to risk and return.

HOW TO COMPOSE A VALUE PORTFOLIO

Value investing relies on fundamental analysis to determine when a stock is trading at less than its intrinsic value. This style is the opposite of growth investing, where investors are willing to chase after stocks that have good growth records and have already risen in value. Value investors are bargain hunters who are looking for companies that have good ideas or products or that have been performing poorly but have good long-term prospects. A good example of value stocks are the home-building companies that have declined in price because of a bubble in the real estate market. The stocks of these companies are trading at around four times their earnings multiples. If interest rates in the economy rise, fewer new homes will be built and sold. Consequently, home-building companies are attractive investments for value investors who are willing to wait until the home-building cycle moves back into an expansionary mode. When a sector of stocks has lagged other stock sectors over long periods, the gap eventually narrows, and the laggard sectors likely will outperform those other stock sectors in the future. This is known as the *regression to the mean*. The flip side of the coin is that stocks that have been outperforming the market likely will revert to the mean and underperform the market at some stage in the future. Thus value investors are always looking for stocks that are considered to be trading below their expected long-term growth rates.

A definition of a value stock is one in which the company's P/E ratio is lower than its earnings growth rate. Chesapeake Energy, for example, is considered a value stock in that its 2007 expected earnings growth rate is 13 percent and its 2007 P/E ratio is 9.6. A stock whose P/E ratio exceeds its growth rate is not considered a value stock.

There is not unanimous agreement on the definition of value stocks. Some definitions center on low P/E multiples or those that are below the market multiples. Others focus on low multiples of cash flow or low price-to-book ratios. The most conservative definition of a value stock is one that has an above-average dividend yield. Out-of-favor stocks are also classified by some as value stocks. For example, when Intel, Cisco, and many other growth stocks fell in value in 2006, many value fund managers bought these stocks as value stocks. Depending, then, on how you define *value*, many investors come up with different sets of value stocks. Some of the bases for determining value stocks are discussed in greater detail below.

Price/Earnings Ratio

The P/E ratio for a stock is calculated by dividing the current market price of the stock by the earnings per share. This can be done using the past four quarters' earnings, which is known as a *trailing P/E ratio*. Alternatively, the P/E calculation can use expected earnings based on forecasts for the upcoming year's earnings. This *future P/E ratio* may be of greater significance to investors because this is an indication of the expectations for the stock in the future.

However, investors should not base their decisions solely on P/E multiples because the type of industry and the capital structure also affect the P/E ratio. Some industries have higher average P/E ratios than others, and it would not necessarily be a meaningful evaluation to compare the P/E ratios across industries. For example, the pharmaceutical companies have much higher multiples than the brokerage stocks. Comparing Schering-Plough Corporation, then, with a trailing P/E ratio of 33, with Goldman Sachs, with a P/E ratio of 11, would be meaningless. Some industries require much greater investments in property, plant, and equipment than others, which means that they are probably much more leveraged in terms of debt. Generally, companies with high debt ratios are much riskier than companies with low debt ratios, and these more highly leveraged companies will have lower P/E ratios.

A low P/E ratio is a relative measure. Some investors might consider Schering-Plough to be a growth stock with a multiple of 33, whereas others would consider this to be a value stock as compared with the high multiples of some of the other stocks on the exchanges.

Price-to-Book Ratio

This measure compares the market price to the book value. The book value per share is computed as assets minus liabilities divided by the number of outstanding shares. Value investors look for stocks with market values that are below their book values. Benjamin Graham, who did the pioneering work on fundamental analysis, has some guidelines for stock pickers, which include buying a company's stock when the stock price is less than two-thirds the book value per share.

There are a number of reasons why a low price-to-book ratio is not reason enough, by itself, to buy a stock. The book value per share is an accounting measure, and it can be distorted by using different accounting methods within the generally accepted accounting principles (GAAP), such as the use of accelerated depreciation versus straight-line depreciation or last in, first out (LIFO) versus first in, first out (FIFO) for valuing inventory. The discrepancy between the historical cost of the company's assets and their market value will make the book value per share diverge from the realizable value per share.

Thus it is a good idea to use more than one measure of value to select value stocks.

Selecting a Value Portfolio

The first step is to select a universe of stocks that you are interested in. This can be done using the Internet to print up the financial information on stocks of interest. You then can narrow the list down to stocks that conform with your criteria of value, namely, the specific price-to-book and P/E ratios and dividend yields. You can find stock screening tools at various online Web sites such as www.yahoo.com and www.cnbc.com that you can use to plug in criteria for screening different stocks to come up with a screen of value stocks (see Table 13–3). These are not recommendations for particular stocks because over time the financial fundamentals for these stocks will change.

Reasons for Selecting these Stocks

Using a stock screen on Barrons' Web site, the list of stocks in Table 13–3 was produced with the following criteria: a dividend yield of greater than 3 percent, return on equity greater than 10 percent, and 3-year EPS growth rates in excess of 10 percent. The list was reduced based on PEG ratios of less than 1, with the exception of Microchip Technology. From this list, the fundamental value for each of the stocks was considered. BP and Chevron were chosen because they are among the largest global companies in their sectors. Future growth in the supply of basic materials and oil would not keep up with the growth in demand from the emerging economies of China, India, Brazil, and Russia. Dow Chemical, an underloved stock, was trading at a lower P/E ratio than its peers in its industry. If valued like its peers, Dow Chemical's stock price would trade in the low $60s. Bank of South Carolina had sales and income growth that exceeded its peers in the regional banking industry. In addition, its debt-to-equity ratio was less than those of banks in its industry. Unilever N.V. is a global consumer goods

TABLE 13-3

Value Stocks Based on Fundamental Factors

Company	Symbol	Sector	Price	Div. Yld.	Return on Equity	Debt-to-Equity Ratio	PEG	EPS Growth	Market Cap
Bank of South Carolina	BKSC	Financial	$15.84	3.5%	17.2%	0.01	0.32	22.32	$62.6 M*
BP PLC	BP	Basic materials	$68.44	3.4%	29.6%	0.24	0.21	79.39	$231.9 B†
Chevron	CVX	Integrated oil	$69.54	3%	25.2%	0.15	0.97	36.61	$153 B
Dow Chemical	DOW	Basic materials	$40.81	3.7%	23.0	0.61	0.96	49.31	$39.9 B
Microchip Technology	MCHP	Technology	$33.30	3.1%	14.7	0.04	3.3	19.72	$7.1 B
Unilever N.V.	UN	Consumer	$26.40	4.2%	40	1.36	0.06	48.49	$44.8 B
Rayonier, Inc.	RYN	Financial REIT	$39.61	4.8%	19.4	0.61	0.05	32.46	$3.09 B
Knightsbridge Tankers, Ltd.	VLCCF	Shipping	$26.81	11.9%	22.3	0.62	0.37	20.61	$461.5 M

*M-millions
†B-billions

pick. The parent company of the Unilever Group is a leading supplier of food, home, and personal care products around the world. Knightsbridge Tankers Limited is a small-cap international stock whose primary business is the transport of crude oil. If the Knightsbridge stock was valued like its peers, it would trade in the low $40s.

Low *PEG ratio* stocks were selected because this measure is an indication of potential value. PEG ratios of less than 1 indicate that the stock might be undervalued because of prevailing expectations that the stock's earnings growth might not be realized. A PEG ratio of greater than 1 indicates that the stock might be overvalued because the earnings growth rate is less than the P/E ratio.

The initial screen of stocks was reduced based on debt-to-equity ratios. With the exception of Unilever, all the stocks in Table 13–3 have low debt-to-equity ratios.

Over long periods, *earnings* drive the growth in stock prices. Look for companies that will be able to sustain increased earnings over long periods of time. Companies with three-year growth rates that were in excess of their P/E ratios were chosen.

The *dividend yield* is another measure of value. All the stocks selected had dividend yields in excess of 3 percent. Stocks with high dividend yields are attractive to value investors, who can collect the dividends while waiting for capital appreciation.

Value investors select stocks that they believe are undervalued relative to their fundamental intrinsic value. These are some of the measures used to determine value stocks.

HOW TO COMPOSE A GROWTH PORTFOLIO

Growth investors look for companies with above-average growth rates. These can be companies with consistently high sales growth. Growth investors are willing to pay high multiples of earnings for companies with high growth rates, which explains why growth stocks generally have high P/E multiples. Stocks such as Google and Starbucks trade at P/E ratios of greater than 40, and these multiples might expand as these companies grow at their expected growth rates. Should growth stocks not be able to sustain their high growth rates, their stock prices are severely punished. This occurred when Cisco Systems could not sustain its growth rate of 35 to 50 percent in 2000; its stock price declined from the mid-$50s to the midteens.

Growth stocks had an incredibly good run of consistent earnings growth in the slow-growth economic environment in the United States during the period 1995 to April 1999. This was in part due to low inflation and declining interest rates. The P/E ratios of the large-cap growth stocks were expanding to historically high levels, suggesting a definition of growth stocks: companies with higher-than-average growth in sales and earnings with high P/E ratios and high price-to-book ratios. The high P/E ratios mean that investors are willing to pay a high premium to buy these stocks. However, if there are disappointments in the sales and/or earnings growth, these stocks get severely punished and therefore are considered to be more risky, with a greater potential for losses. Investors have lower expectations for value stocks. Consequently, any sales or earnings disappointments will cause smaller losses. Generally, growth companies reinvest their earnings to fund more growth rather than paying them out in dividends. If growth companies do pay dividends, they are relatively small with low dividend yields.

Growth Rates
There is no precise definition of the exact growth rate that distinguishes a growth stock from a value stock. Investors can choose any growth rate to determine their universe of growth stocks and then extrapolate their growth rates into the future.

There are a number of measures of growth. Investors can focus on revenue growth, earnings-per-share growth, return-on-equity growth, or cash-flow-per-share growth from year to year.

Selecting a Growth Portfolio
The first step is to determine your criteria for selecting growth stocks from a stock screen. Table 13–4 shows stocks selected using revenue growth rates of greater than 50 percent for the past five years and earnings-per-share growth rates in excess of 30 percent for the past three years. This is not a recommendation to buy these particular stocks because information, financial conditions, and circumstances change over time.

Reasons for Selecting These Stocks
The growth stocks selected for Table 13–4 had relatively low P/E ratios for companies with high sales and earnings growth rates.

TABLE 13-4

Growth Stock Portfolio Based on Growth in Excess of
30 Percent

Company	Symbol	Industry	P/E	5-Yr. Rev Growth	Price	3-Yr. EPS Growth	Beta	Market-Cap
Armor Holdings, Inc.	AH	Defense	14.8	53%	$54.05	39.7%	1.23	$1.9 B*
Ceredyne, Inc.	CRDN	Industrial equip.	13.17	67%	$52.30	84%	1.72	$1.1 B
Chesapeake Energy	CHK	Oil & gas	7.21	53%	$32.51	34%	0.46	$14.1 B
Synergetics USA, Inc.	SURG	Medical appliances	29	50%	$4.33	45%	0.84	$103.6 M†

*B-billions

†M-millions

Another strategy for selecting growth stocks might be to pick industry leaders such as Cisco Systems (telecom equipment), Google (Internet search), Best Buy (retail), Amgen (biotechnology), and Apple Computer (iPod) even though their P/E ratios are higher than the stocks selected in Table 13–4. Cisco Systems does not make the list because its growth declined after the Internet bubble, when communications equipment orders dried up. However, Cisco Systems has recovered in 2006 and managed to grow its sales and earnings for the year. Generally, the leading stocks in their respective industries have sustainable sales and earnings growth.

Growth

A growth investor needs some justification to purchase high P/E ratio stocks, and that justification is growth rates. Generally, investors look for growth stocks with P/E ratios that are less than their growth rates. The time to buy growth stocks is when they have underperformed value stocks, such as in 2006, and they are trading at reasonable P/E ratios. This strategy is known as *growth at a reasonable price* (GARP). The question to answer with growth stocks is, "How much should I pay for the company's earnings?" If the company appears to be able to maintain or increase its growth rate into the future, then paying a higher multiple of earnings might be justified. Google, Inc., is such an example. Google is trading at a lofty P/E multiple, and as long as Google can grow its earnings at the same or greater growth rate, the stock price will continue to rise.

However, any disappointments in sales or earnings growth will punish the stock price severely.

A good starting point to select growth stocks for a portfolio is to look at the fastest-growing sectors of the economy. At the time of this writing, biotechnology and technology sectors were the fastest growers.

Returns

When growth stocks are trading at rich valuations, investors need to look at the returns to justify the lofty prices. For example, Starbucks, a growth company, was punished when it announced quarterly earnings that were shy of analysts' expectations. However, Starbucks announced that it was going to increase its growth through the opening of more stores around the world. Look for companies that have or will post superior earnings returns into the future rather than those with half the picture, namely, tremendous sales growth but flat or decreasing returns.

HOW TO COMPOSE A BLEND OF VALUE AND GROWTH STOCK PORTFOLIO

Instead of concentrating on only one style of investing, investors can choose a blend of value and growth stocks for their portfolios. Within this blend, there may be a bias toward one or the other style or a straight 50 percent allocation to each style. Generally, it is one style that tends to outperform the other style at a single point in time, so by investing in a blend of growth and value stocks, investors can benefit from the winning style. Another advantage of a blend is that investors avoid the question of when to pick the top of the winning style and when to enter the style that is expected to increase. The blend strategy of having exposure to both growth and value stocks lowers volatility risk.

The divergences in returns of the different styles of investing over time suggest that for buy-and-hold investors, who are not willing to time the different sectors, a blended portfolio of value and growth stocks spread among the different stock size categories is the answer. As market conditions change, the leaders in the stock markets eventually become the laggards, and then, over time, this process reverses. By diversifying into the different sectors of the market, investors avoid timing and market performance decisions. By going for a blend of stocks from value and growth styles, investors may be sacrificing on short-term performance, but they reduce their risk of having all their stocks invested in one equity style. For example, when interest rates go up, this has a more devastating effect on growth stocks than on value stocks. The reason is because growth stocks have higher P/E ratios, and with their high expectations, they are punished more severely than value stocks with their low P/E multiples and low expectations.

For example, by investing in an underperforming sector such as growth stocks, investors are taking advantage of the disparity in the markets to create opportunities. Examining what has happened in the market is a case in point. Value stocks have risen in the years after the Internet bubble, and many value stocks are no longer undervalued. This does not mean that investors should change their portfolios whenever there is some economic news. By broadening ownership into stocks that have not contributed to the rise in performance, investors can seek a balance between the leader and laggard stocks in the market.

Table 13–5 lists some value and growth stocks. The stocks were selected based on growth with a bias toward value. Growth stocks selected had either one-year growth rates in sales or earnings of greater than 14 percent. Because growth stocks have been the laggard style, the time horizon for growth in sales and earnings was reduced from three years to one year. The value stocks selected had P/E ratios of less than 12 and the potential to grow their future sales and earnings.

Reasons for Selecting These Stocks

In this blended portfolio of value and growth stocks, the emphasis was on finding stocks that were priced like value stocks but that also had greater growth rates. Stocks were screened, and only stocks

TABLE 13-5

Portfolio of a Blend of Growth and Value Stocks

Company	Price	P/E	Yield	Price/Book	1-Yr. Sales Growth %	1-Yr. Earnings Growth
Amgen	$72.51	29.8	0	4.77	14.5%	−25.7%
Oracle Corp.	$19.46	28.7	0	6.65	29.7%	29.1%
Cisco Systems	$27.15	28.5	0	6.45	24.9%	27.5%
D. R. Horton	$24.96	6.4	2.41%	1.21	−4.2%	−16.1%
Citicorp	$50.66	12.1	3.88%	2.13	27.8%	8.7%
ExxonMobil	$73.08	11.0	1.71%	3.64	−1.10%	15.1%

that had P/E ratios of less than their growth rates were chosen. Cisco Systems was a borderline example, and Amgen an exception. Cisco Systems expanded its business operations through increased market share in the communications network and information technology sectors in addition to acquiring key companies to make the company more competitive. Cisco Systems seems to be a turn-around story after the technology slump in 2000, judging from its one-year growth in sales and earnings. Amgen, a leading biotechnology company, has a stream of successful products (Epogen, Aranesp, Neulasta, Neupogen, and Embrel) on the market, along with a number of promising drugs in the pipeline. Amgen had a disappointing year through November 2006 in terms of sales growth and a decrease in income. However, Amgen's profit margins are higher than those in the industry, and it has the potential to increase its future sales and earnings growth. Oracle acquired four business software companies in 2006, which puts Oracle in a position to expand its market share in its industry.

The last three stocks in Table 13–5 are value stocks. D. R. Horton is a home-building company in the United States. Stocks of home-building companies are cyclical and decline in price when the Federal Reserve raises interest rates. As of November 2006, these stock prices have plummeted from their record highs owing also to fears of an economic slowdown. A patient investor willing to wait out the three- to five-year cycle for these stocks to rebound would find value in the home-building stocks, particularly the larger companies that pay dividends. Citicorp is a diversified financial services company that is growing globally. With close to a 4 percent dividend yield and trading at 12 times trailing earnings, there seems to be little risk of loss for shareholders purchasing the stock. ExxonMobil is a well-run integrated oil company that continues to grow in all types of economic climates. Historically, ExxonMobil managed to expand its earnings despite the price of oil. When oil was trading in the low double digits over a decade ago, ExxonMobil increased its earnings by trimming expenses and continued its profitable trend when oil went up in price in later years. Shareholders have benefited because ExxonMobil has consistently raised its dividends, making it a relatively profitable investment.

A very different portfolio also could be assembled with different interpretations of value and growth definitions. Fifty percent of this portfolio is in low P/E ratio value stocks that have good earnings expectations in the future and the balance of the portfolio put into stocks that are the leaders in their fields and have experienced exceptional growth despite their high P/E multiples.

HOW TO COMPOSE A MOMENTUM PORTFOLIO

Momentum investing is the riskiest of the investing styles discussed in this chapter. Momentum investors look for stocks that are moving up in price, buy them, and settle in for the ride. The time to sell is when a stock's price peaks (before it begins to fall). This definition implies perfect timing on two accounts: The first is to correctly identify stock prices with an upward trend, and the second is to recognize when the stock is trading at or near its peak price. In fact, many momentum investors will continue to buy a stock at its new high price because that is a sign that the stock has broken through a resistance level and will continue to rise in price.

A momentum style of investing is fraught with risk. Buying a stock at its 52-week high price, which then declines in price, will result in a loss of principal. To minimize the amount of potential losses, momentum investors need to be nimble traders. This style of investing favors market timing and a short time horizon for holding a stock.

Profits from this style of investing depend on the accuracy of the investor's decisions on when to buy and when to sell. Profits from this style of investing have the potential to be greater than from the other styles of investing when these decisions are accurate.

Momentum investors are more likely to rely on technical analysis to spot upward price trends.

How to Select a Momentum-Driven Investment Portfolio

The stocks listed in Table 13–6 were selected based on their chart patterns and whether their stock prices had upward trends. Screening stocks with these upward trends for good fundamental factors, such as increasing sales and earnings, can reduce some risk. Another tool is to assess the money flows into the stocks. Stocks with accumulation of money flows indicate that there are more buyers than sellers, whereas stocks with more sellers than

TABLE 13-6

Momentum Stocks

Company	Price	P/E	Volume, in Millions
Nymex Holdings	$133.50	91.1	$1.93
Google, Inc.	$508.01	64.6	$4.5
Corning, Inc.	$21.00	29.2	$17.79
Cisco Systems	$26.91	28.3	$27.15

buyers indicate that the price of the stock is headed south. Look for reasons why a particular stock is rising in price. If you can't find any reasons for the momentum, you probably don't want to buy the stock.

Reasons for Selecting These Stocks
Outperforming Sectors

The exchange sector has been on an upward move, and the stocks in this sector had the highest P/E ratios of any industry sector in November 2006. Consequently, on November 17, 2006, when the New York Mercantile Exchange listed its shares on the NYSE and on its first day of trading more than doubled from $59 to $150 per share, this was a good sign for a momentum investor. Believing that the Nymex's stock price will perform in the same manner as the other exchange-listed stocks is a reason to jump onto the bandwagon. The Chicago Mercantile Exchange came public at $35 per share in 2002 and was trading at $535 per share on November 17, 2006.

Analyst Upgrade

The second stock, Google, Inc., was chosen based on analysts upgrading their price targets to $600 per share. Google, Inc., passed $500 per share on November 21, 2006, and closed for the day at $509 per share. Google's stock hit a low of $331.55 on March 10, 2006, and has been on an upward tear. Such price strength appeals to the momentum-driven investor. However, momentum investors need to be mindful of how long this stock can continue to appreciate, particularly with increasing competition in the online advertising space.

Fundamental Factors

The key to successful investing is to identify companies with accelerating growth in sales and earnings that then translate into appreciating stock prices. This is easier said than done because by the time such a stock is identified, the stock price probably has appreciated significantly. Corning officials had positive announcements on its future quarter's sales, which is a reason for this pick. Corning indicated that for the first quarter of 2007, the company could benefit from increased demand for liquid-crystal display (LCD) glass for TV sets from China and from households in the United States. The company also said that it would protect prices by walking away from lower-priced business.

Cisco Systems was another choice based on fundamental factors. Cisco purchased many businesses within the communications sector, allowing the company to broaden its sales and consolidate its leadership position. The stock price reacted to these fundamental factors but has not risen quite as much as some of the other momentum-driven stocks listed in Table 13-6.

REFERENCES

Capaul, C., I. Rowley, and W. Sharpe. "International Value and Growth Stock Returns." *Financial Analysts' Journal,* January/February 1993.

Coggin, Daniel T., Frank J. Fabozzi, and Robert D. Arnott. *Handbook of Equity Style Management,* 2d ed. New Hope, PA: Frank Fabozzi Associates, 1997.

Farrell, Christopher. "Why Index Funds Can't Be Beat." *BusinessWeek Online,* November 14, 2003.

Farrell, James L., Jr. "Homogeneous Stock Groupings: Implications for Portfolio Management." *Financial Analysts Journal,* May/June 1975, pp. 50–62.

Jensen, Michael C. "The Performance of Mutual Funds in the Period 1945–1964." *Journal of Finance,* May 1968, pp. 389–416.

Martin, Larry L. "The Evolution of Passive versus Active Equity Management." *Journal of Investing,* Spring 1993, pp. 17–20.

Strong, Robert A. *Practical Investment Management* Cincinnati, Ohio 1998 p. 363.

Tam, Pu-Wing, and Patrick McGeeham. "Finding the 'Value' in Value Funds." *Wall Street Journal,* April 16, 1999, pp. C1, C19.

Tergesen, Anne. "Sifting for Clues." *BusinessWeek,* March 29, 1999, pp. 110–111.

CHAPTER 14

Open-End Mutual Funds

KEY CONCEPTS

- Understanding funds and how they work
- Different types of funds
- What to look for in a fund's prospectus before investing in a fund
- The different sources of risk of mutual funds
- Determining when it is advantageous to invest in individual securities or to use the different types of funds discussed in this chapter

---

Investment Snapshot

- The Investment Company Institute estimated that about 55 million U.S. households owned mutual funds as of November 2006.
- As of November 2006, total net assets invested in mutual funds were over $10 trillion in the United States.
- A total of $5.45 trillion was invested in equity mutual funds as of September 2006.
- The total number of stock mutual funds offered in September 2006 was 4,686.

Mutual funds have come close to providing the ideal type of investment for millions of investors who do not want to manage their own investments. The managers of these funds invest shareholders' money in diversified portfolios of stocks, bonds, and money market instruments. Investors receive shares in these mutual funds related to the size of their investments. Thus, even with a modest investment, an investor owns a share of a diversified portfolio of stocks or bonds. An advantage of this type of investment is that investors—who do not have the time to manage their financial investments or knowledge of the individual financial securities—can invest their money in diversified stock, bond, and money market portfolios of mutual funds.

Studies have shown that stock mutual funds have underperformed the market averages over long periods. Research by Standard & Poor's (S&P) on equity mutual funds found that very few mutual funds consistently outperform the markets. The small number of funds that did consistently perform well had a common theme: low expense ratios. For this reason, many investors have turned to exchange-traded funds (ETFs) as a popular investment alternative.

With so many mutual funds to choose from, investors should be as careful in their selection of mutual funds as they are in investing in individual securities. Three steps can facilitate the choice of which fund to invest in

1. Understand how these funds work.
2. Determine what the objectives of the funds are and the types of investments they make.
3. Evaluate the fund's performance from its prospectus and other sources.

FUNDS AND HOW THEY WORK

The investment company that sponsors a mutual fund sells shares to investors and then invests the funds that are received in a portfolio of securities. By pooling investors' funds, a fund manager can diversify the purchase of different securities, such as stocks for stock funds and bonds for bond funds. The objectives of a fund determine the types of investments chosen. For example, if a stock fund's objective is to provide capital appreciation, the fund invests in growth stocks.

Dividends from stocks in the portfolio are passed through to the fund's shareholders (as dividends from the fund). An investor who invests $1,000 gets the same rate of return as another investor who invests $100,000 in the same fund, except the latter shareholder receives a dividend that is 100 times greater (proportionate to the share ownership in the fund).

When prices of securities in the portfolio fluctuate, the total value of the fund is affected. Many different factors—such as the intrinsic risk of the types of securities in the portfolio, in addition to economic, market, and political factors—cause these price fluctuations. The fund's objectives are important because they indicate the type and quality of the investments chosen by the fund. From these objectives, investors can better assess the overall risk the fund is willing to take to improve income (return) and capital gains.

Investment companies offer four different types of funds:

- Open-end mutual funds
- Closed-end funds
- Unit investment trusts (UITs)
- Exchange-traded funds (ETFs)—ETFs are mostly sponsored by brokerage firms and banks.

Closed-end funds and UITs are discussed in Chapter 15, and ETFs are discussed in Chapter 16.

The Different Types of Funds

Two basic types of funds are open-end or closed-end funds. *Open-end funds* issue unlimited numbers of shares. Investors can purchase more shares from the mutual fund company and sell them back to the fund company, which means that the number of shares increases or decreases, respectively. A *closed-end fund* issues a fixed number of shares, and when all the shares are sold, no more are issued. In other words, closed-end funds have fixed capital structures.

Shares are bought in an open-end mutual fund at its net asset value. *Net asset value* (NAV) is the market value of the fund's assets at the end of each trading day minus any liabilities divided by the number of outstanding shares.

Open-end funds determine the market value of their assets at the end of each trading day. For example, a balanced fund, which invests in both common stocks and bonds, uses the closing prices of the stock and bond holdings for the day to determine market value. The number of shares of each of the stocks and the number of bonds that the fund owns are multiplied by the closing prices. The resulting totals of each investment are added together, and any liabilities associated with the fund (such as accrued expenses) are subtracted. The resulting total net assets are divided by the number of shares outstanding in the fund to equal the NAV price per share. Table 14–1 shows how the NAV is determined.

The NAV changes daily because of market fluctuations of the stock and bond prices in the fund. NAVs are important because

1. The NAV is used to determine the value of your holdings in the mutual fund (the number of shares held multiplied by the NAV price per share).
2. The NAV is the price at which new shares are purchased or redeemed.

NAVs of the different funds are quoted in daily newspapers or on the fund's Web site.

Mutual funds pay no taxes on income derived from their investments. Under the Internal Revenue Service Tax Code, mutual funds serve as conduits through which income from investments is passed to shareholders in the form of dividends and capital gains or losses. Individual investors pay taxes on income and capital gains distributions from mutual funds.

Shareholders receive monthly and annual statements showing purchases and sales of shares, interest income, dividends, capital gains and losses, and other relevant data that they should retain for tax purposes. In addition, when investing in mutual funds, investors also should keep track of the NAV prices of shares purchased and sold. This information is used in the computation of gains and losses when shares are redeemed.

TABLE 14-1

How the Net Asset Value (NAV) of a Fund Is Determined

Market value of stocks and bonds in the fund	$100,000,000
Minus total liabilities	−150,000
Net worth	$ 99,850,000
Number of shares outstanding	7,500,000
Net asset value	$ 13.313 (99,850,000/7,500,000)

The value of a mutual fund increases when

- Interest and dividends earned on the fund's investments are passed through to shareholders.
- The fund's management sells investment securities at a profit. The capital gains from the sale are passed through to shareholders. If securities are sold at a loss, the capital loss is offset against the gains of the fund, and the net gain or loss is passed through to shareholders.
- The NAV per share increases.

TYPES OF MUTUAL FUNDS

Investors can invest in stock funds, bond funds, money market funds, hybrid funds, and commodity funds. Table 14–2 shows the different types of equity fund classifications based on investment objectives.

A stock mutual fund specializes in stock investments. Stock funds vary with regard to the types of stocks the funds choose for their portfolios and are guided by the fund's investment objectives. The Securities and Exchange Commission (SEC) requires that funds disclose their objectives. For example, a fund might have the objective to seek growth through maximum capital gains. This type of fund then would appeal to more aggressive investors who can withstand the risk of loss because of the speculative nature of the stocks of the unseasoned, small companies in which the fund invests.

A conservative equity fund's objectives are geared more toward providing current income than capital growth. This type of fund invests in dividend-paying stocks, which also would provide for capital appreciation, even though that might not be a primary objective. Growth and income funds seek a balance between providing capital gains and providing current income.

Equity funds also can be classified according to *investment style*, namely, growth stocks or value stocks or a blend of the two. Value stocks have financial characteristics different from growth stocks. Value stocks generally pay dividends and have low price/earnings (P/E) ratios, whereas growth stocks have high P/E ratios, and the companies tend to have high sales growth rates for a specified period.

Investing in equity funds does not immunize you from the volatility in the markets. In a market downturn, the more speculative

TABLE 14-2

Types of Equity Mutual Funds

Fund Type	Objectives
Aggressive growth	Seek maximum capital gains; invest in stocks of companies in new industries and out-of-favor companies.
Growth	Seek an increase in value through capital gains; invest in stocks of growth companies and industries that are more mainstream than those chosen by aggressive growth funds.
Growth and income	Seek an increase in value through capital gains and dividend income; invest in stocks of companies with a more consistent track record than companies selected for growth and aggressive growth funds.
Income equity	Invest in stocks of companies that pay dividends.
Index	Invest in securities that replicate the market, for example, Standard & Poor's (S&P) 500 Index, Dow Jones Industrial Average (DJIA).
International equity	Invest in stocks of companies outside the United States.
Global equity	Invest in stocks of companies both inside and outside the United States.
Emerging market	Invest in stocks of companies in developing countries.
Sector	Invest in stocks in the sector of the economy stated in the fund's objectives, for example, energy, health care sector, technology, and precious metals.
Balanced	Seek to provide value through income and principal conservation; invest in common stocks, preferred stocks, and bonds.
Asset allocation	Invest in securities (stocks, bonds, and money market) according to either a fixed or variable formula.
Hedge	Invest in securities (stocks and bonds) and derivative securities to hedge against downturns in the market, interest-rate changes, and changes in currency values.

stocks in the funds' portfolios generally decline more than established blue-chip stocks. Share prices of aggressive funds are therefore much more volatile than share prices of conservative stock funds.

An *index fund* is a mutual fund that includes a portfolio of securities designed to match the performance of the market as a whole. An index fund tracks an underlying market index and seeks to match the returns of that particular market index. For example, the S&P 500 Index Fund invests in the stocks of the S&P 500 Index.

This strategy does not require active management of the assets in the fund because turnover is low. The stocks are held in the fund until they drop out of the index. Only then are changes made to the fund. The enthusiasm for index funds has spurred growth into other areas, such as mid-cap and small-cap stocks, emerging markets, Europe, Asia, and the Pacific Rim.

A combined stock and bond fund is called a *balanced fund*. Balanced funds invest in a mixture of stocks and bonds. The equity portion of a fund aims to provide capital growth, and the fixed-income investments provide income for shareholders. The range of percentages allocated to stocks and bonds are stated in the prospectus of the fund.

Generally, the riskier the securities held in a fund, the greater is the potential return and the greater is the potential loss. This statement is true for all types of funds, including stock funds.

Much has been written about hedge funds since the disaster at Long Term Capital Management, a Connecticut hedge fund that had to be bailed out by 14 financial institutions. Long Term Capital Management suffered heavy losses in its positions on Russian bonds because of adverse swings in the prices in the currency markets. Yet, in 2001, the Dow Jones Total Market Index of U.S. stocks declined by 12 percent, whereas hedge funds gained 4.4 percent, as measured by the CSFB/Tremont Index (Clements, 2002, p. C1). Table 14–3 defines hedge funds and lists some of their characteristics.

AN ANALYSIS OF THE PROSPECTUS CAN ASSIST IN THE CHOICE OF A FUND

The best place to learn more about a particular fund is from its prospectus. The SEC requires that investors receive a prospectus before investing or soon afterward. A *prospectus* is a formal written document listing relevant information about the fund, the goals of the fund, the strategies for achieving the goals, securities held by the fund, risk, historical returns, fees charged, and financial data.

A prospectus contains the following information:

- Objectives
- Strategies for achieving the objectives
- Overall risk
- Performance
- Fees

TABLE 14-3

What Is a Hedge Fund?

A hedge fund is not a mutual fund. Hedge funds with fewer than 99 investors are *not* required to register with the SEC. Hedge funds cater to wealthy investors who have a significant net worth ($1.5 million) and are willing to invest $1 million or more. With the negative stock market returns in 2001 and 2002, hedge funds attracted large amounts of new capital and a broader-based clientele. Although returns for hedge funds were low (1 to 2 percent) or flat for 2001, they were nevertheless much better than the double-digit losses posted by most mutual funds for the same period. The reason is that hedge funds can take both long and short positions in stocks, whereas mutual fund managers can only take long positions. In addition, hedge fund managers can use borrowed money, which can increases their returns. These positive returns resulted in the introduction of mini-hedge funds in 2002, a new investment product offered by Wall Street. This type of fund requires a relatively low investment of $250,000, even though investors still must have significant assets to withstand any potential risk of loss (Clements, 2002, p. C1). However, the combination of long and short positions of hedge funds did not perform as well as mutual funds in a rising stock market.

A hedge fund is a specialized open-end fund that allows its manager to take a variety of investment positions in the market to seek higher-than-average potential gains with exposure to greater-than-average risk. U.S. hedge funds, which have been in existence for almost 50 years, typically take the form of limited partnerships. Hedge funds have numerous investment styles, such as market-neutral strategies, in addition to the high- and low-risk strategies. Hedge funds, because they are not as heavily regulated as mutual funds, do not have the same limits on the types of investments they can make and have less stringent disclosure requirements. Investors are limited in how they can withdraw funds. Many hedge funds allow investors to withdraw money only at the end of the year. Others may allow investors to withdraw money at the end the year or at the end of each quarter (Scholl and Bary, 1998, p. 19).

Before investing in a hedge fund

- Read the offering documents.
- Evaluate the hedge fund's risk and use of leverage.
- Understand how long your money is tied up before you can redeem your funds.
- Ask whether there are any side-letter agreements that offer some investors lower fees and other benefits (Maxey, 2006, p. B4).

Objectives

A fund's objectives can be broadly phrased; the most common are

1. To seek long-term capital appreciation through growth of the fund's value over a period of time
2. To seek current income through investments that generate dividends and to preserve investors' principal

Strategies

A fund's strategy reveals the steps its fund manager might take in achieving the fund's objectives. For example, the manager of a stock fund might buy growth stocks or value stocks of companies with a particular size capitalization (small-cap, mid-cap, or large-cap stocks).

Overall Risk

A fund's objectives describe the types of securities in which the fund invests in addition to the risk factors associated with the securities. For example, if a prospectus states that its fund invests in growth securities, you should not be surprised to find that most of the stocks will have high P/E ratios and can include riskier small-cap stocks. Consequently, a decline in growth stock prices would cause investors in this fund to lose money. A fund's investment policies outline the latitude the fund manager has to invest in other types of securities, including options to hedge bets (on the direction of interest rates or the market) and derivative securities to boost the yield of the fund. Many conservative funds, which supposedly only hold blue-chip stocks, have resorted occasionally to investing in small-company and offshore stocks to boost returns. The greater the latitude fund managers have in investing in these other types of securities, the greater is the risk. The types of securities in which the fund invests outline the overall risk of the fund.

Another measure of risk is how diversified the fund is. If the fund cannot invest more than 5 percent of its assets in the securities of one company, it is a diversified fund. However, if a fund has no limits, the fund manager can choose to invest in a few securities, which greatly increases the risk of loss if one of these investments declines significantly.

Performance

The overall performance of a fund pertains to these concepts:

- Total return
- Expenses

Funds are required by the SEC to provide annualized returns. These returns can be presented in a table or graphically, showing results for one year, five years, or ten years. New funds provide their returns from the date of inception. These returns are presented on a before-tax basis and an after-tax basis, which shows how tax efficient the fund is. Funds also must compare their returns to an appropriate market index.

Many funds can boast that they have attained the number-one position in some area of performance at some point during their existence. Note, however, that good past performance may not be indicative of good future performance. Some funds that did well in the past no longer even exist.

Several business magazines track the overall performance records of many mutual funds during up and down markets. These performance results are a better yardstick to use than the advertising messages of the mutual funds themselves. From these publications, you can see how well funds have performed in up markets and how the funds protected their capital during periods of declining prices. New funds do not have track records, which means that their performance during a period of declining prices may not be available. This statement is especially true for funds that come into existence during a bull market.

Organizations such as Morningstar (www.morningstar.com) rate a mutual fund's performance relative to other funds with the same investment objectives. However, this rating can be misleading when you are trying to choose a fund. First, the funds may not be comparable, even though they have similar objectives. For example, one fund might have riskier assets than another. Second, past performance may not be a reliable indicator of future performance.

In choosing a fund, you should look at what the fund invests in (as well as can be determined) and then try to determine the volatility in terms of up and down markets.

Total Return

Yield is a measure of a fund's dividend distribution over a 30-day period. It is only one aspect of the fund's *total return*, however. Mutual funds pass on to shareholders any gains or losses, which can increase or decrease the fund's total return.

Another factor that affects total return is the fluctuation in NAV. When the share price increases by 6 percent, it effectively increases the total return by an additional 6 percent. Similarly, a decline in the NAV price of a fund decreases the total return. This concept explains why funds with positive yields can have negative total returns.

Interest on reinvested dividends is another factor that also might be included in the total return. When dividends paid out by a fund are reinvested to buy more shares, the yield earned on those reinvested shares boosts the overall return on the invested capital.

The total return of a mutual fund includes the following three components:

- Dividends and capital gains or losses
- Changes in net asset value
- Dividends (interest) on reinvested dividends

Expenses are a key factor in differentiating the performances of different funds. By painstakingly looking for funds with the highest yields, you are looking at only half the picture. A fund with a high yield also may be the one that charges higher expenses, which could put that fund behind some lower-cost funds with lower yields. Fees reduce total returns earned by funds. You cannot count on future performance projections unless the fees and expenses charged by mutual funds are fairly consistent. A mutual fund prospectus has a separate table with a breakdown of expenses. This table typically shows the different charges paid for either directly by shareholders or out of shareholders' earnings in the fund: load charges, redemption fees, shareholder accounting costs, 12(b)–1 fees (explained below), distribution costs, and other expenses.

The mutual fund industry has been criticized for its proliferation of fees and charges. Granted, these are all disclosed by the mutual funds, but you need to know where to look to find the less obvious fees.

Load Funds versus No-Load Funds

A *no-load* fund is a fund whose shares are sold without a sales charge. In other words, you do not pay any fees to buy or sell shares in the fund. With an investment of $10,000 in a no-load fund, every cent of the $10,000 is used to buy shares in the fund. No-load funds sell directly to investors at the NAV per share.

A *load fund* is a fund whose shares are sold to investors at a price that includes a sales commission. The selling price or offer price exceeds the NAV. These fees can be quite substantial, ranging to as much as 8.5 percent of the purchase prices of the shares. The amount of the sales (load) charge per share can be determined by deducting the NAV price from the *offer price*. Table 14–4 illustrates how to determine the effective load charge of a fund. Some funds give quantity discounts on their loads to investors who buy shares in large blocks. For example, a sales load might be 5 percent for amounts less than $100,000, 4.25 percent for investments between $100,000 and $200,000, and 3.5 percent for amounts in excess of $200,000. Investors buying load funds need to determine whether a load is also charged on reinvested dividends.

Funds also can charge a *back-end load* or *exit fee*, which affects investors selling shares in the fund. A back-end load is a fee charged when shareholders sell their shares. The back-end load can be a straight percentage, or the percentage can decline the longer the shares are held in the fund. For example, if you sell $10,000 in a mutual fund with a 3 percent back-end (redemption) fee, you only receive $9,700 [10,000 − (0.03 × 10,000)].

The ultimate effect of a load charge is to reduce the total return. The effect of a load charge is felt more keenly if the fund is held for a short time. For example, if a fund has a return of 6 percent and charges a 4 percent load to buy into the fund, your total return for the year is sharply reduced. If you must pay a back-end load to exit a fund, this charge could be even more expensive than a front-end load when the share price has increased. This is so because the load percentage is calculated on a larger amount.

TABLE 14-4

How to Determine the Effective Load Charge

A mutual fund quotes its load charge as a percentage of its offer price, which understates the real charge paid by investors in load funds. For example, for a mutual fund with a load charge of 5 percent and a NAV as quoted in the newspapers of $25 per share, the load is based on the offer price, which must first be determined.

$$\text{Offer price} = \text{NAV}/(1 - \text{load percent})$$
$$= \$25/(1 - 0.05)$$
$$= \$26.32$$

The investor pays a load fee of $1.32 per share ($26.32 − $25.00), which is a 5 percent charge of the offer price. However, this load charge as a percentage of the NAV is higher than 5 percent.

$$\text{Effective load charge} = \text{load charge}/\text{NAV}$$
$$= \$1.32/\$25.00$$
$$= 5.28 \text{ percent}$$

You should not be fooled by funds that tout themselves as no-load funds and assess fees by other names that come right out of investors' pockets like loads. These fees are not called loads, but they work exactly like loads. Their uses are to defray some of the costs of opening accounts or buying stocks for the fund's portfolio. The fees vary from 1 to 3 percent among the different fund groups. From an investor's point of view, the lofty purpose of these fees should not matter. They reduce the amount of the investment.

Why, then, do so many people invest in load funds when the commissions eat away so much of their returns? Some possible answers are

- Investors do not want to make decisions about which funds to invest in, so they leave those decisions to their brokers and financial planners.
- Brokers and financial planners earn their living by selling investments for which they are paid commissions. These investments include only load funds and funds that pay commissions out of 12(b)–1 fees. These funds are promoted as the best ones to buy.
- No-load funds and funds that do not pay commissions to brokers and financial planners are not promoted or sold by brokers and financial planners.

No evidence exists to support the opinions expressed by many brokers and financial planners that load funds outperform no-load funds. According to a study on the long-term performance of mutual funds, there was no statistical difference between the performance of no-load funds and load funds over a 10-year period (Kuhle and Pope, 2000). However, after adjusting for sales commissions, investors would have been better off with no-load funds.

A *12(b)–1 fee* is a charge a mutual fund can take from investment assets to cover marketing expenses. A 12(b)–1 fee is less obvious than a load. This type of fee is charged by many funds to recover expenses for marketing and distribution. This type of fee, assessed annually, can be steep when added to a load fee. Many no-load funds boast the absence of sales commissions and then tack on 12(b)–1 fees, which resemble hidden loads. A 1 percent 12(b)–1 fee might not sound like much, but it results in $100 per year less in your pocket on a $10,000 mutual fund investment.

In addition to the above-mentioned charges, funds have *management fees* that are paid to the managers who administer the portfolio of investments. These fees can range from a 0.5 to 2 percent of assets. High management fees also take a toll on an investor's total return.

All fees bear watching because they reduce yields and total returns. Critics of the mutual fund industry have cultivated a sense of awareness regarding the proliferation of these charges. Indeed, do not be deceived by funds that claim to be what they are not. Lowering or eliminating front-end loads doesn't mean that a fund cannot add fees somewhere else. Many new funds waive some of their fees. Check to see whether and when these waivers are set to expire or whether they can be revoked.

A fund has to disclose its fees. You can find management fees, 12(b)–1 fees, redemption fees (back-end loads), and any other fees charged somewhere in the fund's prospectus.

Selected Per-Share Data and Ratios

Table 14–5 summarizes a typical fund's performance over the periods shown, and this information can be found in the fund's prospectus or annual report. Although the selected per-share data vary in detail from fund to fund, the format is essentially the same.

The "Investment Activities" section of Table 14–5 shows the amount of investment income earned on the securities held by the fund; this income is passed on to the fund's shareholders. For instance, in 2006, all of the net investment income of $0.37 was distributed to the shareholders (line 4), but in 2005, only $0.30 of the $0.31 of net income was paid out to shareholders. In 2005, the $0.01 that was not distributed to shareholders increased the NAV (line 7) in the "Capital Changes" section. (The capital loss and distribution of gains were reduced by this $0.01 because it was not distributed.)

Capital gains and losses also affect the NAV. Funds distribute their realized capital gains (line 6), but the unrealized capital gains or losses also increase or decrease the NAV.

Changes in the NAV from year to year give some idea of the volatility in share price. For instance, for the year 2005, the NAV decreased by $1.01, which is a 9.17 percent decrease. If you invest $10,000 knowing that it could decline to $9,082.65 (a 9.17 percent decline), how comfortable would you feel with this investment in the short term?

The portfolio turnover rate gives prospective investors an idea of how actively the investment assets in a fund are traded.

TABLE 14-5

Selected Per-Share Data and Ratios

	2006	2005	2004
NAV			
Beginning of the year	$10.02	$11.01	$10.73
Investment Activities			
Line 1: Income	0.40	0.35	0.55
Line 2: Expenses	(0.03)	(0.04)	(0.05)
Line 3:Net investment income	0.37	0.31	0.50
Line 4: Distribution of dividends	(0.37)	(0.30)	(0.47)
Capital Changes			
Line 5: Net realized and unrealized gains (losses) on investments	1.00	(0.75)	1.50
Line 6: Distributions of realized gains	(0.70)	(0.25)	(1.25)
Line 7: Net increase (decrease) to NAV	0.30	(0.99)	0.28
NAV beginning of the year	10.02	11.01	10.73
NAV at end of year	10.32	10.02	11.01
Ratio of operating expenses to average net assets	0.53%	0.56%	0.58%
Ratio of net investment income to average net assets	0.45%	0.46%	0.84%
Portfolio turnover rate	121%	135%	150%
Shares outstanding (000)	10,600	8,451	6,339

A turnover rate of 100 percent indicates that the investment assets are sold an average of once during the year. For example, if a fund holds stocks with a value of $100 million, that means $100 million of stocks are traded once a year with a 100 percent turnover rate. According to Morningstar Mutual Funds, as reported by the Vanguard Group (1999), the average stock mutual fund turnover was 86 percent. High portfolio turnover (more than 200 percent) might not necessarily be bad for shareholders in that the fund might be generating high capital gains.

High turnover is an indication, however, for shareholders to expect capital gains distributions by the end of the year. In accounting terms, the amount of the distribution per share is deducted from the NAV of the shares in the fund.

Index funds have extremely low turnover, around 5 percent (The Vanguard Group, 1999). The advantages of lower turnover are decreased costs and greater tax efficiency. A fund also might have low turnover because it has been holding low-performing stocks for a long time in the hopes of a turnaround. This situation has occurred with many value funds where value stocks did not participate in the stock market rally of the three years from 1996 to 1999.

The ratio of operating expenses to average net assets is fairly low in the example in Table 14–5 (close to one-half of 1 percent).

You can determine an average total return by considering the three types of returns on a mutual fund—dividends distributed, capital gains distributed, and changes in share price—by using the following formula:

$$\text{Average total return} = \frac{\dfrac{\text{dividend} + \text{capital gains distributions} + \text{ending NAV} - \text{beginning NAV}}{\text{number of years}}}{\dfrac{\text{ending NAV} + \text{beginning NAV}}{2}}$$

$$\text{Average total return for 2006} = \frac{\{(0.37 + 0.70) + [(10.32 - 10.02)/1]\}}{[(10.32 + 10.02)/2]} = 13.50\%$$

This simple 13.5 percent yield indicates that an investor in this fund received double-digit returns mainly because of gains realized and increases in the NAV share price. The more volatile the NAV of the fund is, the greater the likelihood there is of unstable returns.

THE RISKS OF MUTUAL FUNDS

The major risk of investing in a mutual fund is the *risk of loss of principal* owing to a decline in NAV. Many types of risk exist: interest-rate risk, market risk, and quality of the securities, to name a few. Rising market interest rates tend to depress both the stock and the bond markets, resulting in a decline in the NAVs of stock and bond funds. A decline in market rates of interest results in an appreciation of stock and bond prices (and the NAVs of stock and bond funds).

The *quality of securities* determines the volatility of the fund's price swings. Stock funds that invest in small-company stocks and emerging growth stocks see greater upward swings in price during bull markets and greater downward swings during bear markets than conservative income equity funds, which invest in the stocks of larger, more established companies. Some small-cap funds have invested in small-cap stocks of dubious value, which has caused some losses to their funds.

With bank failures in the past and the shaky financial status of some savings and loan associations in the United States, investors are naturally concerned about the *risk of insolvency* of mutual funds. A mutual fund can always "go under," but the chance of it happening is small. The key distinction between banks and mutual funds is the way in which mutual funds are set up, which reduces the risk of failure and loss owing to fraud.

Mutual funds typically are corporations owned by shareholders. A separate management company is contracted by shareholders to run the fund's daily operations. Although a management company oversees the fund's investments, the company does not have possession of the assets (investments). A custodian, such as a bank, holds the investments. Therefore, if a management company gets into financial trouble, it does not have access to the fund's investments. Yet, even with these checks and balances, the possibility of fraud always exists. The SEC cleared two mutual funds whose prices were quoted in the financial newspapers along with all the other mutual funds, but they turned out to be bogus funds.

A transfer agent maintains shareholders' accounts and keeps track of shareholders' purchases and redemptions. In addition, management companies carry fidelity bonds, a form of insurance to protect the investments of the fund against malfeasance or fraud perpetrated by its employees.

Along with these safeguards, two other factors differentiate mutual funds from corporations such as banks and savings and loan associations:

- Mutual funds must be able to redeem shares on demand, which means that a portion of its investment assets must be liquid.
- Mutual funds must be able to price their investments at the end of each day, which is known as *marking to market*. This adjustment of market values of investments at the end of the trading day reflects gains and losses.

For these reasons, mutual funds cannot hide their financial difficulties as easily as banks and savings and loans can.

The SEC regulates mutual funds, but as noted earlier in this chapter, fraudulent operators can always find a way into any industry. Although the risk of fraud is always present, it is no greater in the mutual fund industry than in any other industry. Above all, you should be aware that you can lose money through purchasing a fund whose investments perform poorly on the markets.

THE TAX CONSEQUENCES OF BUYING AND SELLING SHARES IN A MUTUAL FUND

Tax reporting on mutual funds can be complicated. At the end of the year, the mutual fund sends to each mutual fund shareholder a Form 1099 showing the amount of dividends and capital gains received during the year. Individual shareholders pay taxes on their dividends and capital gains. When you automatically reinvest your dividends and capital gains in your funds, these amounts need to be added into the cost basis when you sell shares in the fund.

Suppose that you invested $10,000 in a fund two years ago and reinvested a total of $2,000 in dividends and capital gains in the fund to date. You then sell all shares in the fund and receive $14,000. Your cost basis is $12,000 (not $10,000), and the gain on the sale of the shares is $2,000 ($14,000 − $12,000).

When you sell only a portion of your total shares, the calculation is different and can be tricky. It is further complicated when you actively buy and sell shares as though the fund were a checking account. In fact, many mutual funds encourage you to operate your funds like a checking account by providing check-writing services. Every time you write a check against a bond or stock fund, a capital gain or loss tax consequence occurs. This does not include money market funds, which have a stable share price of $1. These actions can cause a nightmare at tax time and produce extra revenue for your accountant for the additional time spent calculating gains and losses. Consequently, you need to keep records of your mutual fund transactions by saving all the monthly statements showing purchases and sales of shares, dividends, and capital gain distributions.

From these records you can determine the cost basis of shares sold using an average-cost method, the FIFO method, or the specific identification method.

The FIFO method (which stands for first in, first out) uses the cost of the first shares purchased in the fund as the first to be sold. Table 14–6 illustrates the FIFO method of calculating a capital gain or loss on the partial sale of shares in a mutual fund. The example shows that the earliest shares purchased are the first to be used in the sale of shares. After all the shares of the invested funds are sold, the basis of the dividend and capital gain shares is used to determine any gain or loss. During periods of rising share prices, using this method results in a higher tax liability than the average-cost method.

The average-cost method is an accounting method in which the average cost per share is determined by dividing the number of shares available into the total cost of the shares in the fund. Several funds provide the gains and losses on an average-cost basis when investors sell shares. The average-cost method allows shareholders to average the cost of the shares in the fund. The average-cost basis can get quite complex with additional sales and purchases of shares. Consequently, some funds don't provide average-cost data after shareholders redeem shares in the fund.

The specific identification method allows shareholders to identify the specific shares that they want to sell. You can minimize

TABLE 14-6

Calculation of Gains/Losses on the Sale of Shares

Summary of Growth and Income Fund					
Date	Transaction	Dollar Amount	Share Price	No. of Shares	Total No. of Shares
6/14	Invest	$15,000	$10.00	1,500	1,500
11/26	Invest	4,500	9.00	500	2,000
11/30	Redeem (sell)	18,600	12.00	(1,550)	450
12/31	Dividends	1,000	10.00	100	550

To Calculate Gain/Loss on a FIFO Basis

Sold: 1,550 shares at $12.00 per share

Sale price: $18,600

Cost basis

06/14 1,500 shares at $10.00 = $15,000

11/26 50 shares at $9.00 = $450

Total cost: $15,450

Gain $3,150

Cost Basis of the Growth and Income Fund after Sale					
Date	Transaction	Dollar Amount	Share Price	No. of Shares	Total No. of Shares
11/26	Invest	$4,050	$9.00	450	450
12/31	Dividends	1,000	10.00	100	550

your gains by choosing to sell shares with the highest cost basis first. However, to get Internal Revenue Service (IRS) acceptance of this method, you must specify to the fund in writing which shares are to be sold and must receive a written confirmation of the sale by the fund. If the specific shares are not identified, the IRS assumes that the shares sold are the first acquired.

The specific identification method works as follows: Suppose that you buy 100 shares at $7 per share and six months later buy another 100 shares at $14 per share. You decide to sell 100 shares at $20 per share. If you specifically identify the shares bought at $14 per share, the capital gain is $6 per share ($20 − $14). Using the average-cost method, the cost basis is $10.50 per share ($2,100/200 shares), and the capital gain is $9.50 per share. Using FIFO, the shares sold are those purchased first at $7 per share, resulting in a gain of $13 per share.

If you use the average-cost method to sell shares in a fund, you cannot switch to the specific identification method for subsequent sales. This limitation does not preclude investor from choosing other methods to sell shares in any other funds that you own.

For individual stocks, investors cannot use the average-cost method, but specific identification and FIFO methods are acceptable.

To minimize the complexities of computations, you are better off not writing checks on your stock or bond funds for your short-term cash needs. This practice only creates gains or losses. You are better served by investing the money needed for short-term purposes into a money market fund, which alleviates any complex tax calculations.

Hidden Capital Gains

You have no control over the distribution of hidden capital gains from mutual funds, which can upset careful tax planning. Because investment companies do not pay taxes, all income and capital gains in the fund are passed through to shareholders. If a fund has bought and sold investments at a gain, these gains are passed on to shareholders when the fund distributes its gains. Shareholders are liable for the taxes on these capital gains even if the share price of the fund has dipped below the purchase price.

The following example illustrates this concept: Suppose that you purchase 1,000 shares in a mutual fund at $10 per share. The next day the mutual fund distributes capital gains of $2 per share. The share price declines to $8 per share ($10 – $2 capital gain per share). You now have 1,250 shares at an NAV of $8 per share ($2,000 capital gain ÷ $8 NAV = 250 shares). If you continue to hold the shares until year-end, you are liable for the taxes on the $2,000 distribution of capital gains. If you decide to sell all the shares in the fund when the distribution is made at the NAV of $8 per share, you receive $10,000 and experience a loss of $2,000 ($10,000 in proceeds minus the adjusted cost basis of shares is $12,000). This loss is offset by the capital gains distribution, and no tax consequences occur.

In another scenario, suppose that you hold the shares and the share price declines below $8 per share. You are still faced with $2,000 of capital gains, even though the principal is now less than the $10,000 invested. This happened at the end of 2001 when the stock market declined during the latter half of the year. Investors were saddled with capital gains distributions while their principal diminished because of the decline in their funds' NAVs.

New investors should avoid buying into a mutual fund toward the end of the year because they can increase their tax burden from hidden capital gains. Before buying into a fund, investors should investigate whether the fund has accumulated any capital gains distributions that have not been distributed to shareholders. These gains are passed on to shareholders at the end of the year through a capital gains distribution, even if the shareholders did not own the fund when the gains were incurred.

Hidden Capital Losses

Hidden capital losses have the opposite effect from hidden capital gains. For example, a mutual fund with an NAV of $10 per share at the beginning of the year might accumulate capital losses of $3 per share because of a declining market in which investments are sold at a loss during the year. If you purchased the shares at $10 per share and sell them at $7 per share, you have a capital loss of $3 per share. You can use this loss to offset capital gains or income up to the allowable limit ($3,000 for 2005). However, if you buy shares at $7 per share and then sell them later at $14 per share, you have a capital gain of $4, not $7, per share. The reason is that the fund has accumulated a $3-per-share loss, which means that the adjusted cost basis of the shares in the fund is $10 (the capital loss is added to the cost of the shares).

Unrealized capital losses in a mutual fund offer potential tax savings for investors in a fund in the same way that unrealized

TABLE 14-7

Tax-Efficient Investing Strategies

Successful investing requires building a portfolio of securities that can generate healthy after-tax returns for long periods of time. This is more than merely minimizing taxes on dividends received and capital gains. For stock investments, a tax-minimization strategy would be to buy stocks that pay dividends and offer the prospects of long-term capital gains because both dividends and long-term capital gains (if held for more than one year) are taxed at lower rates than interest income. However, in the early 2000s, with the decline in the stock market, there has been a greater focus on dividend-paying stocks, which tend to drop less in price than growth stocks that don't pay dividends. Thus one approach to a declining stock market is to focus on quality stocks that pay dividends.

Hold appreciated stocks for at least one year to take advantage of the favorable capital gains tax rates. If the stock has appreciated and the future prospects for the stock do not look good, sell the stock even if you have held it for less than one year. It is better to have short-term gains than long-term losses.

If you have stocks with losses and the stocks' future prospects are not good, sell them to take the losses. You can use these losses to offset capital gains. In addition, you can use losses exceeding capital gains to offset income up to $3,000 (married filing jointly) or carry the losses forward indefinitely to offset future gains. Timing your gains and losses can reduce the amount of your taxes. If you have large capital losses, you can sell stocks with large capital gains to offset those losses.

---

capital gains offer tax liabilities to investors in a fund. Table 14–7 summarizes investment strategies that take advantage of the existing tax treatment of investment income.

SHOULD AN INVESTOR INVEST IN INDIVIDUAL SECURITIES OR USE FUNDS?

Stock and bond mutual funds have been popular among investors, and record amounts have been invested in them over the years. The advantages of mutual funds, as stated earlier in this chapter, are the use of professional management, diversification, the freedom to invest small amounts of money, and the ease of buying and selling. For many investors, these advantages far outweigh the disadvantages of mutual funds.

Mutual funds might be the most practical way for investors to buy many types of securities, including bonds that sell in high denominations (minimum investments of $50,000) and to build a diversified portfolio of stocks. The decision of which individual stocks to invest in can be avoided by choosing equity mutual funds.

Diversification achieved by mutual funds minimizes the effect of any unexpected losses from individual stocks in the portfolio. Also, the professional managers of these funds have quicker access to information about the different issues. The managers might react sooner in buying or selling the securities in question.

However, in certain cases, a strong argument exists for buying individual securities over mutual funds. The rates of return on individual stocks and bonds are often greater than those earned from mutual funds. This statement is true even for no-load funds because in addition to sales commissions, other fees, such as 12(b)–1 and operating fees, reduce the returns of mutual funds. By investing in individual securities, you avoid these fees. A study by Malkiel (1995, pp. 549–572) during the period 1971–1991 on the performance of equity mutual funds indicates that on a yearly basis throughout this period, the top-performing funds in one year could easily become underperforming funds in the next year. This phenomenon occurred more in the 1980s than in the 1970s.

If you have a small amount of money to invest, mutual funds are a better alternative. A $2,000 investment in a stock fund buys a fraction of a diversified portfolio of stocks, whereas for individual securities this amount might allow for buying only the shares of one equity company. Investing in mutual funds is good strategy if you do not have enough money to diversify your investments and do not have the time, expertise, or inclination to select and manage

TABLE 14-8

Characteristics of Individual Securities versus Mutual Funds

	Individual Securities	Mutual Funds
Diversification	Achieved only if a large number of securities is purchased.	Achieved with a small investment.
Ease of buying and selling	Easy to buy and sell stocks at real-time prices during the trading day. More difficult to buy bonds	Easy to buy and sell shares. Trades occur only at the closing price at the end of the day
Professional management	No	Yes
Expenses and costs to buy and sell	Brokerage fees to buy and sell.	Low to high expenses depending on fund.
Tax planning	Easier to predict income and plan capital gains and losses.	Can upset careful tax planning owing to unpredictable distributions of income and capital gains.

individual securities. In addition, a number of funds offer you the opportunity to invest in the types of securities that would be difficult to buy individually.

Table 14–8 compares some characteristics of investing in individual securities versus mutual funds.

REFERENCES

Clements, Jonathan. "Wall Street's Latest: Mini-Hedge Funds." *Wall Street Journal*, March 26, 2002, p. C1.

Kuhle, James L., and Ralph A Pope. "A Comprehensive Long-Term Performance Analysis of Load versus No-Load Mutual Funds." *Journal of Financial and Strategic Decisions* 13 (Summer 2000): 1–11.

Malkiel, Burton G. "Returns from Investing in Equity Mutual Funds 1971–1991." *Journal of Finance* 50 (June 1995): 549–572.

Maxey, Daisy. "At Hedge Funds, Study Exit Guidelines." *Wall Street Journal*, September 23, 2006, p. B4.

Scholl, Jaye, and Andrew Bary. "A Lousy New Year." *Barron's*, October 12, 1998, p. 19.

The Vanguard Group. "FUNDamentals: Turnover." www.Vanguard.com; accessed March 11, 1999.

CHAPTER 15

Closed-End Funds

KEY CONCEPTS

- What closed-end funds are and how they work
- The different types of closed-end funds, unit investment trusts, and real estate investment trusts
- The different sources of risk of closed-end funds
- Times when it is advantageous to invest in individual securities or to use mutual funds or closed-end funds

---

Investment Snapshot

- According to the Investment Company Institute (www.ici.org), closed-end funds had a total of $285.8 billion invested as of September 2006.
- For the third quarter of 2006, there were 196 closed-end stock funds.
- Shares of closed-end funds are traded on the stock exchanges.
- Shares of closed-end funds can trade at a discount or a premium to their net asset values.

A *closed-end* fund issues a fixed number of shares, and when all the shares issued are sold, no more are issued. In other words, closed-end funds have fixed capital structures. Investors who want to invest in closed-end funds after all the shares are sold (for the first time) have to buy them from shareholders who are willing to sell them in the market. Shares of closed-end funds are listed on stock exchanges and over-the-counter (OTC) markets, whereas shares of open-end mutual funds are bought from and sold to the investment company sponsoring the fund. As a result, share prices of closed-end funds are a function not only of their net asset values but also of the supply of and demand for the stock in the market.

A unit investment trust (UIT) is another type of closed-end fund. A *unit investment trust* issues a fixed number of shares, which are sold originally by the sponsor of the trust. The proceeds from the sale are used to buy stocks or bonds for the trust, which are held to maturity. Unlike an open-end or closed-end fund, no active trading of the securities in the portfolio takes place. Consequently, no active management of the trust takes place, which should translate into lower management fees, although this is not always the case. A trust has a maturity date, and the proceeds are then returned to the shareholders of the trust.

All UITs charge sales commissions, whereas investors in open-end funds have a choice between the purchase of a fund that does or does not charge a sales commission. Table 15–1 illustrates the differences between open-end and closed-end funds.

TABLE 15-1

Closed-End versus Open-End Funds

Closed-End Funds	Open-End Funds
1. Issue a fixed number of shares, which are sold to original shareholders.	1. Issue an unlimited number of shares.
2. Shares (after issue) are traded on the stock exchanges.	2. Shares (including new shares) may be bought (and sold) from (and to) the fund.
3. Shares may trade at, above, or below net asset value.	3. Shares trade at net asset value.
4. Share prices depend not only on the fundamentals but also on the supply of and demand for the shares.	4. Share prices depend on the fundamentals of the assets in the fund.
5. Closed-end funds do not mature; UITs do.	5. Open-end funds do not mature except for zero-coupon funds

CLOSED-END FUNDS

Closed-end funds issue a fixed number of shares that are traded on the stock exchange or OTC market. When the shares are sold, the fund does not issue more shares. These funds have professional managers who assemble and manage the investment portfolios according to the goals and objectives of the funds. Unlike open-end funds, closed-end funds do not trade at their net asset values (NAVs). Instead, their share prices are based on the supply of and demand for their funds and other fundamental factors. Consequently, closed-end funds can trade at premiums or discounts to their NAVs as shown in Table 15–2. Closed-end fund prices can be obtained from financial newspapers or from Web sites on the Internet.

Shares of closed-end funds are bought and sold through brokers. You should be aware of the following facts about the purchase of closed-end funds:

- Brokerage firms underwrite and sell newly issued shares of closed-end funds.
- The brokerage fees on these newly issued shares can be quite high, which then erodes the price of the shares when they trade on the market. For example, if a closed-end fund sells 1 million shares at $10 per share and there is a brokerage commission of 7 percent, the fund receives

TABLE 15-2

Closed-End Fund Premiums and Discounts

Company	NAV	Market Price*	Premium/Discount
Gabelli Equity Trust	9.44	9.57	1.4%
ASA Bermuda, Ltd.	73.59	64.11	−12.9%
How to Calculate the Discount or Premium			
Premium (discount) = (market price − NAV)/NAV			
Gabelli Trust premium = (9.57 − 9.44)/ 9.44			
= 1.4%			

* Prices as of December 4, 2006.

$9.3 million to invest ($700,000 is deducted from the $10 million proceeds). The share price drops in value from the $10 originally paid and trades at a discount to the offer price.

- Another reason not to buy newly issued shares in a closed-end fund is that the portfolio of investments has not yet been constituted, so investors do not know what the investment assets are and, in the case of bond funds, the yields on those investments.

UNIT INVESTMENT TRUSTS

UITs are registered investment companies that sell units (shares) of a relatively fixed investment portfolio consisting of bonds or stocks. UITs have a stated termination date when the investments either mature or are liquidated. The proceeds are then returned to the unit-holders (shareholders). Consequently, these trusts are well suited to bonds, with their streams of income and maturity of principal. With stock UITs, the stocks are sold at the termination date, and the proceeds are returned to the unit-holders. The majority of UITs sold consists of tax-exempt municipal bonds, followed by taxable bond trusts and then equity (stock) trusts.

UITs are bought through brokers who sponsor their own trusts and through brokerage firms that represent the trusts. If you do not want to hold your trust through maturity, you can sell it back to the sponsor of the trust. The trust sponsors are required by law to buy the shares back at their NAVs, which can be more or less than the amount the investor paid initially. Under certain conditions, shares of these trusts can be quite illiquid, particularly for bond trusts when interest rates are rising.

The same caveats apply for buying initial public offerings (IPOs) of UITs as for closed-end funds:

- Investors do not know the composition of the portfolio's investments.
- Investors pay sales charges or loads, which may be as much as 4 to 5 percent higher than the NAVs.

In a UIT, the portfolio of investments generally does not change after purchase. In other words, no new securities are bought or sold. Theoretically, therefore, management fees should be lower on UITs than on closed-end funds because the portfolio remains unmanaged. The only time securities are sold in a UIT is generally when a severe decline in the quality of the issues occurs. Consequently, no management fees should be incurred on a UIT. In most instances this is not the case, and fees can be high.

REAL ESTATE INVESTMENT TRUSTS

A *real estate investment trust* (REIT) is a fund that buys and manages real estate and real estate mortgages. REITs offer individual investors the opportunity to invest in real estate without having to own and manage individual properties. REITs were popular during the middle of the 1990s when inflation was expected to surge. In 2001–2002, when the stock market declined, investors again turned to REITs as safe-haven investments. When interest rates declined in 2005–2006, REITs were among the top-performing sectors of the stock market.

A REIT is a form of closed-end mutual fund in that it invests in real estate the proceeds received from the initial sale of shares to shareholders. REITs buy, develop, and manage real estate properties and pass on to shareholders the income from the rents and mortgages in the form of dividends.

REITs do not pay corporate income taxes, but in return, they must, by law, distribute 95 percent of their net income to shareholders. Consequently, not much income remains to finance future real estate acquisitions.

Following are three basic types of REITs:

- *Equity REITs* buy, operate, and sell real estate such as hotels, office buildings, apartments, and shopping centers.
- *Mortgage REITs* make construction and mortgage loans available to developers.
- *Hybrid REITs*, a combination of equity and mortgage REITs, buy, develop, and manage real estate and provide financing through mortgage loans. Most hybrid REITs have stronger positions in either equity or debt. Few well-balanced hybrid REITs exist.

The risks are not the same for each type of REIT, so you should evaluate each type carefully before investing. Equity REITs generally tend to be less speculative than mortgage REITs, although the risk level depends on the makeup of the assets in the trust. Mortgage REITs lend money to developers, which involves a greater risk. Consequently, shares of mortgage REITs tend to be more volatile than shares of equity REITs, particularly during a recession.

Equity REITs have been the most popular type of REIT recently. Their cumulative performance of 55 percent total returns since year-end 1999 through August 2002 have outpaced the Standard & Poor's (S&P) 500 Index, which declined by 35 percent for the same period (Clements, 2002, p. D1). Equity REITs derive their income from rents received from the properties in their portfolios and from increasing property values.

Mortgage REITs are more sensitive than equity REITs to changes in interest rates in the economy. The reason is that mortgage REITs hold mortgages whose prices move in the opposite direction of interest rates. Although equity REITs may be less sensitive to changes in interest rates, they too suffer the consequences of rising interest rates. Mortgage REITs generally do well when interest rates fall. Because of the different property holdings in mortgage REITs, they tend to be more income oriented in that their emphasis is on current yields, whereas equity REITs offer the potential for capital gains in addition to current income. For example, Annaly Mortgage Management, Inc. (a mortgage REIT), paid a dividend yield of 9 percent in the first quarter of 2005, which was a premium dividend rate to stock and bond yields.

REITs can have either finite or perpetual lives. Finite-life REITs, also known as *FREITs*, are self-liquidating. In the case of equity REITs, the properties are sold at the end of a specified period. In mortgage REITs, profits are paid to shareholders when the mortgages are paid up.

Little correlation exists in the performance of REITs and the stock market. Consequently, investors should hold a small percentage (no more than 5 percent) of their investment assets in REITs. Table 15–3 lists some of the guidelines for buying REITs.

TABLE 15-3

Guidelines for Selecting REITs

- Investigate a REIT before buying into it. Get the REIT's annual report from a broker, or call the REIT directly. You also can get additional information from the National Association of Real Estate Investment Trusts, 1101 17th Street N.W., Washington, D.C. 20036.
- Look to see how long the specific REIT has been in business. How long have its managers been in the real estate business, and how well do they manage the REIT's assets? How much of a personal stake do its managers have in the REIT? According to Byrne (1994, p. 32), insiders should own at least 10 percent of the stock.
- Look at the REIT's debt level. The greater the level of debt, the greater is the risk because more of the revenue is needed to service the debt. If a downturn in revenue occurs, interest payments become harder to service. Look for REITs with debt-to-equity ratios of less than 50 percent (Byrne, 1994, p. 32).
- Don't choose a REIT because it has the highest yield. The higher the yield, the greater is the risk. In some cases, underwriters raise the yields to hide poor fundamentals (Zuckerman, 1994, p. 35).
- Select REITs that have low price-to-book values (1:1 or less).
- Check the REIT's dividend record. Be wary of REITs that have recently cut their dividends. Check the source of cash for the payment of dividends. Cash for dividends should come from operations, not from the sale of properties.
- Location is everything in real estate. Look at the locations of the properties in the trust. Avoid REITs that have invested in overbuilt or depressed locations.

Caveats

- Avoid REITs that are blind pools. These might be set up by well-known management firms that raise funds to invest in unidentified properties. Before investing in any project, it is important to see what the real estate assets and liabilities in any project are.
- Investors should not invest more than 5 percent of their total investment portfolio in REITs.

WHAT ARE THE RISKS OF CLOSED-END MUTUAL FUNDS AND UITS?

Both closed-end bond funds and UITs are subject to *interest-rate risk*. When market rates of interest increase, generally prices of stock issues held in both UITs and closed-end funds decline. This means lower fund share prices. Moreover, this is a double-edged sword in that if there is selling pressure on the fund's shares, the decline in share prices will be even greater than the decline in NAV. The opposite is true in that if interest rates decline, there will be appreciation in the assets and, of course, in the share price. For both closed-end funds and UITs, there is the risk that share prices will fall way below NAVs owing to excess selling pressure in the stock markets. Then, of course, the danger arises of not being able to recoup the original price paid for the shares when selling. This is a common phenomenon experienced by closed-end funds and UITs.

For UIT shareholders, there is the added risk of not getting back the full amount of their original investments at maturity. This can be caused by a number of factors. The composition of the trust's assets, commissions, high management fees charged to the trust; and the use of leverage are all factors that can add to the risk of loss of principal. The managers of UITs and closed-end bond funds charge in many cases very generous annual fees, in addition to their up-front commissions on the original sale of the shares. This means that these funds will have to earn spectacular returns in order for the managers of these funds to be able to collect their fees without eroding yields significantly; also, they will have to rake up some capital gains to be able to recoup the sales commissions in order to return to the shareholders their entire investments at maturity. This explains why many UITs use leverage and resort to derivative securities as ways to try and boost their returns.

The types of investments that a fund or trust holds has a marked effect on the NAV, as well as the volatility of the share price. Unfortunately for the original shareholders of closed-end bond funds and UITs, there is no way of knowing the composition of the portfolio investments when they originally subscribe to the shares of the fund/trust. This is so because only after the original shareholders invest their money to buy the shares do the managers of the fund or trust buy the investment assets. Thus original shareholders may not be able to evaluate the levels of risk of the assets until the portfolio has been constituted. The composition may include the stocks of highly risky companies. Investors then trying to exit the fund or trust may experience losses from the decline in share price. If there is an exodus of shareholders from UITs and closed-end funds, shareholders may find it difficult to sell their shares without taking large losses.

SHOULD AN INVESTOR INVEST IN INDIVIDUAL SECURITIES OR USE FUNDS?

Stock closed-end funds offer investors the opportunity to invest in diversified portfolios of different sectors of the economy and foreign countries, just like mutual funds. The advantages of both closed-end funds and mutual funds are the use of professional management, diversification, the freedom to invest small amounts of money, and the ease of buying and selling. For many investors, these advantages far outweigh their disadvantages. Decisions of which individual stocks to invest in are avoided by choosing equity mutual funds and closed-end funds.

An advantage of a closed-end fund over a mutual fund is that closed-end funds can trade at a discount to their NAVs. This is akin to buying a dollar's worth of assets for less than a dollar. This strategy appeals to value investors, who have the patience to wait for the assets to rise in value.

Mutual fund managers can experience liquidity risk from excessive sales of shares by shareholders. Fund managers would have to sell some of their stock holdings to raise enough cash to be able to redeem the shares sold by shareholders. This does not happen in closed-end funds, allowing their managers to invest in less liquid investments, such as real estate and foreign company shares.

Investing in individual stocks and closed-end funds allows investors to choose their purchase and selling prices during the trading day. Mutual fund transactions are enacted at the NAV price as of the close of the trading day. Similarly, there are no minimum investment amounts stipulated with closed-end fund investments as there are with mutual funds. An investor can buy or sell a single share or in round lots of shares.

However, in certain cases, a strong argument exists for buying individual securities over mutual funds and closed-end funds. Returns on individual stocks could be greater than those earned from mutual funds and closed-end funds owing to fees charged by the funds. This statement is true even for no-load funds because in place of sales commissions, other fees, such as 12(b)–1 and management fees, reduce the returns of mutual funds. By investing in individual securities, you avoid these fees. Closed-end funds do not charge 12(b)–1 fees, but management fees can be high.

Investing in mutual funds and closed-end funds is a good strategy if you do not have enough money to diversify your investments and do not have the time, expertise, or inclination to select and manage individual securities. In addition, a wide range of funds offers you the opportunity to invest in the types of securities that would be difficult to buy individually.

Table 15–4 compares some characteristics of investing in individual securities versus mutual funds and closed-end funds.

TABLE 15-4

Characteristics of Individual Securities versus Mutual Funds and Closed-End Funds

	Individual Securities	Mutual Funds	Closed-End Funds
Diversification	Achieved only if a large number of securities is purchased	Achieved with a small investment	Achieved with a small investment
Ease of buying and selling	Easy to buy and sell stocks at real-time prices during the trading day. More difficult to buy bonds	Easy to buy and sell shares. Trades occur only at the closing price at the end of the day	Easy to buy and sell liquid closed-end funds
Professional management	No	Yes	Yes
Expenses and costs to buy and sell	Brokerage fees to buy and sell	Low to high expenses, depending on fund	Low to high expenses, depending on fund
Tax planning	Easier to predict income and plan capital gains and losses	Can upset careful tax planning owing to unpredictable distributions of income	Can upset careful tax planning owing to unpredictable distributions of income and capital gains

REFERENCES

Byrne, Thomas C. "Beyond Yield." *Individual Investor,* July 1994, p. 32.

Clements, Jonathan. "Its Not Too Late: Despite Recent Gains, REITs Can Still Generate Tidy Returns." *Wall Street Journal,* September 4, 2002, p. D1.

Clements, Jonathan. "Wall Street's Latest: Mini-Hedge Funds." *Wall Street Journal,* March 26, 2002, p. C1.

Kuhle, James L., and Ralph A. Pope. "A Comprehensive Long-Term Performance Analysis of Load vs. No-Load Mutual Funds." *Journal of Financial and Strategic Decisions* 13 (2000): 1–11.

Lauricella, Tom. "Is It an Offer Investors Can't Refuse?" *Wall Street Journal,* July 19, 2002, pp. C1, C15.

Malkiel, Burton G. *A Random Walk Down Wall Street.* New York: W.W. Norton, 1996.

Scholl, Jaye, and Andrew Bary. "A Lousy New Year." *Barron's,* October 12, 1998, p. 19.

The Vanguard Group. 1999. "FUNDamentals: Turnover," www.Vanguard.com; accessed March 11, 1999.

Young, Lauren. "ETFs: What the Buzz Is About." *BusinessWeek,* March 1, 2004, pp. 124–126.

Zuckerman, Lawrence. 'A Look Under the Hood at Realty Stocks." *New York Times,* July 16, 1994, p. 35.

Exchange-Traded Funds (ETFs)

KEY CONCEPTS

- Understanding ETFs
- The advantages and disadvantages of ETFs
- Should you invest in ETFs or pick individual stocks?

Investment Snapshot

- As of October 2006, there were 315 ETFs in the United States, of which 309 were stock ETFs (www.ici.org).
- The number of ETFs on the market grew by 57 percent for 10 months of 2006.
- ETFs are traded on the stock markets and not through investment companies.

Exchange-traded funds (ETFs) are baskets of stocks or bonds that track a broad-based index, sector of an index, or stocks in countries. ETFs are similar to closed-end mutual funds in that investors buy these listed shares on the stock exchanges. The predominant listings are on the American Stock Exchange (AMEX). These shares represent ownership in a portfolio of stocks or bonds that track a broad index or sector indexes. Investors buy or sell these shares through brokers just like they do with individual stocks. ETFs are priced based on the types of securities that they hold in addition to the supply of and demand for the shares. These shares can be sold short or bought in margin accounts, and they can be traded using market, limit, or stop orders.

The greatest competition to mutual funds has come from ETFs. ETFs have become popular investment alternatives to mutual funds for many investors who want diversification and low-cost investment options. The typical costs charged to investors in equity ETFs are 0.4 percent of assets annually compared with 1.4 percent of assets for the average equity mutual funds, according to Standard & Poor's (Young, 2004, p. 124).

There are over 300 ETFs to choose from; this number has grown significantly since the first ETF, the Standard & Poor's (S&P) Depository Receipts (known as *Spiders*) was introduced in 1993. Table 16–1 lists a few of the many ETFs traded on the market.

Some of the more popular ETFs are the SPDRs (Spiders) that track the S&P 500 Index; Diamonds, ticker symbol DIA, that track the 30 stocks in the Dow Jones Industrial Average; and the Qubes, ticker symbol QQQQ, that track ownership in the 100 largest stocks on the Nasdaq. There are numerous ETFs that are specialized in

TABLE 16-1

List of Some Exchange-Traded Funds

Name	Ticker Symbol	Category/Index
SPDRs	SPY	S&P 500 Index (large-cap)
Diamonds	DIA	Dow Jones Industrial Average (large-cap)
Nasdaq 100 Trust	QQQQ	100 Largest stocks on Nasdaq
iShares MSCI EAFE Index	EFA	International index (large-cap)
Semiconductor HOLDRs	SMH	Semiconductor stocks
BLDRS Asia 50 ADR	ADRA	Pacific/Asia stocks
BLDRS Europe 100 ADR	ADRU	European stocks
iShares Lehman TIPS Bond	TLT	Inflation government bonds
Pharmaceutical HOLDRs	PPH	Pharmaceutical stocks
Financial Select Sector	XLF	Financial stocks in S&P 500 Index
iShares Russell 2000	IWN	Small-cap stocks in Russell 2000 Index
iShares MSCI Spain	EWP	Spanish stocks

Note: For a complete list of ETFs visit the following Web sites: www.amex.com, www.ishares.com, www.yahoo.com and click on "Finance" and then on "ETFs."

sectors of the broad indexes (financial, technology, and industrials, for example) and in foreign stock market indexes [i Shares, which tracks the Morgan Stanley Capital International indexes (MSCI) for 20 countries and many regional sectors around the world]. Visit the AMEX Web site at www.amex.com for information on the various ETFs listed. See Table 16–2 for a description of spiders, diamonds, and the Nasdaq 100 tracking stock.

The description of the net asset value (NAV) implies that the share price of an ETF can trade above or below its NAV. This discrepancy generally will not occur because of the issuance by the

TABLE 16-2

More About Spiders, Diamonds, and Nasdaq 100 ETFs

There is a family of ETFs that is based on the S&P 500 Index and its component sectors, such as technology, energy, and financials, for example. The SPDR Trust holds shares of all companies in the S&P 500 Index. The purchase of a single share in this trust gives its owner a share of the 500 companies in the S&P 500 Index. Several select, specialized SPDRs allow investors to track, for example, the financials in the S&P 500 Index or the 79 tech stocks in the S&P 500 Index. Investors also can track the utilities, industrials, and five other sectors in the S&P 500 Index. These sector ETFs are traded just like the main SPDR (SPY).

The ETF that tracks the 30 stocks of the Dow Jones Industrial Average (DJIA) is called a Diamond (DIA). The purchase of a single share in this fund gives its owner a share of the 30 DJIA stocks.

The ETF that mirrors the 100 largest stocks in the Nasdaq is called a *Qube* (QQQQ). The purchase of a single share in this ETF gives its owner a share of these Nasdaq 100 stocks.

Following is a list of some of the features of these ETFs:

Trading. These ETFs are traded on the AMEX.

Approximate share price ratio. The values of shares of a Spider, Diamond, and Qube ETF in relation to the respective indexes tracked are 1/10 the value of the S&P 500 Index for 1 SPY share, 1/100 the value of the DJIA for 1 DIA share, and 1/20 the value of the Nasdaq 100 Index for 1 QQQQ share.

Dividends. Dividends are paid quarterly (in January, April, July, and October)

Risks. The risk for these ETFs is the same as experienced by individual stocks, namely, price fluctuations. There is also the additional risk that the fund may not replicate the exact performance of the underlying index because of expenses incurred by the fund.

Net asset value. The NAV per ETF is calculated at the close of each business day. The value represents the market value of the stocks in the underlying index, plus any accrued dividends and minus any expenses on a per-share basis.

Short selling. Investors can sell short these ETFs and on a downtick.

Source: American Stock Exchange, www.amex.com.

ETF of shares in kind. Whenever a discrepancy in price occurs and an institutional investor wants to exploit this price differential with large blocks of shares (a minimum of 50,000), the ETF trust redeems the shares with the underlying stocks in the index rather than paying cash. The institutional investor then sells the shares of the underlying stocks in the index, not the shares of the ETF, to realize the price discrepancy. This concept emphasizes the similarities between open-end mutual funds and ETFs. An ETF buys and sells shares and issues new shares when necessary. However, ETF investors can buy or sell shares at any time during the day on the stock exchanges, whereas transactions involving open-end mutual funds take place only at the end of the day at the closing NAV price. The major difference between an open-end mutual fund and an ETF is that when shareholders in mutual funds sell their shares, the mutual fund may have to sell securities to raise enough cash to pay shareholders, resulting in capital gain or loss transactions. With ETFs, traders buy the shares sold by investors, and this leaves the portfolio intact.

ADVANTAGES AND DISADVANTAGES OF ETFS

Because of the passive management of ETFs, fees are low, and the turnover of securities is low, which (similar to index mutual funds) results in low capital gains taxes. See Table 16–3 for the advantages and disadvantages of investing in ETFs.

SHOULD AN INVESTOR INVEST IN INDIVIDUAL SECURITIES OR USE ETFS OR FUNDS?

The diversification achieved by mutual funds, closed-end funds, and ETFs minimizes the effect of any unexpected losses from individual stocks and bonds in a portfolio. Also, professional managers of mutual and closed-end funds may have quicker access to information about the different issues and may react sooner in buying or selling the securities in question. ETFs are similar to index funds and are not actively managed.

For investors willing to manage their own portfolios, a strong argument exists for buying individual securities over mutual funds. The rates of return on individual stocks have the potential to be

TABLE 16-3

The Advantages and Disadvantages of Investing in ETFs

ETFs bear similarities to open-end mutual funds, index funds, and closed-end funds. Knowing the advantages and disadvantages of ETFs will help you to determine which type of investment is more suitable to your needs.

- ETFs offer diversification (similar to mutual funds), but they trade as stocks. Even though the stock prices of ETFs that track the different indexes fluctuate when markets are volatile, the effect of the fluctuations on each of the indexes may be more muted than in a portfolio of individual stocks.
- ETFs charge low fees and generally are tax efficient in the management of these securities, making them similar to index funds. (Some newly introduced ETFs to the market have increased their fees, which suggests that investors should check the fees charged before investing).
- ETFs are bought and sold through brokers, just like any other stocks on the market at real-time price quotes during the day. Mutual funds can only be traded once a day at their closing prices.
- Investors do not need large amounts of money to be able to buy ETFs, which gives them broad exposure to a market index, a sector of the market, or a foreign country.
- The disadvantage of ETFs is that investors incur commissions to buy and sell shares, whereas no-load mutual funds charge no transaction fees to buy or sell shares. These transaction costs to buy ETFs make it uneconomical for investors who typically invest small amounts of money on a frequent basis.
- Sector ETFs may be too concentrated in their sectors to share in the gains of their sectors. In 2006, the telecommunications sector had large returns that were not shared by some of the telecommunications sector ETFs (Salisbury, 2006, p. C11).

greater than those earned from mutual funds. This statement is true even for no-load funds because in addition to sales commissions, other fees, such as 12(b)–1 and operating fees, reduce the returns of mutual funds. By investing in individual securities, you avoid these fees. ETFs generally have lower management fees than mutual funds. However, commissions are charged to buy and sell individual stocks, ETFs, and closed-end funds.

If you have a small amount of money to invest, mutual funds and ETFs are better alternatives. A $2,000 investment in a stock fund buys a fraction of a diversified portfolio of stocks, whereas for individual securities, this amount might allow for buying only the shares of one equity company. Investing in mutual funds is good strategy if you do not have enough money to diversify your investments and do not have the time, expertise, or inclination to select and manage individual securities. In addition, a number of funds offer you the opportunity to invest in the types of securities

TABLE 16-4

Characteristics of Individual Securities versus Mutual Funds, Closed-End Funds, and ETFs

	Individual Securities	Mutual Funds	Closed-End Funds	ETFs
Diversification	Achieved only if a large number of securities is purchased	Achieved with a small investment.	Achieved with a small investment.	Achieved with a small investment.
Ease of buying and selling	Easy to buy and sell stocks at real-time prices during the trading day. More difficult to buy bonds.	Easy to buy and sell shares. Trades occur only at the closing price at the end of the day.	Easy to buy and sell liquid closed-end funds.	Easy to buy and sell ETFs at real-time prices during the day.
Professional management	No	Yes	Yes	Replicates a market index.
Expenses and costs to buy and sell	Brokerage fees to buy and sell.	Low to high expenses, depending on fund.	Low to high expenses, depending on fund.	Brokerage fees to buy and sell and low fees.
Tax planning	Easier to predict income and plan capital gains and losses.	Can upset careful tax planning owing to unpredictable distributions of income and capital gains.	Can upset careful tax planning owing to unpredictable distributions of income and capital gains.	More tax efficient than mutual funds.

that would be difficult to buy individually. ETF investors are not hampered by the minimum investment amounts set by mutual funds. Investors can buy a single share of stock in an ETF.

Table 16–4 compares some characteristics of investing in individual securities versus mutual funds, closed-end funds, and ETFs.

REFERENCES

Salisbury, Ian. "Telecom Gains Often Elude ETFs." *Wall Street Journal,* November 22, 2006, p. C11.

Young, Lauren. "ETFs: What the Buzz Is About." *BusinessWeek,* March 1, 2004, pp. 124–126.

CHAPTER 17

Investing in Foreign Stocks

KEY CONCEPTS

- Why should you invest in foreign stocks?
- The risks of foreign stocks
- How to invest in foreign stocks
- Is international investing good for me?

Investment Snapshot

- Foreign currency volatility can erase gains from investing in foreign stocks.
- Global investing has become easier for investors.
- China Life Insurance Company announced that it planned to sell 1.5 billion shares in an initial public offering (IPO) on the Shanghai exchange. Shares of China Life are listed in Hong Kong and as American depository receipts (ADRs) in the United States.

Investing in international stocks has become very much easier and more popular with many investors. European, Asian, and Latin American stock markets have provided investors with growth opportunities not matched by the American markets in the late 1970s through early 1990s and 2003 through 2006. This process of investing abroad has been facilitated by technological advances. There is an almost instantaneous flow of information about financial events, which also has increased the correlation of the foreign markets with the U.S. markets. In earlier years there was a low correlation between the foreign markets and the U.S, stock markets. However, a precipitous decline in the Hang Sen Index on the Hong Kong Stock Exchange affects not only the other Asian stock markets but also the European and American stock markets. Similarly, an early morning rally on Wall Street can spur stock markets in Europe to close at higher levels.

While economic and financial events around the world may be interconnected and move stock markets in the same direction at several points over time, over longer periods of time there is a relatively low correlation with stock market price movements. This correlation, however, has been increasing over the years.

WHY SHOULD YOU INVEST IN FOREIGN STOCKS?

There are several compelling reasons why investors should consider adding foreign stocks to their portfolios. Foreign stocks as a group have outperformed U.S. stocks during the period 2003 through 2006. Moreover, there will always be some equity markets abroad that will outperform U.S. stocks in any particular year. Because economic cycles in different countries move separately from each other, investors can take advantage of the different stock market situations. This is indeed confirmed by the fact that the majority of the stocks traded in the world originate outside the United States.

Investing in foreign stocks gives investors the opportunity to diversify their portfolios, which reduces the overall risk and volatility of the portfolio. If stocks in one country decline, there is a good chance that stocks in another country will increase to even out the variability in stock prices.

Investing in foreign stocks provides a hedge against a slump in the U.S. stock market or any other economic woes, such as inflation or rising interest rates. The same factors apply to foreign stock prices as to American stock prices. The earnings and economic health of the company are reflected in the stock price, as well as the economic and political conditions of the country.

Foreign stock markets may not be as efficient as the U.S. markets in pricing their stocks. The U.S. stock markets generally are characterized by relatively fast flows of information on stocks, large amounts of capital, and many traders, which make the pricing of stocks relatively efficient. In smaller foreign markets, there may be more opportunities to exploit pricing inconsistencies because there are fewer traders, smaller amounts of capital chasing stocks, and possibly slower information flows. Hence the potential gains to be had in these markets may be larger than those in the U.S. markets. This is certainly reflected in the growth of foreign stock markets. The U.S. share of the total world's market capitalization is expected to decline as foreign stock markets become more accessible.

WHAT ARE THE RISKS OF FOREIGN STOCKS?

Investors need to understand the additional risks they face from investing in foreign stocks. As mentioned earlier, all companies face business and financial risks, but additional risks pertain to foreign stocks.

Currency fluctuations can adversely affect the value of stock for U.S. investors. If the value of a foreign currency moves sharply relative to the U.S. dollar, the value of the stock will either produce spectacular gains or very large losses, even if the stock price remains unchanged.

When buying foreign stocks, dollars are converted into the foreign currency of the stock. When the stock is sold, the proceeds in that currency are converted back into dollars. For example, the dollar has recently fallen against the Euro, which has provided rather large gains for U.S. investors in European stocks. However, if the dollar strengthens against the Euro, these gains could be reversed.

Political risk is another important factor. The São Paulo stock market in Brazil plunged over 50 percent during the early part of 1994 when the socialist presidential candidate showed an initial lead in the polls. Thereafter, when the conservative candidate took the lead, the Brazilian stock market soared. The Mexican Bolsa also was badly shaken not only by the assassination of the leading presidential candidate before the elections but also by a peasant uprising.

Many foreign countries tend to be less stable politically than the United States, and any political upheavals in these countries can erode foreign investments.

Another factor facing foreign investors is the information gap. Foreign companies whose shares are not traded on the U.S. stock exchanges do not have to follow U.S. accounting and reporting standards. Not being familiar with the accounting and financial standards of foreign companies can lead to inaccurate conclusions about a company. In countries where companies are not strictly regulated with regard to their adherence to accounting and financial standards, there is the additional risk of fraud. Many Russian investors lost their investments in the mutual fund called MMM when it turned out to be a pyramid scheme. For many foreign companies, information may be scarce, and even if there are reports in the financial newspapers, interested investors could miss them because they might not be feature news items.

Foreign companies whose stocks trade as American depository receipts (ADRs), explained in the next section of this chapter, on the U.S. exchanges are required to recast their financial statements using U.S. accounting standards. This can explain some of the differences in the reporting of accounting standards of foreign countries. When Daimler Benz, the German auto company, initially requested a listing on the U.S. stock exchange, it reported profits of $294 million in Germany. When their financial statements were converted into U.S. generally accepted accounting principles (GAAP), the profit was reduced by $60 million (Glasgall and Lindorff, 1994, p. 102). With less information available on foreign companies and different accounting procedures, investment decision making on foreign stocks becomes more complex than investing in American stocks.

Quotes on some of the thinly traded foreign stocks (and the pink sheet ADRs that trade on the bulletin board) may be difficult to get, which can make it difficult to buy and sell at predetermined prices. However, this is changing as more of the computer online services go global and as more investors become interested in foreign stocks.

Transaction costs of trading foreign stocks are much higher than American traded stocks. In addition, because of the lower volume of stocks traded, a large order by foreign standards, although reasonable by American standards, could cause a trading imbalance. This could result in larger price swings for the stock. This then poses the risk of liquidity. If there are no takers for a large sell order of stocks, then there could be increased bid and ask spreads in the bidding for these stocks.

These risks need to be weighed against the advantages of investing in foreign stocks. Despite the foreign-exchange risks over the long term, foreign stocks can balance a portfolio in terms of safety and can increase overall returns.

HOW TO INVEST IN FOREIGN STOCKS

During the early 1990s, American investors rushed to invest globally at a time when the U.S. stock market had hit an impasse, and the foreign stock markets were flourishing. This was particularly true of emerging markets, where investors saw spectacular returns over short periods of time. However, with the political and economic turmoil in Asia and Latin America, these gains turned into spectacular losses, which tempered the flow of money abroad. This scenario changed in the 2000s, when foreign stocks have outperformed many of their U.S. counterparts.

There are a number of different ways for U.S. investors to invest abroad:

- Buy foreign stocks listed on foreign exchanges.
- Buy foreign stocks trading in dollars as ADRs.
- Invest in ETFs.
- Invest in international and global mutual funds.
- Invest in country funds, mostly closed-end mutual funds.

Foreign Stocks on Foreign Exchanges

Investors can buy shares of foreign companies that list on foreign exchanges, which is the riskiest of the four methods to invest internationally. The additional risk, over and above the different types of risk mentioned in the preceding section, include differences in trading regulations of foreign brokers and their exchanges. There is little recourse open to U.S. investors as to the protection of their investments from unscrupulous practices in many foreign countries. High fees (transaction costs, which are higher than those charged for trading U.S. stocks, and other additional fees such as foreign withholdings taxes) may be imposed, which could erode potential profits. In addition, lags in time and information may make it difficult for investors to determine when to buy and sell. Without the benefits of daily information about these foreign companies and industries, investors may not be able to make timely transaction decisions. This pertains particularly to companies whose stocks are not quoted in U.S. newspapers. For example, some of the smaller South African mining companies that are quoted on the Johannesburg Stock Exchange in rands (the local currency) are not reported in the U.S. financial newspapers. With the lack of daily information (unless a call is placed on a daily basis to the foreign broker), an investor might miss any news announcements, making it difficult to buy or sell on a timely basis.

A few major brokerage firms are making it easier for investors to buy shares listed on foreign exchanges. E*Trade Financial Corporation plans to make it possible for its investors to trade stocks listed in Japan, Canada, Hong Kong, and European countries in local currencies in 2007. Charles Schwab Corporation cut its brokerage fees for investors buying foreign stocks, and Fidelity Investments increased its brokerage services to facilitate customers' orders of foreign stocks (Lucchetti, 2006, p. B1).

Another development that has made it easier for customers to invest directly in foreign stocks is the merger activity of the stock markets. For example, the New York Stock Exchange (NYSE) proposed a merger with Euronext NV, the European exchange operator (Lucchetti, 2006, p. B1).

Nevertheless, buying foreign stocks listed on foreign exchanges should be left to more experienced investors who not only are knowledgeable about the foreign companies and their industries but also have access to daily information about them and are familiar with the different trading practices. Japanese stocks, for instance, trade at very much higher price/earnings (P/E) multiples than American stocks, and industry statistics in foreign countries are not easy to come by. It is difficult enough for most investors to select stocks trading on the American exchanges; direct investment in foreign stocks may be likened to navigating a mine field in the dark while riding on the back of an elephant.

Buying Foreign Stocks Trading as ADRs

An easier way to invest in foreign stocks is to buy American depository receipts (ADRs), or shares of foreign companies traded in U.S. dollars. ADRs are negotiable receipts that represent ownership of the shares of foreign companies traded on the American securities markets. The ADRs are issued by American banks, which hold in trust the shares representing the ADRs. Each ADR certificate represents a percentage ownership of the securities held in trust.

ADRs work in the following way: When a broker receives an order to buy 100 shares of an ADR such as Glaxo Smith Kline, the British pharmaceutical company, the broker will pass this order on to either the brokerage firm's London trading desk or another

British firm's trading desk. The foreign firm will buy the stock, which is then deposited with the custodian bank. The custodian bank authorizes the American depository bank to issue an ADR certificate, which is then sent to the brokerage firm. The broker sends the certificate to the investor in the same way as it would be done for the purchase of a domestic stock.

For actively traded ADRs, brokers don't need to fill the orders from abroad because there are so many ADR certificates in circulation in the United States. Large brokerage firms often can match the buy and sell orders of the large, actively traded ADRs from their own inventories. When selling ADRs, the process described earlier is completed in reverse.

ADRs give U.S. investors the opportunity to buy and sell foreign companies' stocks with the same ease as the stocks of U.S. companies. ADR buy and sell transactions are completed in the same period of time (three days) it takes for American stocks.

ADR holders have voting rights and may participate in the rights offerings if the company registers with the Securities and Exchange Commission (SEC). If the company does not register with the SEC, the ADR bank will sell the rights and remit the value to the ADR shareholders.

There are two forms of ADRs: sponsored and unsponsored. *Sponsored ADRs* are those issued through banks by the foreign companies that have registered with the SEC. *Unsponsored ADRs* are of companies that have not fully registered with the SEC; their shares trade on the over-the-counter (OTC) markets.

Even though investors can trade ADRs on the markets as easily as they can domestic stocks, they are still exposed to many of the risks outlined earlier. ADRs trade in dollars on the U.S. markets, which eliminates the need to exchange dollars for a foreign currency. However, the value of the ADR is influenced by exchange rates. When the dollar declines relative to a foreign currency, a foreign company's stock is worth more when it is converted into dollars. Conversely, when the value of the dollar increases, the foreign currency is worth less. When dividends are paid, the issuing bank receives and distributes them to the ADR holders minus their fees.

Information on the companies issuing ADRs is increasing owing to demands of U.S. investors to diversify their portfolios (see Table 17–1 for a list of some of the ADR stocks). However, information on these companies is still not as readily available as it is for domestic companies.

TABLE 17 - 1

Some Selected ADRs

Company	Country	Industry	Symbol	Exchange
Danone	France	Food products	DA	NYSE
Glaxo Smith Kline	Britain	Pharmaceuticals	GSK	NYSE
Nice Systems	Israel	Telecom equip.	NICE	Nasdaq
Volvo	Sweden	Trucks and vehicles	VOLV	Nasdaq
SAP	Germany	Software	SAP	NYSE
Ahold	Netherlands	Food retailer	AHO	NYSE
Siemens	Germany	Electronic equip.	SI	NYSE

Exchange-Traded Funds

Investors can use ETFs to invest in foreign stocks. There are ETFs that specialize in single countries such as South Africa, China, Taiwan, India, and Korea. These are country-specific index investments that are traded on the AMEX. Table 17–2 presents a list of country ETFs and their trading ticker symbols. These ETFs are offered by Barclays Global Investors. There are other groups that offer foreign ETFs such as State Street Global Advisors and the Vanguard Group's Vipers.

Each ETF represents a basket of foreign stocks of that particular country that appeals to investors wanting to invest in that country.

ETFs are purchased like individual stocks through a broker, discount broker, or online broker. The stocks trade on the AMEX with the corresponding ticker symbols for each country.

TABLE 17 - 2

Single-Country ETFs

Country	Ticker Symbol	Country	Ticker Symbol
Australia	EWA	Austria	EWO
Belgium	EWK	Canada	EWC
France	EWQ	Germany	EWG
Hong Kong	EWH	Italy	EWI
Japan	EWJ	Malaysia	EWM
Mexico	EWW	Netherlands	EWN
Singapore	EWS	Spain	EWP
Sweden	EWD	Switzerland	EWL
United Kingdom	EWU	Taiwan	EWT

As with closed-end funds, the net asset values (NAVs) are calculated at the end of each business day. Dividends from investment income and capital gains realized from the sale of securities are paid out at least once a year. These payouts would be net of fees and transaction costs incurred by the country ETFs.

The advantage of investing in foreign ETFs is that they provide a lower-cost passive approach to investing in the stocks of specific countries. The goal for each country ETF is to provide the same performance as that of the particular index of that country. However, many of these country funds do not have diversified portfolios because most of their investments are in a few companies. For example, the South Africa Index Fund had over 20 percent of its investments in two stocks (13 percent of its investments in Sasol, Ltd., and 7.8 percent invested in Standard Bank) (Salisbury, 2006, p. B4).

The risks are the same as those outlined earlier in this chapter for international investing, in addition to the specific risks that pertain to ETFs. Foreign ETFs might be subject to greater volatility because of the political and economic risks of the particular foreign country, in addition to the risks of withholding taxes, imposition of restrictions on the expatriation of capital, and the lower liquidity of the stocks. Single-country ETFs are also not considered to be fully diversified investments because in many countries there is a concentration of investments in certain industries.

International Mutual Funds

An even easier way to invest internationally is through mutual funds that specialize in foreign investments. Investors invest in international mutual funds in the same way as they choose domestic stock and bond funds. International mutual funds invest in the stocks of foreign countries.

Some funds invest in a mixture of countries, including U.S. companies. Depending on their mix of foreign holdings, mutual funds may be classified as follows: international, global, regional, and country.

International funds invest in the securities of companies whose stocks trade on foreign exchanges. *Global funds*, as the name implies, invest in securities around the world, including those of U.S. companies. *Regional funds* specialize in the securities of companies located in a specified geographic area of the world. For example, there are funds that specialize in the Pacific Rim area, Latin America, Europe, and the emerging economies. Many of these may be closed-end funds that trade on the exchanges as opposed to the open-end mutual funds that are bought and sold through investment companies or through brokers in the case of load funds. Only *country funds* invest in the securities of a specified country. Some examples include Japan funds, Spain funds, Portugal funds, Switzerland funds, Chile funds, and India funds. As with regional funds, there are open-end and closed-end funds.

Open-end mutual funds and closed-end funds are discussed in detail in Chapters 14 and 15, respectively. Investors should be aware of the nuances, risks, advantages, and disadvantages of these types of funds before they invest.

One of the advantages of choosing international mutual funds over investing in individual foreign stocks is that with a mutual fund, the investor owns a part of a broadly diversified portfolio. To obtain such diversification with individual stocks, investors would need larger amounts of money. International funds are more diversified than sector and country funds. However, when the markets of sector and country funds are "hot," they can easily outperform the more broadly diversified international funds. The converse is true when these markets slump.

The results of international, global, regional, and country funds depend on their holdings in the funds. If, for example, the bulk of an international fund's holdings are concentrated in European countries, that fund may not experience the benefits of the worldwide growth of the Pacific Rim and Latin America. European economies are somewhat connected and may have similar economic cycles. Many international and global funds concentrate on certain sectors of the globe and are not broadly diversified.

Investors should read the fund's prospectus with a list of the fund's country holdings before investing. By identifying the mix of stocks in the different countries, an investor can allocate investments on a geographic basis. For example, an investor who wants a broadly diversified portfolio might have to invest in two different international mutual funds to get this broad diversification.

Investing in international mutual funds is advantageous for investors who do not have the time or the inclination to research individual foreign stocks. The portfolio managers of these funds select the foreign stocks after researching the companies and economic climates of the countries.

Another advantage of investing in international mutual funds over individual foreign stocks is that portfolio managers of international funds may be able to reduce the risks of unfavorable currency fluctuations by using hedging strategies. These involve the use of foreign currency options and futures contracts.

Not all the international funds use these strategies, and some use them only on an occasional basis. The objective of international investing is not only to invest solely in foreign stocks that increase in price but also to take advantage of the devaluation of the dollar relative to these currencies. For long-term investors in foreign stocks and/or funds, the currency effects tend to even out over longer periods of time.

Investors need to be aware of the objectives of the funds, the stated returns, the risks, and the fees charged. Invest in funds with low expense ratios.

Country Funds

Country funds specialize in the securities of a particular country. Country funds can be open-end or closed-end, but most country funds are closed-end. Examples of these are the Korea fund, the Italy fund, the Thai fund, the Japan fund, and ASA, Ltd., which specializes in South African gold mining companies.

Many of the securities in these portfolios are thinly traded stocks, which points to an advantage of choosing a closed-end fund over an open-end country fund. With closed-end funds, portfolio managers do not have to sell stocks in their portfolios to meet the redemption needs of their shareholders. The number of shares is fixed at the initial offering, and after they are all sold, they trade on the exchange or the OTC market. Open-end portfolio managers have to sell some of their portfolio holdings to raise cash to buy back shares from shareholders at NAVs.

Closed-end funds could trade at large discounts or premiums to their NAVs depending on the supply of and demand for their stocks and other factors. Potential investors in closed-end funds should be aware of their NAVs so that they do not end up buying a fund that is trading at a healthy premium over the NAV.

Country funds make it very easy for investors to invest in markets about which they have very little knowledge and information. For instance, stock markets in Turkey, India, New Zealand,

South Africa, and Singapore have outperformed many other markets. For investors who do not have the time or inclination to research these markets for promising individual stocks, there is the convenience of a county fund. In selecting country funds, investors still need to be aware of the country's potential economic outlook, political stability, and exchange rates. Country funds are specialized to those countries and, as a result, may be quite volatile.

When the Japanese stock market rose to its 10-year high, Japanese country funds were trading at large premiums to their NAVs. Then the Japanese stock market plummeted, and Japanese country funds traded at deep discounts to their NAVs.

IS INTERNATIONAL INVESTING SUITABLE FOR ME?

Foreign investments involve additional risks to those facing domestic investments. The risks of loss from political turmoil and/or currency exchange rates can wipe out any profits and produce losses on foreign investments that were carefully selected using the most up-to-date information available.

The difficulty in obtaining information about individual foreign securities may prompt many American investors to use mutual funds to make their foreign investments. Global and international mutual funds minimize some of the business, financial, economic, and political risks by investing in a broadly diversified portfolio of investments around the world. An investment in the more specialized regional and country funds has increased risks and rewards.

Investors need to weigh the risks against the potential returns. Overseas stock markets have over various periods of time outperformed the American stock markets. Thus, over long periods of time, investors should be rewarded, assuming that increasing worldwide growth and trade continue. By diversifying your investments to cover many different economies, you are helping to even out the fluctuations in your overall portfolio and participating in the larger returns of the faster-growing foreign economies.

Investors who do not want to take the added risks of foreign investments might consider diversifying their portfolios to include the common stocks of U.S. multinational corporations. Corporations such as PepsiCo, Coca-Cola, McDonald's, ExxonMobil, and Microsoft achieve a large percentage of their sales and earnings outside the United States. If the American stock markets decline, investors still may be able to obtain positive rates of return from their foreign investments.

Investors who can tolerate the additional risks of foreign investments should invest directly in foreign stocks or indirectly through international mutual funds.

REFERENCES

Glasgall, William, and Dave Lindorff. "The Global Investor." *BusinessWeek*, September 19, 1994, pp. 96–104.

Lucchetti, Aaron. "Global Investing Made Easy." *Wall Street Journal*, August 12–13, 2006, p. B1.

Salisbury, Ian. "Do You Know What's in Your ETF?" *Wall Street Journal*, August 12–13, 2006, p. B4.

CHAPTER 18

Portfolio Management and Evaluation

KEY CONCEPTS

- Investors' objectives
- Asset allocation
- Selection of individual investments

Investment Snapshot

- With a portfolio of diverse investments, total returns can be increased and total risk lowered more than with individual investments.
- The number of stocks held in a portfolio determines the level of risk and return characteristics of the portfolio.

INVESTOR'S OBJECTIVES

The aim of portfolio management is to assemble individual investment securities in a portfolio that conforms to the investor's level of risk and rate of return. The investor's objectives are the most important guidelines to managing an investment portfolio. The main types of objectives for a portfolio are preservation of principal, providing income, or seeking capital growth. For example, an investor pursuing capital growth for a portfolio might allocate a greater portion of the portfolio's assets toward growth stocks, small-cap stocks, and real estate. From time to time the investor would evaluate the performance of the portfolio with regard to risk and return as to whether the portfolio is meeting his or her investment objectives.

An investor seeking income with some capital growth from a portfolio would allocate a greater portion of the portfolio to bonds, along with some stock investments. For example, a total portfolio amount of $600,000 might be invested in the following manner: $500,000 in bonds yielding 6 percent, which would generate income of $30,000 per year, and $100,000 in 4 percent dividend-yielding stocks, which would bring in an additional $4,000 in income per year. By investing a small percentage of the portfolio in stocks rather than 100 percent in bonds, this investor is seeking potential capital growth to the portfolio and also minimizing the total risk of the portfolio. If large-cap stocks increase by 8 percent for the year, the value of the stock portfolio would grow to $108,000, which would more than offset the reduction in income from investing in lower-yielding stocks than bonds.

Investors continually must be aware that not only do their objectives and individual characteristics change over time, but their investments must be monitored owing to financial conditions and markets. Companies change, and their securities may no longer fulfill the criteria for which they were purchased. Not all investments in the portfolio realize their projected returns, so investors managing their portfolios might need to sell and replace them with other investments. This does not mean that all or most of the investments in the portfolio should be turned over continuously. Only those investments that are unlikely to achieve the objectives specified should be liquidated.

ASSET ALLOCATION

Asset allocation is a plan to invest in different types of securities (stocks, bonds, and money market funds) so that the capital invested is protected against adverse factors in the market. This, in essence, is the opposite of an investor putting all his or her eggs in one basket.

Diversification is the other balancing tool in a portfolio. For example, a portfolio might have investments in different asset classes according to a well-balanced asset allocation plan, but all the stocks and bonds might be invested in companies in the same economic sector, which would not insulate the portfolio from the risk of loss. By investing in the stocks of different companies in various sectors of the economy and different types of bonds, the portfolio would be better insulated against the risk of loss.

The risk of loss has been spread over a number of securities. Increasing the number of stocks and bonds held in a portfolio decreases the volatility. However, by increasing the number of stocks and bonds held in a portfolio, investors are also reducing the potential performance of that portfolio. Diversification seeks a balance between the risk/return tradeoff. The return on a portfolio depends on the types of investments held in the portfolio.

Classifying some of the different types of investments on a continuum of risk, common stocks are considered to be the most risky (in terms of variability in share price), followed by long-term bonds, with the shorter maturities on the low-risk end. Bear in mind that there are many other types of investments that are riskier than common stocks, such as commodities and futures contracts. Similarly, there is a great variation in quality among common stocks. The common stocks of the well-established blue-chip companies are considered to be less risky than the bonds of highly leveraged companies with suspect balance sheets.

Common stocks are considered to be the most risky owing to the volatility of stock prices. However, over long periods of time where the ups and downs of the stock market can be averaged out, stocks have provided higher returns. Common stocks provide the growth in a portfolio and should be included among the investment assets to accomplish long-term growth goals. The percentage allocated to common stocks depends on the investor's objectives and personal characteristics. As mentioned earlier, a retired widow who depends on the income generated from the investments in the portfolio may not have any common stocks in the portfolio. However, if the portfolio generates more than a sufficient level of income for the widow's current needs, a small portion of the portfolio could be invested in common stocks to provide some growth in the portfolio for later years.

There isn't a rigid formula for asset allocation. Rather, it is a good idea to think about the concept as a guideline when investing money. Some investors may tilt toward an aggressive portfolio, whereas others require a conservative portfolio. The mix of investment assets depends primarily on the levels of risk that investors are willing to take and their time horizons. The percentage allocated to the different types of assets always can be changed depending on circumstances. As individual circumstances change, so will the investor's objectives. If the emphasis shifts, for example, to greater income generation and preservation of capital from capital growth, the percentage of the investments in the portfolio can be changed accordingly. The most important aspect of investing is having an asset allocation plan that signifies the broad mix of assets to strive for. Once these broad categories are determined, the individual assets are purchased. When considering the different types of securities to choose for a portfolio, investors should weigh the characteristics of the types of investments along with the risks to assist them in their overall choice.

Investors need to revisit their asset allocation mix from time to time to determine whether to rebalance their mix and realign it with their investment objectives. The frequency with which the asset allocation plan is rebalanced also depends on the investor's portfolio management investment style. A *passive investment style* suggests leaving the portfolio alone, in other words, buying and holding the investments without regard for factors that affect them. An *active portfolio investment style* involves changing the investment assets within the portfolio whenever external circumstances have the potential to influence performance. The management of bond portfolios is very different from the management of stock portfolios. Bonds provide regular flows of income and have fixed lives, whereas stocks do not mature, might not provide regular flows of income if they do not pay dividends, and do not have maturity dates, which means uncertainty with regard to future stock prices. This means that in the management of stock portfolios there is a greater emphasis on stock selection (buying stocks that will appreciate the most).

Table 18–1 illustrates the need for rebalancing a portfolio. If the investor's objectives and personal characteristics have not changed one year later, the asset allocation mix should be realigned to the original mix. Both advantages and disadvantages arise from rebalancing a portfolio. The advantages are

- The relative weighting of the portfolio assets are aligned with the individual's objectives, personal characteristics, risk tolerance, and rate of return.
- The risk of loss is reduced by selling appreciated assets to realize capital gains.

The disadvantages of rebalancing a portfolio are

TABLE 18-1

Rebalancing a Portfolio

1. Begin with an asset allocation plan.

    The investor started with the asset allocation illustrated in Figure 18–1.

2. Revisit the asset allocation plan after a period of time.

    One year later with the rapid appreciation of the equity portfolio, the asset alloca-tion mix has changed to the percentages shown in Figure 18–2.

3. If necessary, rebalance the portfolio.

    The investor needs to determine whether this new asset allocation mix is consis-tent with his or her objectives, personal circumstances, and risk tolerance. With appreciation of the equity assets, the new equity mix is now 50 percent of the total portfolio value, and the bond mix has dropped from 50 percent to 35 percent. This may not be suitable for an investor who relies more on income-generating assets than on growth assets. Rebalancing requires selling off some stocks and buying more bonds with the proceeds in order to realign the asset allocation mix closer to an acceptable asset allocation mix.

4. Proposed asset allocation plan after rebalancing.

    Figure 18–3 shows the current and proposed asset allocation mixes.

Current Asset Allocation Mix		Proposed Asset Allocation Mix	
Money market securities	15%	Money market securities	15%
Money market mutual funds	$45,000	Money market mutual funds	$45,000
Stocks	50%	Stocks	35%
Large-cap stocks	$150,000	Large-cap stocks	$52,500
Bonds	35%	Mid-cap stocks	$52,500
		Bonds	50%
Intermediate municipal bonds	$50,000	Long-term treasury bonds	$75,000
Intermediate-term agency bonds	$55,000	AAA corporate bonds	$75,000
Total	$300,000	Total	$300,000
Before-tax return	5.10%	Before-tax return	6.15%
After-tax return	3.15%	After-tax return	4.5%
Risk (standard deviation)	9.00%	Risk (standard deviation)	7.65%

- Rebalancing a portfolio incurs trading costs (commissions) and advisory fees.
- Investors run the potential risk of loss that comes from selling the winners in the portfolio to buy more of the losing assets.
- Selling securities involves tax implications in taxable accounts.

FIGURE 18-1

Original Asset Allocation Mix

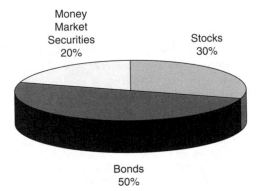

FIGURE 18-2

Asset Allocation Mix One Year Later

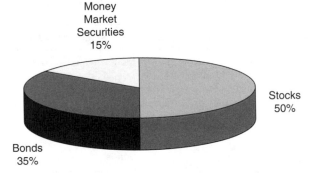

FIGURE 18-3

Current and Proposed Asset Allocation Mixes

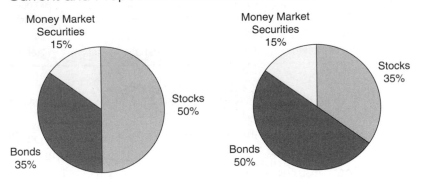

The most important aspect of investing is having an asset allocation plan that signifies the broad mix of assets to strive for. Once these broad categories are determined, the individual assets are purchased. Table 18–2 presents examples of different asset allocation plans for investors with different investment objectives.

TABLE 18-2

Asset Allocation Models for Different Investment Objectives

A *conservative portfolio* is one in which the investment goals are to preserve capital, allowing for some growth to the portfolio. The weighting is geared toward high-quality bonds and some common stocks for growth. See Figure 18–4.

A *balanced portfolio* includes a larger percentage allocated to common stocks, which provide capital growth for the portfolio, and another large percentage of fixed-income securities, which provide the income for the portfolio. See Figure 18–5.

An *aggressive portfolio* is overweighted in common stocks in order to provide capital growth without any regard for generating income for the portfolio. See Figure 18–6.

The allocation plan of a young couple, both professionals who are not dependent on income from their investments and are investing for long-term growth, could break down their stock investments into the categories shown in Figure 18–7. This is a second example of an aggressive portfolio allocation.

FIGURE 18-4

Asset Allocation for a Conservative Investor

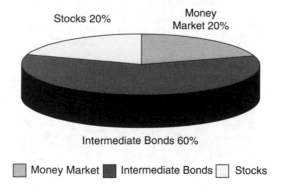

Stocks 20% Money Market 20%

Intermediate Bonds 60%

☐ Money Market ■ Intermediate Bonds ☐ Stocks

FIGURE 18-5

Asset Allocation for a Balanced Portfolio

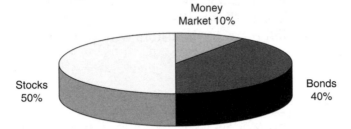

FIGURE 18-6

Asset Allocation for an Aggressive Portfolio

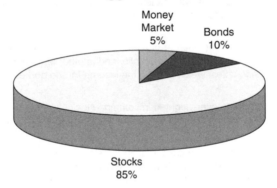

FIGURE 18-7

Stock Portfolio Allocation for a Couple Seeking Long-Term Growth

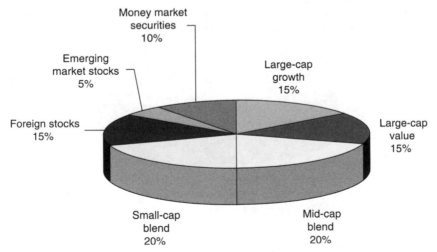

SELECTION OF INDIVIDUAL INVESTMENTS

In order to match your objectives with specific investments, you need to identify the characteristics of the different investments and their risks. Funds for immediate needs and emergency purposes should be liquid, in other words, able to be converted easily into cash without incurring a loss of principal. Such investments are money market mutual funds, checking accounts, and savings accounts. These are readily convertible into cash. By increasing the time horizon from immediate needs to short-term needs, investors could increase marginally their rates of return by investing in certificates of deposit (CDs), Treasury bills, and commercial paper. However, of these, only Treasury bills are marketable, meaning that they can be sold on the secondary market before maturity.

Savings accounts, CDs, money market mutual funds, Treasury bills, and commercial paper provide some taxable income, are liquid, but do not offer the possibilities of capital gains or losses. Although investors might not lose any of their principal by investing in this group of investments, there is a risk that the returns from these investments may not keep up with inflation.

The financing of intermediate-term objectives that stretch several years into the future—such as the purchase of a car, a house, or an appliance or the funding of a child's education—requires investments that generate income and the return of principal. These investments need to produce a greater rate of return than a savings account or short-term money market securities. Short- to intermediate-term bonds offer increased rates of return over money market securities as well as the possibility of capital gains or losses if the investor needs the money before maturity. Although investors receive increased rates of return from intermediate-term securities over money market securities, investors need to be aware that their principal invested in intermediate-term bonds is not as liquid as short-term securities.

An investment plan to finance a child's education in five years requires a relatively safe investment, which would not include investing in stocks. Most people would not gamble with the money earmarked for their children's education in the event of a declining stock market when the money would be needed.

Long-term objectives such as saving for retirement or for an infant's college education in 18 years require investments that offer long-term growth prospects as well as greater long-term returns. Stocks provide larger long-term returns than bonds or money market securities, but stock prices are more volatile. The level of risk that can be withstood on stock investments depends on the individual investor's circumstances.

A more conservative long-term portfolio might consist of long-term bonds, blue-chip stocks, and conservative-growth stocks. The emphasis of this strategy is to invest in good-quality bonds and the stocks of established companies that pay dividends and offer the prospect of steady growth over a long period of time. Securities offering capital growth are important even for conservative portfolios in order to provide some cover against any potential erosion in future purchasing power from inflation.

A growth-oriented part of a portfolio seeks the generation of long-term capital gains and the monetary growth in value of the stocks in the portfolio. A more speculative portfolio, where an investor can absorb greater levels of risk to strive for greater growth and returns, would include growth stocks, stocks of emerging companies, foreign stocks, emerging market stocks, convertible bonds, junk bonds, real estate, options, commodities, and futures. Bear in mind that including the last three types of investments—options, commodities, and futures—is not an endorsement that these securities should play a major role in a portfolio. For a speculative investor who understands the nuances of these investments, these securities could account for no more than 5 percent of the total portfolio. The other assets mentioned offer investors the opportunity for large gains, but the risks of loss are also greater. Foreign bonds and stocks also should be considered, but investors should do their homework first so that they understand the risks fully. International mutual funds might be more helpful to spread some of the risk, although in the short term there is always currency risk when investing in off-shore investments. Over the long term, however, exchange-rate fluctuations tend to even out and are not a significant factor.

Investors who are not comfortable buying individual bonds and stocks could choose mutual funds, exchange-traded funds, or closed-end funds. Investors willing to make their own investment decisions on individual securities can eliminate the fees and expenses charged by mutual funds and closed-end funds. When considering the different types of securities to choose for a portfolio, investors should weigh the characteristics of the type of investment along with the risks. (See Table 18–3 for a summary of the strategies to reduce the different types of risk.)

TABLE 18·3

Summary of Strategies to Manage Risk

Investment	Risk	Strategy
Common stock	Market risk	Invest for a long period of time.
	Financial risk	Diversification: invest in companies with low leverage.
	Interest-rate risk	Active or passive strategy, depending on the investor's time horizon
	Declining market rates of interest	Increase the percentage of the portfolio allocated to stocks.
	Increasing market rates	Decrease the percentage of the portfolio allocated to stocks.
	Credit risk	Invest in good-quality stocks.
	Purchasing power risk	Requires active portfolio management; invest in stocks that (when inflation increases) will weather the effects of inflation better, such as gold stocks, oil, and commodity stocks.

As mentioned throughout this book, diversification reduces risk without decreasing returns. A portfolio should include at least 12 to 15 stocks in order to lessen the risk of loss. In other words, an investment in one company should not account for more than 10 percent of your portfolio. If that investment declines significantly, you would be limiting the total amount of your loss to at most 10 percent of your portfolio. One method of building a portfolio is to invest equal amounts in different stocks. For example, if you want to invest in 20 stocks, the amount invested in each stock would be 5 percent of your total capital. However, you might identify some of the 20 stocks that have the potential to perform better with lower risk, and you would want to allocate greater amounts to those stocks and lesser amounts to stocks that might not be as attractive.

Investors who assume that the stock markets are efficient strive to build portfolios that are well diversified with risks and returns that match those of the market. In order to earn returns that are greater than those of the market, investors would need to invest in securities with higher risks than the market indexes. Passive investment strategies of matching market returns involve indexing and long-term buy-and-hold investing strategies.

Investors who think that they can beat the market averages are more likely to choose their own stocks and are also likely to have shorter holding periods for their stocks. Market timers buy and sell stocks as market trends and economic factors change. Some industries are more sensitive to the economy than others. Industries that move in the same direction as the economy are referred to as *cyclical industries*. The sales and earnings of these companies generally are aligned with the economic cycle. The stage in the business cycle of the economy becomes important to the timing of the investments in these cyclical companies. For example, you would not want to invest in the stocks of automobile companies at the peak of an economic expansion because their stock prices would be at their upper limits, and they would face a downturn in earnings when the economy slows down. During a period of economic expansion, the stock prices of cyclical companies traditionally increase; during an economic recession, the prices decline. Cyclical companies are in industries such as automobiles, building and construction, aluminum, steel, chemicals, and lumber. Because these stocks are sensitive to changes in economic activity, investors should time their purchases of cyclical stocks to the early phases of an expansionary period. Figure 18–8 illustrates the timing of the different industries in the business cycles of the economy.

FIGURE   18-8

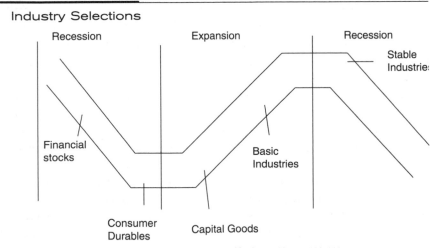

Source: Susan E. Kuhn, "Stocks Are Still Your Best Buy," *Fortune*, March 21, 1994, pp. 130–144.

Coming out of a recession, financial stocks tend to do well because of lower interest rates, whereas at the expansionary phase, stocks of consumer durable goods companies are the ones to buy. During a recession, consumers delay purchases of automobiles, large appliances, and houses. Cyclical stocks fluctuate with the state of the economy and are always hit hard by rising interest rates. Into an expansionary cycle, capital goods companies benefit from increased sales in the business sector, which result in an increase in the demand for raw materials and commodities. Stable industries include health care stocks, beverage stocks, food retailers, food companies, consumer services, and household non-durables.

This pattern is typical in most business cycles, but exceptions always exist. During the recession of 2000–2002, for example, auto companies saw sales of cars rise significantly because of sales and marketing incentive programs, such as zero-percent financing and considerable price discounts. This increase improved auto companies' sales but did not improve their profits. By timing stock purchases in these different industries, investors might be able to improve their returns.

Anticipating changes in interest rates could prompt investors to reallocate the types of investments in their portfolios. If higher rates of interest are anticipated, an investor has a number of different options. Profits may be taken by selling stocks that have appreciated, or the investor may decide to sell stocks in the interest-sensitive industries, such as financial stocks, cyclical sector stocks in the automotive and home-building industries, and utility stocks. Some investors might buy stocks in the pharmaceutical and food industries, which tend to weather the effects of higher market interest rates better than other sectors of the economy. Other investors might decide to hold their existing stocks but not invest any new money in the stock market until interest rates start to level off. True market timers might liquidate their entire stock positions and wait on the sidelines for more favorable conditions.

Purchasing power risk, or inflation, hurts all financial investments to some degree or another. However, traditionally, returns on stocks tend to outperform those of bonds and money market securities during low to moderate rates of inflation. Mining stocks, such as gold and platinum, and aluminum stocks have been good hedges against inflation.

Even a passively managed portfolio should be examined at various intervals with regard to returns on different investments as well as the changing economic conditions. Not all investments achieve their anticipated returns, and if they turn out to be poor performers, they might need to be liquidated.

Investors who do not have the knowledge and skills to manage their portfolios might turn to professional advisors. Financial planners and accountants offer advice on the planning and management of portfolios. For investors who do not wish to be involved in the management of their assets, there are professional money managers and trust departments of various institutions. Their fees are often a stated percentage of the total dollar amount of the portfolio, which often requires that the portfolio be substantial in dollar terms.

The key to long-term successful investing is to allocate investments into bonds, stocks, and money market securities suited to the investor's particular objectives and circumstances.

Index